Disclaimer and Warning

This book is intended to give moral and ethical guidance on the subject of self-defense, which necessarily includes citations of law and various legal principles. However, the citations and examples used in this book apply only to the specific situations herein and must not be construed as legal advice in or for any specific situation. Furthermore, the recommendations, descriptions of weapons, tactics or actual use-of-force accounts must not be undertaken or used without first obtaining professional legal and self-defense advice from experienced lawyers and certified instructors IN YOUR OWN STATE. Self-defense laws and the legality of owning various weapons differ from state to state (and county to county and city to city in some states), including state and federal laws governing legal transportation of various weapons. The reader is encouraged to study the recommended works cited to gain a better understanding of use-of-force principles and methods, and then seek out hands-on training from qualified instructors before attempting to actively defend himself or others. Self-teaching or unskillful use of active defensive weapons and martial arts can result in serious injury or death. Self-defense is an individual decision. The reader has a personal, moral, and legal obligation to use power and knowledge responsibly and legally and is personally liable for improper use-of-force.

Therefore, the editor, the publisher, their contractors and employees, along with the author and his heirs and assigns, and any distributor (wholesale or retail) of this book accept no liability (expressed or implied) for damages of any kind resulting from reliance on any teaching, opinion, legal citation, or any other aspect of this book, including but not limited to consequential damages. This book is to be used as a moral and ethical guide ONLY and is not to be considered, construed, or used as legal advice.

Gregory N. Hopkins
Attorney at Law

Library of Congress Control Number 2019941966

ISBN 978-1-7322707-7-0

Printed in United States of America
Published in Florence, Alabama

MINDBRIDGE PRESS

A Time to Kill
The Bible and Self Defense

Greg Hopkins

MINDBRIDGE PRESS

Florence, Alabama

Dedication

To Matt Payne and all other Shepherds – civilian, police, and military;
past, present, and future – who sacrifice to keep us safe and free.

Contents

Author's Preface
In Defense of Self-Defense

Since God shows us the difference between good and evil, between life and death, we can make decisions in a godly manner. So why are so many Christians unsure about self-defense? There has always been a vague notion of pacifism in Christianity, centered on what I believe to be a misconception of Jesus' words and actions. Sincere, well-intentioned, loving Christians take that misconception and the Bible's clear commands to take care of and show kindness to others and convince themselves that they cannot justifiably take a life under any circumstances. Taking the Bible's admonitions to preserve innocent life and some of Jesus' statements, they extrapolate that to an aversion to take the life of the guilty as well.[1] Their intentions are noble and they mean well, but their understanding of Scripture on the subject is lacking, and the results can be tragic. Despite their intent to hold life precious, their stance amounts to a refusal to protect innocent life. "There is a way which seems right to a man, but its end is the way of death" (Proverbs 14:12). If you are a pacifist and the latest version of the Manson "family" breaks into your house, they will kill you and step over your body to take out any possible witnesses as well. Sheep do not survive wolf attacks unless the shepherd is there to stop it. "Thorns and snares are in the way of the perverse. He who guards himself will be far from them" (Proverbs 22:5). Despite the good intentions of many, pacifism kills.

I believe the major reason Christians are vague on pacifism and self-defense is ignorance. This is not unusual. In a *Washington Post* article, Elizabeth Tenety points out that many religious people lack understanding of even the basic doctrines of their faith.[2] The Bible says, "My people are destroyed for lack of knowledge, because you have rejected knowledge" (Hosea 4:6a). Some people do not know what the Bible says on a given subject. Some do not want to know. However, if God addresses self-defense, then would it not be a good thing to know which side He comes down on? If God forbids it, then we must, in faith, stand by and let evil have its way. However, if He says self-defense is okay, we can keep the innocent from being destroyed.

Another reason we are vague on this issue is our own disobedience. Despite many passages that encourage us to study and to apply the Bible in our lives, we do not.[3] Are we afraid that knowledge produces obligation? Is it possible we think that if we do not know a command is there, we can claim we are not responsible? That attitude does not work in court: "ignorance of the law is no excuse." The next time a police officer pulls you over for speeding, say, "But officer, I didn't know there were such things as speed limits!" Let me know how that works out for you.

Let's face it, too often we simply do things because it is what we want to do, regardless of God's opinion. For example, a Christian who is also a gun owner might not study the Biblical view of self-defense because he is afraid he will find that self-defense is forbidden. He would rather "take his chances with God" than give up the right to defend himself, collect guns, or hunt. When we refuse to consult God's will because of fear that it will contradict our pleasures, then we clearly love our "rights" more than we love God. A pacifist Christian might refuse to study the subject because of his impression that pacifism makes him "more spiritual" than others. The idea of martyrdom may even feed his ego. Both of these attitudes are wrong. As Jesus told the disciples, "If you know these things, you are blessed if you *do* them" (John 13:17, emphasis mine). To refuse to determine God's will on a subject near and dear to us is the same as knowing His will and refusing to conform. In either case, it amounts to practical atheism.

Practical atheists are those who profess belief in God but deny His sovereignty over part of their lives. That is why Jesus asks, "And why do you call me, 'Lord, Lord' and do not do what I say?" (Luke 6:46). The Bible is our owner's manual, written by Him who made us. We ignore it at our peril, just as if we disregarded our car manual's recommendations to change the oil every 5000 miles. This was the Pharisees' problem. They cherry-picked the parts of God's Word they liked and made up rules to get around those they didn't like (see Matthew 15:1-9; 23). They did not recognize Jesus as Messiah because He did not meet their preconceptions.

Today, some people see the Bible only as ancient literature and praise the beauty of some of its passages. Some parts are indeed poetic, but God gave us His Word to practice, not just to praise. Like the Pharisees, we forget that we should read the Bible as servants, not merely as students. The student learns to gather information that he can use later at his discretion. The servant learns to dedicate his life to his master's service and to help others as his master directs.

It is All About Stewardship

Whether we are concealed-carry permit holders, police, or soldiers, we have accepted the same obligation as shepherds: to protect, preserve, grow, and defend the good in this world. A shepherd is a kind of steward. *Steward* is an Old English/Scottish term for one who stands responsible to care for the belongings and/or family of another. Placed in a Biblical context, stewardship is responsible caretaking based on the idea that I own nothing – I just manage it for God. I can hear you thinking now, "Uh-oh, he's gonna start talking about tithing or giving my time and talent to the church." Calm down, my friend! I already got into your wallet for this book, and I am not going to beg for more. What I am asking you to do is to look inside at why you would carry a gun. Consider this: "Or do you not know that your body is a temple of the Holy Spirit Who is in you, Whom you have from God, and that you are not your own? For you have been bought with a price: therefore glorify God in your *body*" (1 Corinthians 6:19-20, emphasis mine). Could it be that preserving your life (which belongs to God) is proper stewardship?

Honoring God with my body encompasses how I think, act, spend, opine, and relate. It includes my every attitude, word, action, or deed. Jesus spelled it out in Mark 8:34 when He said: "If anyone wishes to come after Me, let him deny himself, and take up his cross, and follow Me." As a steward, I offer to God all of *who I am*; not just the sum total of what I *have.* Remember, we are made in His image to reflect His character. Jesus explains this concept with His parable in Luke 12:42-48:

> And the Lord said, "Who is the faithful and sensible steward whom his master will put in charge of his servants, to give them their rations at the proper time? Blessed is that slave whom his master finds so doing when he comes. Truly I say to you, that he will put him in charge of all his possessions. But if that slave says in his heart, 'My master will be a long time in coming,' and begins to beat the slaves, both men and women, and to eat and drink and get drunk; the master of that slave will come on a day when he does not expect him, and at an hour he does not know, and will cut him in pieces and assign him a place with the unbelievers. And that slave who knew his master's will and did

not get ready or act in accord with his will shall receive many lashes, but the one who did not know it and committed deeds worthy of a flogging, will receive but few. And from everyone who has been given much, much shall be required; and to whom they entrusted much, of him they will ask all the more."

Jesus describes a steward as both faithful *and* sensible when he takes care of others' needs at the proper time. This servant is the man who takes the 2 A.M. feeding of his new daughter to let his wife sleep. She is the teacher who stays after school with kids who need help with a concept. It is the youth minister who, instead of always entertaining them, leads his charges into service projects so they can learn the joy of giving. It is the waitress who gives her best service and smile even with non-tippers who have been there before. It is the hospice nurse who helps a family through the final days of a loved one. It is the grown child who gladly diapers an aged, infirm parent. It is the scoutmaster, the preacher, the bricklayer, the prayer warrior, and the electric lineman. A steward is anyone who gives his best effort because they see Jesus in everyone they meet. It certainly includes the armed citizen, the police officer, the firefighter, and the soldier who stand between danger and evil to protect lives. Each of these is dedicated to give others what they need, when they need it.

So stewardship is the basis for self-defense. The steward's job is to be conscious of a duty to preserve and increase what is good and what is God's. As a husband and father, it is clearly my duty to first preserve my life so I am available to my family as long as possible, and then to love and nurture my wife and children and preserve their lives. If necessary, it means I will give up my life to save theirs. Not only that, but the longer I am here, the more good I can do and the more people I can introduce to Jesus.

Think about your own life in relation to how Jesus ends the parable: "To whom much has been given, much will be required." Don't make the common mistake of interpreting this in solely material terms, as in "Wow! I need to guilt trip Bill Gates about this verse so he will give me a grant," or "Rats! God's gonna take most of my hard-earned stuff." That leads to envy and covetousness, concentrating on the stuff you do not have instead of on your riches in Christ. Have you ever stopped to think that if all Jesus *ever* did for you was provide the opportunity to be His child forever, that He had already given you a gift greater than the whole universe *and* that He is under no obligation to give you anything else? (Does that help put your five-year-old Ford in perspective with the new red Lexus that passed you this morning?)

Yet, in addition to salvation, God supplies us with uncountable blessings (both materially and spiritually), including the ability to withstand all the trials of life. David says, "Bless the Lord, O my soul; and all that is within me, bless His holy name. Bless the Lord, O my soul, and *forget none of His benefits …*" (Psalm 103:1-2, emphasis mine). Job, who had spent his life trusting God and being a godly steward, was materially and spiritually blessed and shared his wealth and wisdom with those in need (Job 4:3-4; 29:11-17). Yet when Job saw his wealth and his family destroyed, he said, "Though He slay me, I will hope in Him" (Job 6:10; 13:15). Job had not placed his life and trust in his stuff and family, so when they were destroyed, he was not. Satan distracts us daily to keep us from being the good stewards we could be. He constantly reminds us of all we do not have, causing us to be envious in violation of the 10th commandment ("Thou shalt not covet …" Exodus 20:17). As a result, we become frustrated and angry at God, forgetting to concentrate on all that He has blessed us with. By this stratagem, Satan reduces the blessings we could share with others by ruining our attitudes. So what is the answer?

The Attitude of Gratitude

Here is how stewardship works in the self-defense realm. In the 49 states with concealed carry laws, only two to seven percent of the adult population carry a handgun. Yet in his book *More Guns, Less Crime*, John Lott has demonstrated that even that small a percentage of legal concealed carriers significantly lowers violent crime in those states.[4] That small group of legal carriers has a cumulative effect in preventing violent crime far out of proportion to the numbers involved. There are many reasons why a person would carry a concealed firearm. As a Christian, I believe it flows naturally from gratitude for all the blessings God has given me: salvation, life, family, country, and freedom. If I truly appreciate and value something, I will spend time and treasure to ensure that I keep it and increase it. I have to stay in God's Word and meditate on His blessings so that I am motivated to value them properly and to keep them. Some of those blessings are victory over death (1 Corinthians 15:56-57; 2 Corinthians 9:15), the ability to witness about Jesus (2 Corinthians 2:14-16), enthusiasm in our concern for others (2 Corinthians 8-9, especially 2 Corinthians 8:16), brothers and sisters in Christ who help and support us (Philippians 1:3-11; 1 Thessalonians 3:9), a purpose for our lives (Colossians 3:12-17), a just government and an ordered society (1 Timothy 2:1-3), and the ability to make a judgment based on God's Word (John 8:31-32). The next time you get a case of the "dumb-uglies" ("I'm dumb, I'm ugly, and my momma dresses me funny"), meditate on some of those verses (there are hundreds more), and see if they do not change your perspective.

In light of those verses, we should try to lead grateful lives in all that we do. Gratitude gives us purpose, focus, and goals worth achieving. It gives us perspective when times are tough. It also gives us endurance by keeping our eyes on the prize. Gratitude convinces us of what we are fighting for and why. Gratitude helps us stay on the straight and narrow (which also minimizes our chances of running into criminals). The "attitude of gratitude" is one of our foremost weapons against sin, passivity, and despair: it motivates us to be good shepherds of all that is valuable in God's eyes. When we look into the eyes of our spouse and children, gratitude for God's blessings and the reasons for defending them become real.

So let us investigate what God says about self-defense, realizing that He has our best interests in mind. "For I know the plans I have for you, declares the Lord. Plans for welfare and not for calamity, to give you a future and a hope" (Jeremiah 29:11). If God means for us to have a secure, happy future, does that mean that part of His provision for that future includes allowing us to defend ourselves? Let's see.

Introduction

This book is about decisions. Not the everyday kind such as "What should I wear today?" or "Where shall we eat tonight?" but decisions dealing with life, death, and protecting the innocent. The issue of self-defense concerns decisions of survival for the individual. It can also decide the fate of a nation and its citizens. Survival is the most basic of instincts. Without it, there is no family, community, culture, or state. Unless a person survives, he cannot pass down his genes, ideas, or beliefs. And religious beliefs can affect survival.

The arguments and conclusions in this book reflect my own struggle with this issue. When I was 16, a man called our home and threatened to kill my mother with a .22 rifle. The only weapons my two brothers (ages 15 and 11) and I had to defend her was a 25 pound bow with target arrows and a WWI bayonet. She called the police, who took a report and patrolled frequently. Two neighbors with shotguns came over to sit with us until dad got home. He was working 100 miles away but made it home in an hour-and-a-half through blowing snow and black ice. Our neighbor left a shotgun, and we all calmed down when dad arrived. Within a week, an uncle dropped off a Smith & Wesson .38 and a .22 revolver. We boys got our first handgun training from Dad the next weekend. The police put a trap on our phone, and when the person called to threaten again, he was caught. He turned out to be a harmless psychiatric patient and was returned to the state mental hospital. The fear he sowed passed quickly, and the demystified revolvers held no fascination for us. But the memory of the helpless feeling along with the natural rightness of defending my family stayed with me.

As a college student, I thought little about personal safety other than to make sure that the girls I knew did not walk around campus alone at night. But just after graduation, I read *In Cold Blood* by Truman Capote. Capote's novel forced me to confront the fact that there were truly evil people who would kill me just for the fun of it. I decided I did not want to be a victim, especially like those in Capote's book. I determined I would not die helplessly trussed up while some psycho had his way with me and my family. I would go either running or fighting – but never quietly. Thus, I began to learn seriously about self-defense. In 1983, I joined the police auxiliary in my hometown of Waverly, Ohio. Our captain, a

Christian and an elder in my congregation, began our use-of-force training by quoting Romans 13:4: "The government (police) does not bear the sword (guns, the power of capital punishment) in vain (it works to deter criminals)." This was my first exposure to the idea that there might be a Biblical basis for self-defense. Later that same year, I read Massad Ayoob's book *The Truth About Self-Protection*. His chapter "The Will to Resist" was the first serious treatment I had seen on the ethics/morals of use-of-force against criminals and during war.

At that point, I began my own study on the Bible and self-defense. As a Christian, I realized that my decision not to be a victim was spiritually sinful if Jesus condemns it. My purpose was to find every relevant passage concerning self-defense and analyze it in context until I had an answer. I based this study on my belief that the Bible is the inspired, complete Word of God. I hold that the Holy Bible is the final word on all matters of theology, faith, and practice. In the end, I will not be judged by what I thought or hoped the Bible said, but by the very standards God set forth in it. As I started law school, I began to compare the Bible passages with the law, and I was able to apply them as a city prosecutor, city judge, police trainer, and expert witness on firearms and self-defense.

Some might say that the right to self-defense is a given, yet many people do not think about the basics of survival. Most have never taken a first-aid course, owned a home-fire extinguisher, or if they own a gun, have never attended a training course on how to use a firearm safely and legally. If they ever consider a criminal assault possible, most people have no idea how to prevent the crime other than to say, "Stay out of the bad side of town."

Those who have given serious thought to survival include many Christians. Most Christians see no conflict between following God and applying passive self-defense measures, such as door locks, alarm systems, and dogs. However, when it comes to the use of weapons, they are troubled by a tradition of pacifism in Christian history. They are torn between their God-given moral sense of survival and the pacifism (supposedly based in the scriptures) espoused by various theologians and denominations through twenty centuries. Faced with this dilemma, most Christians will do one of two things: go with passive defense only or embrace using weapons and trust that God will forgive them if they are forced to harm a criminal.

This book proposes a third way: study the Bible, see if God has addressed self-defense, decide what His will is on the basis of Scripture, and then proceed with our hearts and minds at rest.

A person using this book and any English version of the Bible can study and compare my arguments with Scripture and make an informed decision about matters of self-defense. I hope this book will give you a basic understanding of the biblical justification for self-defense. Once you understand that God gives permission and even commands that we defend the innocent, you can arm yourself and train to be effective without moral qualms.

This book includes chapters concerning the use of force by the police and military. When I was a prosecutor working with police officers, many of them asked me to address how a Christian police officer should conduct himself. While I have tried to describe Biblical conduct for the police and for the military, I have a second goal: to help reduce the incidence of post-traumatic-stress disorder (PTSD). In our current war against radical Islamic terrorists, our military has suffered the highest rates of PTSD in its history. Many factors contribute to this, but certainly one of the biggest is the moral uneasiness about killing. Human beings have a God-given aversion to killing other people, but the Bible tells us that evil people and nations sometimes force us to do so. I hope that the Scriptures I cite and the arguments I present will help police officers and soldiers understand that taking a life in justifiable law-enforcement situations or to protect our country is not murder. God knows the difference between the two. I pray that this book will give police officers and soldiers confidence as they go about their duties and that it will provide healing in the aftermath.

And certainly, I hope this book will help civilians who are undecided about self-defense as well as those who are pacifists to make a biblically informed decision about using justifiable force. In a criminal attack, moral uncertainty causes hesitation, and hesitation can spell disaster. Finally, to readers who are not Christians, my prayer is that this book will help you see that God cares for you and your physical, mental, and spiritual well-being; that He addresses self-defense in a logical, reasonable, and loving manner; that Jesus Christ is the embodiment of His love; and finally, that you may come to faith in Him.

As I said previously, this book is about making a decision concerning self-defense, a decision that might be one of the most important you ever make.

Greater love has no one
than this, that one lay down
his life for his friends.

John 15:13 NASB

Self-Defense

God's Pattern for Self-Defense in the Old Testament

"The wicked spies upon the righteous, and seeks to kill him. The Lord will not leave him in his hand, or let him be condemned when he is judged" (Psalms 37:32-33). Interesting, huh? These verses describe a scenario repeated throughout human history: (1) Predators seek targets of opportunity, and (2) their targets turn the tables on them. Put yourself in the following scene.

You follow your wife home one night after meeting her at an after-work function. She stops at the drive-up ATM, so you park and get out about 20 yards away. As you watch, you hear shoes grinding on asphalt and see a man coming around the corner of the bank. He heads toward your wife's car. So do you. In his left hand is a large knife. As he closes in, he yells, "Give it up!" at your wife. One-fifth of a second passes before your right hand sweeps back your jacket to grab your gun – a move you have practiced a thousand times. Time and movement seem to slow radically now that the situation is real. You yell, "Don't move! Drop that weapon!" in your best command voice. He is now only five yards from her, spinning to face you as you raise your gun to point at his chest. He clumsily tries to change direction and charge you. You could swear he is on top of you, and you hear two small pops as the muzzle flashes in the night. His arms flail. The knife seems to fly from his hand in slow motion as he stumbles sideways, falling about three yards away. You realize that your wife has backed out of the ATM and is okay. By sheer will and training, you rip your attention away, shifting your feet 90 degrees and sweeping the gun to your left. Over your sights, you see a second guy standing 20 yards away in front of an Accord. All at once, he drops a ball bat, raises his hands, and screams, "Don't shoot!"

A woman waiting for her turn at the ATM sees the whole thing. Your wife dials 911 while you control the scene. The second mugger lies down at your command to wait for the police. The cops and EMS arrive. They arrest the accomplice and take the injured robber to the emergency room. Later that night, you will thank God for that shooting school, the legal use-of-force class, and the instructors at both. Right now, though, you thank Him that your wife is alive.

Days later, based on the witnesses' testimony and the physical evidence, the police clear you of any wrongdoing. You have restless nights for a couple of weeks, but the adrenaline eventually flushes out of your system, and the nightmares pass. Your gun-savvy preacher helps you through it, reminding you of verses like Psalms 37:32-33. Like a thousand other times since you became a Christian, you have literally lived out God's Word – in a different way than ever before, but it was not unexpected. You were prepared because God's Word and common sense told you that predators are out there.

Psalm 37 and many other verses in the Old Testament remind us that the Lord will help the righteous defeat the wicked (as in my hypothetical situation above). However, some folks believe that the defeat will be accomplished by God alone. In other words, they expect that the righteous will be saved by a miracle. That is possible. I would never say God could not or would not do that for someone, but that kind of care is usually reserved for special people of God. When three companies of soldiers were sent by King Ahaziah of Israel to capture Elijah, the prophet called down lightning to burn up the first two companies (2 Kings 1). When his successor prophet, Elisha, was surrounded by Syrian troops coming to capture him, Elisha had God strike them temporarily blind. Then Elisha handed them over as prisoners to King Joram (2 Kings 6:8-23). There are other examples. In each case of divine intervention, however, God protected a special person for a special purpose. I am not a great prophet like Elijah or Elisha. I am not special. I am just a person serving Jesus the best I can. So barring a miracle for God's own reasons and without personal guarantees, I am on my own regarding self-defense.

Did God mean for His people to rely solely on His divine intervention when home invaders kick down their doors? If so, why does Exodus 22:2-3 say we are allowed to kill the burglar? I have never seen a verse backing the assumption that God is obligated to miraculously save us. If so, then when we consider all the godly people who are harmed by criminals each day, we must conclude that God is not holding up His end of the bargain. That assumption cannot be true because "God is not slow about His promise" (2 Peter 3:9a) nor is He able to lie (Hebrews

6:18; Titus 1:2). The fact is, God never promised that He would shield us from every physical threat (Luke 13:1-5). He does, however, guarantee that we will never be tempted beyond what we can personally stand (1 Corinthians 10:13).

From the principles and history of the Bible, it is certain that we must exercise self-reliance in these matters. God could have easily provided for and promised our physical safety by miraculous intervention. Instead, verses such as Exodus 22:2-3 and Leviticus 19:16b say that He authorizes us to defend ourselves and others.

By the way, did you ever notice that people who reject firearms and other means of active resistance on principle never advertise the fact? When was the last time you saw a pacifist's house with a sign out front that read: "Christians here! No guns, dogs, locks, alarms, or martial artists. Everyone welcome! Come on in and take what you want!" If they were consistent, they would have such signs. Should we reject guns and other modern defensive innovations that make us equal to the greater size, strength, or superior numbers of criminals? If so, how could we plan for our family's future in the chaotic society that would result? We would surely have to employ far more police, but all of them would have to be non-Christians (if Christians must be pacifists). But if we are pacifists, should we allow armed people to protect us? Would we not be sending them to Hell by proxy? It is an interesting puzzle.

There is a society where all weapons are totally banned, the police are constantly patrolling and never more than a few yards away. And all the houses have state-of-the-art security. Yet, this society has a higher per capita rate of violent crime than any other. This society is found in our American prisons. Nobody wants to be in there, yet it is the most controlled environment in the nation. Without the equalizer of guns, the bad guys would improvise weapons and rule by force-of-numbers just as they do in prison. This is a completely different societal outcome than that predicted by gun banners and pacifists. It sounds an awful lot like the pre-flood world. Did God intend such an outcome?

So starting with the Mosaic Law, let's consider what God has to say on the subject of self-defense and base our conclusions on His attitude about it.

General Examples of Self-Defense in Old Testament

The only verses in the Bible that specifically address killing in self-defense are in Exodus 22:2-4 as part of the general criminal/civil code listed in Exodus 20-23. These verses state specifically:

> If the thief is caught while breaking in, and is struck so that he dies, there will be no blood guiltiness on his account. But if sun has risen on him, there will be blood guiltiness on his account. He shall surely make restitution. If he owns nothing, he shall be sold for his theft. If what he stole is actually found alive in his possession, whether an ox or a donkey or a sheep, he shall pay double.

The Mosaic Law allows killing a burglar for a burglary at night, (verse 3) but not during daylight (verse 4). Jesus later addresses in parables the common sense of armed home defense (Luke 11:21-22).

Exodus 22:2-4 allows killing a burglar at night but not by day. Why the distinction? Killing at night is justified because of the necessity of hand-to-hand combat in the dark with foes of unknown number and weaponry. In addition, the homeowner would fear for women and children in the house if he were overcome or distracted while fighting and outflanked by the burglar's gang. The victim would need to strike quickly and decisively. All these factors make attempts at merely apprehending the intruders extremely dangerous for the homeowner. Yet, by daylight, the number of assailants, their whereabouts, and their weapons could be readily ascertained. Neighbors would be awake. As in English common law, the "hue and cry" could be raised to summon neighbors to help and pursue in daylight. The suspects could easily be identified as they fought or fled, then captured and turned over to the Mosaic judicial system. Daylight made quick escape unlikely, especially since horses were never common in Israel.

In this instance, God allows killing to prevent a night burglary. Burglary is generally defined in modern statutes as "breaking into an occupied dwelling with intent to commit a crime therein."[1] A "dwelling" is a building normally used for lodging, sleeping, or living. Exodus 22:2 allows a burglar to be killed even when his only intent is theft (the text calls him a "thief"). As in the modern statute, the burglar has broken into a dwelling to commit a crime. Yet, it is logical to assume that at night the homeowner cannot be sure whether the burglar's intent is theft, murder, rape, kidnapping, arson, or another life-threatening act. Common law since Anglo-Saxon times has held that a "man's home is his castle." It is an extension of us, not just mere property; therefore, the law traditionally allows deadly force to defend ourselves from burglars. It is well-known in law enforcement circles that anyone who knowingly breaks into an occupied home is almost certainly there to inflict bodily harm on the occupants, notwithstanding any intent he may have toward their property.[2] During a home invasion such as described in Exodus 22:2-4, deadly force is clearly the proper response.

Depending on the state, deadly force is often justified simply by the act of burglary, regardless of whether the actual intent of the burglar is merely to take property. Alabama is one of these states. The self-defense statute says, "A person may use deadly physical force if the actor reasonably believes that such other person is committing or about to commit a ... burglary *in any degree* ... (emphasis added).[3] Alabama has three degrees of burglary. First degree burglary is entering a dwelling with intent to commit a crime therein while armed, causing injury, or threatening immediate use

If the thief is caught while breaking in, and is struck so that he dies, there will be no blood guiltiness on his account. But if sun has risen on him, there will be blood guiltiness on his account. He shall surely make restitution. If he owns nothing, he shall be sold for his theft. If what he stole is actually found alive in his possession, whether an ox or a donkey or a sheep, he shall pay double.

of a dangerous instrument.[4] Second degree burglary includes unlawful entry of a building (a non-dwelling, such as an office) with the same dangerous behaviors as in First degree, but also including unlawful entry of a dwelling to commit a property offense or any felony.[5] Third degree burglary includes unlawful entry of a building, (not a dwelling) whether occupied or not, to commit *any* crime therein.[6]

Note that Alabama's self-defense statute allows deadly force regardless of the degree of burglary and regardless of whether any person is intentionally or directly threatened by the burglar's activity. Other states such as Alaska, Florida, New York, and North Dakota have similar statutes.[7] Exodus 22:2 states the same, *with* the condition that deadly force was for *night* burglaries only (although the daylight bloodguilt on the homeowner assumes the burglar is unarmed). Alabama and many other states, however, have no such daylight/dark restrictions, even though only property is jeopardized because of the common law view that your house or place of work is an extension of yourself. In Moses' day, burglars were limited to hand-held, sharp, or blunt weapons (bows would be too cumbersome in the narrow space of a home). Given the range and deadliness of firearms in our present day, allowing the victim to use deadly force day or night is logical. A burglary victim could easily end up dead if he does not react quickly to a felon who is armed with a firearm or even with an impact or blade weapon at common room distances. Mike Corwin, the captain who taught my auxiliary police officer use-of-force class in 1983 (and an elder in my congregation) gave this instruction: "If a burglar is in your house, and you can clearly see he has a gun – *don't hesitate to shoot him in the back!*"

"Why?" we asked, "Aren't you supposed to give him a chance to surrender?"

"No!" he replied, "Because he's already got adrenaline and/or drugs pumping through him. Your reaction delay will be two-tenths of a second from the instant you perceive he's turning on you before you can begin to react. Warn him, and he will spin and fire. A tie in this gunfight means you *lose!*" Massad Ayoob, world famous police/civilian use-of-force instructor echoes this analysis in both his outstanding *Judicious Use of Deadly Force Class* and his book *In the Gravest Extreme.*[8] I teach my students the same.

In my classes, I point out that Alabama law (and the law in most states) clearly distinguishes property crimes from crimes that endanger life and limb and allows only reasonable, appropriate non-deadly force to protect it (13A-3-26). If a thief is stealing your car from your driveway, you cannot run out and shoot him. This is a problem for the police and for the insurance company. (Ditto for shoplifting, pick-pocketing, and so forth.) As Massad Ayoob has said, if the burglar is only there to steal and not harm, is killing the burglar to keep your stuff more moral than him killing you to take yours?[9] This is the sentiment of life-over-mere property expressed in Exodus 22:2-4.

Exodus 22:3-4 says that when caught, the thief must make restitution. If the thief has nothing to repay, though, he would be sold into slavery (in effect, imprisoned), which lasted six years (Exodus 21:2). The slavery would be to another Israelite, and slavery of fellow countrymen under the Mosaic law was never permanent (unless the slave liked his life with his master so much that he agreed to stay for life, Exodus 21:2-6). There were no prisons in ancient Israel, hence the slavery sentence. This six-year sentence compares favorably with modern statutes. In Alabama, Burglary 1st is a Class-A felony, with a punishment range of 10 years to life. Burglary 2nd is a Class-B felony with a punishment range of 2 to 20 while 3rd degree is a Class-C with a range of 1 year and a day up to 10 years. With time off for good behavior, the felon routinely serves one-third of his sentence in prison, the rest on probation. Like many states, Alabama has a habitual offender law, which allows the judge to enhance sentence on repeat offenders up to life without parole in certain circumstances.

Many studies have found that habitual offender laws keep the most dangerous offenders in jail longer.[10] In addition, the cost of incarceration is far less than the total cost of letting them out. When they are released, the costs of hospital bills for new victims; replacing lost/destroyed property; and capture, trial, and appeals for multiple crimes are many times greater than keeping them in prison. Fundamental fairness requires giving bad guys a chance to learn from their mistakes and get on the right path. But for those who will not change, Proverbs 29:1 says: "A man who remains stiff-necked after many rebukes will suddenly be destroyed without remedy." Habitual felons can have their sentences enhanced until they die in prison. Others push their luck in repeat offenses until one night an armed store-clerk ends their life and career. Based on Exodus 22:1-4 plus the stories of Abraham and Moses, it is logical to conclude that God allowed the Israelites to use deadly force to defend their lives, those of others, and their homes when necessary.

The Mosaic Law was specifically designed to encourage lawful and discourage unlawful behavior by coming down hard on criminals: "They that forsake the law praise the wicked, but those who keep the law strive with them" (Proverbs 28:4). This verse is one among several that say we are to resist evildoers, starting with Leviticus 19:16. We are not to stand by and allow our neighbors to be harmed. That is not "loving your neighbor" as Leviticus 19:18 commands. God intended that we individually participate in defeating evil people.

Psalm 82:2 says that we judge unjustly when we show partiality to the wicked. One way we show partiality is to let the unjust get away with crimes. Psalm 82:3 says, "Vindicate the weak and fatherless; do justice to the afflicted and destitute."

Then Psalm 82:4 commands positive action: "*Rescue the weak and needy; deliver them out of the hand of the wicked*" (emphasis mine). God's command is that we intervene to prevent crime!

God did not leave the Israelites to guess about His intent in this matter. He had Solomon, the wisest man who ever lived, address it. Read Proverbs 3:27-28: "Do not withhold good from those to whom it is due, when it is in your power to do it. Do not say to your neighbor, 'Go, and come back and tomorrow I will give it.'" If government gives me the legal right to carry concealed weapons and I have the training and skill to help, this verse leaves no question as to my moral obligation. It is clearly "in my power" to help. Moreover, verse 28 says that my help is due now! My help must be timely. I cannot say, "Well, I called 911; is it my fault if they didn't get there in time?" God says it certainly is my fault.

Solomon further dismisses the "Who, me?" mentality in Proverbs 24:11-12.

Deliver those who are being taken away to death, and those who are staggering to slaughter, O hold them back. If you say 'See, we did not know this,' does He not consider it who weighs the hearts? And does He not know it who keeps your soul? And will He not render to man according to his work?

These are tough words and high standards based on inescapable responsibility. Delivering those taken to be slaughtered reminds me of the story of a Vietnam vet in Anniston, Alabama, in the early 90s. A three-man team had robbed two Shoney's restaurants in Birmingham the previous month. With each incident, they became increasingly brutal toward the employees and customers. When they hit the Anniston Shoney's, they pistol whipped a couple of patrons and started forcing everyone into the walk-in fridge (usually a prelude to execution). The veteran had dived under his table when they entered the restaurant and announced the robbery. One of the perpetrators saw him as the others herded the victims. He came toward the vet, pointed his gun at him, and ordered him out. As he stood up, the vet drew his .45 automatic and shot the would-be robber. The other two robbers high-tailed it for the door, but the vet wounded one on the way out. The cops caught the third soon after. This armed hero ended the careers of three violent felons, saving not only the people in that restaurant but potential future victims as well. He embodied God's will as stated by Solomon.

Pacifist Christians should think carefully about Proverbs 24:12. Pleading ignorance about self-defense with all the information available today does not please God. He will render to each of us according to our work. On judgment day, would you rather be that Vietnam vet or just another helpless victim being marched to death without a clue how to save yourself, let alone others? God is clear in the Old Testament. He commands the godly to be prepared and active in aiding those in need, be it food, clothing, first-aid, or self-defense.

Corporate Self-Defense

God allowed His people the corporate means to resist evil by force (Joshua 1:1-9). God does not equate all killing with murder, so He allowed them to conquer Canaan and to defend themselves thereafter. By *corporate self-defense,* I mean individual self-defense expanded by numbers of family, tribes, or countrymen to form de-facto "vigilance committees" or militias to enforce the law. They did not have police forces back then. Today, we practice corporate self-defense with professional police forces and legally armed citizens.

An example of corporate self-defense occurs in the book of Esther. Esther was the new queen of Persia, wife of King Ahasereus (better known as Xerxes to history). One of Xerxes' highest ministers was Haman. He had an implacable hatred for the Jews, possibly because he was descended from the Amalekite royal family (Esther 3:1). Neither he nor Xerxes knew Esther was a Jew. Haman, incensed at not receiving his due respect from the Jewish gatekeeper, Mordecai (Esther's uncle and foster-father), devised a plot to exterminate all the Jews in the empire (Esther 3:1-7).

Esther exposed Haman's plot to the king who then wrote a decree that allowed the Jews to defend themselves from their enemies on the appointed day. He granted them permission to form militias and to defend themselves from anyone who might attack them and to alert all the citizens of his empire. He further gave the Jews permission to plunder their enemies and to enslave their families

Deliver those who are being taken away to death, and those who are staggering to slaughter, O hold them back. If you say 'See, we did not know this,' does He not consider it who weighs the hearts? And does He not know it who keeps your soul? And will He not render to man according to his work?

(Esther 8:9-11). The Jews scared many of their enemies into inaction simply by preparation, causing some to convert to Judaism (Esther 8:15-17). For those enemies who chose to try their chance in battle anyway, the Jews killed 75,000 foes across the empire, but they did not plunder their goods or harm or enslave their families. Their sole motive was self-defense (Esther 9:15-16).

Note that the Jews cowed most of their enemies without having to fight. Modern studies show that criminals are deterred by victims who may be armed or who are willing to fight back.[11] Other studies have shown that about 93 percent of the time when a cop or civilian pulls a gun on a criminal, he doesn't have to shoot.[12] Instead, the bad guy runs away or stays put until the police come. Thus, like the Jews in Esther, simply demonstrating the determination and ability to use deadly force when threatened can be the greatest factor in *not* having to employ it.

Nehemiah had to deal with a similar problem, which he solved by use of corporate defense to rebuild Jerusalem's walls. They had many enemies around them: Samaritans, Ammonites, and Arabs. If the Jews fortified their capital, it would turn the balance of power against these marauders. These enemies tried all kinds of psychological warfare and espionage, and they even mustered troops to demonstrate outside the walls to stop the rebuilding (Nehemiah 2:19-20; 4:1-3, 6-12, 6:1-4). When the Jewish people became discouraged, Nehemiah reacted.

Nehemiah had all the workers carry their weapons to the worksites. He reminded them that they were building and fighting for their families and homes (Nehemiah 4:14). Half wore their swords while working, and the other half stood guard by shifts (Nehemiah 4:15-23). Their motto became "Our God will fight for us" because self-defense is God's idea (Nehemiah 4:20). When their enemies saw their armed watchfulness, they slunk away, and the wall was finished in only 52 days (Nehemiah 4:15; 6:15-16). Nehemiah gives an example of what Proverbs 14:19 says: "The evil will bow down before the good, and the wicked at the gates of the righteous."

Improper Self-Defense in the Old Testament

The sons of Jacob give us a good example of improper use of force. This story comes from Genesis 34. While Jacob and his family were camped near a Canaanite city, Shechem saw Jacob's daughter Dinah and kidnapped and raped her. However, he wanted to take her for his wife and asked his dad to pay the bride price so he could marry her. Jacob's boys pretended to agree, but with one condition: circumcision. If the men of Shechem would agree to be circumcised, then Dinah would marry Shechem.

Shechem convinced the townspeople that if they did the deal with these nomadic hayseeds, eventually the smart city boys would inherit, buy, or steal all their property. The promise of wealth convinced them, so all the Shechemite males were circumcised.

Dinah's full-blood brothers, Simeon and Levi, waited three days until the Shechemites were too sore to move. Carrying swords, they sneaked into town (I suppose at night) and moved from house to house, murdering all the men. Their brothers followed, grabbing the women and children and plundering the town. I assume they were aided by their servants. By the laws then and now, this was vengeance and premeditated murder.

Unlike Abram's pursuit and slaughter of the kidnappers in Genesis 14, the acts of Jacob's boys were neither legal nor moral self-defense. Yes, Shechem kidnapped and raped their sister, but according to the custom of the day, his offer to pay their price for her and honorably marry her was the accepted way of settling such offenses. Simeon and Levi were condemned by their own father on his deathbed:

> Simeon and Levi are brothers. Their swords are implements of violence. Let my soul not enter into their council. Let not my glory be united with their assembly because in their anger they slew men, and in their self-will they lamed oxen. Cursed be their anger, for it is fierce, and their wrath, for it is cruel. I will disperse them in Jacob, and scatter them in Israel (Genesis 49:5-7).

In modern self-defense, deadly force can only be used when the felon is in the act of rape. You cannot shoot your daughter's rapist as he runs up the street. That is vengeance. The crime is over. You can capture him and hand him over to the police, but you cannot just kill him.

Righteous Self-Defense in the Old Testament

A story of righteous self-defense is found in 2 Samuel 2 in the account of the civil war between King David and King Saul's loyalists after Saul's death. Saul's son Ishbosheth claimed the kingship. His general was Abner who had served Saul. David's general was Joab, with his brothers Abishai, a captain, and Asahel, a private soldier.

2 Samuel 2:12 tells the story of the battle of the Pool of Gibeon. Instead of a pitched battle, Joab and Abner agreed to a duel to decide the issue. They each selected 12 of their best fighters, but the fight ended in a tie with all 24 warriors killed. Enraged, both armies joined combat, and Joab's men put Abner's men to flight. Asahel, Joab's younger brother, pursued Abner himself.

At this point, Abner's men were no longer a coherent fighting force and, having demonstrated by running that they no longer wanted to fight, my opinion is that any confrontation thereafter became an individual fight – a matter of self-defense. Asahel (who was very fast) caught up to Abner and ordered him to stand and fight. (Joab and Abishai were warriors of long experience who had shared David's exile and battles during that seven year period. This is the first we hear of Asahel, so I assume he was a young and relatively inexperienced fighter.) Abner kept running but warned Asahel to take on someone of his own age lest Abner be forced to slaughter him with his superior strength and skill. Asahel wouldn't listen and sped up until he was right behind Abner, who warned him again, saying he would be ashamed to have to kill Joab's brother. But Asahel closed in. Abner stopped abruptly, held his spear horizontally, and Asahel ran into the sharpened bronze buttspike.[13] Asahel's momentum drove the spear through his chest and out his back. Abner's trick proves an old lawyer's saying: "Experience and treachery beat youth and enthusiasm every time." A truce was declared at dusk. Joab lost only 19 men, but Abner lost 360.

Abner's killing of Asahel was clearly legitimate self-defense. First, it was war. Every combatant on the field was fair game. Second, Abner twice warned his attacker before striking. When tactically possible, both citizens and cops should warn attackers before employing force. Abner even went the second mile by warning a combatant on a battlefield, which he had no legal or moral duty to do.

Third, he struck only when there was no other reasonable, safe alternative to defend his life. Fourth, Asahel's motive had changed from that of an individual soldier to an opportunist. When Abner warned Asahel, he said, "turn yourself to your right or your left, and take hold of one of the young men for yourself, and *take for yourself his spoil*" (verse 21, emphasis mine). Like the warriors in *The Iliad*, Asahel's incentive was the glory he would gain from killing the commander of the rebel army and for the value of stripping Abner's apparently glorious armor and weapons. Asahel's motives were those of a murderous thief, not a soldier advancing his cause. Therefore, Abner slaying him in one-on-one combat was clearly legal and moral self-defense, both in his day and ours.

The lesson for us is that to be justifiable, any force must be reasonable and necessary. *Necessary* means there was no *safe* alternative. Abner could no longer retreat without fighting, since Asahel was faster and refused to quit. But motives of vengeance (as with Levi and Simeon), illegal gain, or preserving some macho image (as with Asahel) are never acceptable to God or society. Self-defense must be legal and moral.

Mindset and Preparation

Never make the mistake that crime is a random chance or an isolated incident. German General Karl von Clauswitz, the 19th century theorist on war, said that war is not an act isolated from the goals of the nation starting the war.[1] The aggressor nation makes a calculated decision to go to war based on a cost/benefit analysis. Seventeen years of dealing with criminals has led me to the same conclusion about them: criminals do a cost/benefit analysis before committing crime (Proverbs 1:10-19). The criminal assailant reaches a decision that the crime benefits him: sexually, emotionally, socially, financially, or materially. "The soul of the wicked desires evil. His neighbor has no favor [gets no mercy] in his eyes" (Proverbs 21:10). His thought process usually is not deep, and it is usually based on instant gratification. But he quickly decides that making you his prey will make his life better, and his chances of getting caught or harmed are low. The initiative (and often surprise) is usually his. He knows what he is about to do. You do not know. Consequently, self-defense is reactive. If you are going to react successfully to a predator, simply hoping for a dumb crook and a lucky outcome are not wise. You must mentally prepare, or the first (and possibly the last) thing that goes through your mind will be, "I can't believe this is happening to me!"

Analyze that phrase a moment: "I can't believe ...." Though you know it is a tough world out there, you really thought people like you were immune from criminal violence. Why are you so special? "This is happening to *me.*" You thought robbery, rape, and kidnapping were outside the spectrum of misfortunes that could touch nice people like you. Sure, you are special. God explicitly promised you special protection (or you figured you could assume so). Of course, other normal bad things have happened to you: an appendectomy, the car wreck where you broke your ankle, that unexpected layoff – "But *this,* to *me?*" Consider the chances. Grasp reality. Study the facts. "Every prudent man acts with knowledge, but a fool displays folly" (Proverbs 16:13), and "Before destruction the heart of man is haughty, but humility goes before honor" (Proverbs 18:12). Good swimmers wear life jackets in boats because they could knock themselves cold as they fall off the boat. The vest is designed to keep your head above water, conscious or not. Embrace the possibility of victimization, and you will achieve the first level of self-defense: *awareness.*

Awareness

Awareness creates alertness. It encourages education and creates resolve. "A wise man is strong, and a man of knowledge increases power. For by wise guidance you will wage war, and in an abundance of counselors there is victory" (Proverbs 24:5). Read a few classic books on the subject of self-defense. Start with Massad Ayoob's book *The Truth about Self-Protection.*[2] It covers a multitude of subjects from locks and alarms to dealing with lawyers and learning first aid. You should learn the color-code of awareness popularized by the late Jeff Cooper, the father of modern gun fighting. In his book *The Principles of Personal Defense,* Cooper advises you to train yourself to notice suspicious things, actions, and the people around you.[3] With a little preparation, you are able to describe and monitor the teenager 20 yards behind you. When driving, you know that the white Cadillac CTS just moved into your blind spot on your left, and you are gaining too fast on the semi ahead. So you slow down and stay in your lane until the CTS passes. You practice walking with purpose and confidence, like you own your space, which sends a clear message to any would-be attacker that you are not worth the trouble. As you walk into a convenience store (police call them "stop and robs" and "murder marts"), you scan its layout and inhabitants. You learn to sit facing the door in restaurants. If you are elderly, you should read *Surviving the Age of Fear* by hero-cop Bill Langlois.[4] Your whole manner must force a potential predator to assume that not only are you aware of him, you are also at the next level: *physical preparedness.*

Physical Preparedness

Physical preparation is a combination of several factors. Physical fitness is the first. You should achieve a level of musculature that will allow you to throw an effective punch or kick without pulling or tearing your own muscles (which would keep you from continuing the fight beyond the first punch). Your wind should be good enough to get you through the fight or escape. You should be flexible enough to jump a fence or make an evasive turn without pulling a hamstring or tearing an ACL.

The second part of physical preparedness is actual proficiency with your chosen weapon or martial art. Six months in a dojo does not accomplish proficiency in the martial arts nor will one NRA gun safety course make you competent to defend yourself. Years of mastery will not stay with you unless you keep up some practice. Physical skills are perishable and practice improves both technique and speed. Do you really know how to use your pepper spray? Did you buy two canisters so you can practice with one? Is it in a place where you can get to it easily? Ditto for your gun. Have you had professional training? Can you conceal your gun effectively? Can you hit your target under stress? Can you draw and present it effectively? Is it powerful enough with enough shots to stop one or more attackers? Do you know when you can and cannot use force legally? Be honest with yourself about this because your life and freedom and that of others may one day depend on it. The Bible is clear that we should be willing to learn the law: "He who turns his ear from listening to the law, even his prayer is an abomination" (Proverbs 28:9) and "he who scorns instruction will pay for it, but he who respects a command is rewarded" (Proverbs 13:13).

The following is a true story of what can happen when you do not think things through. It is from an appellate case that I handled at the Alabama Court of Criminal Appeals. An old man ran a country convenience store where he cashed checks on Fridays. Two guys in their early twenties decided to rob him. They broke the padlock on the door to a bedroom in the mobile home where one lived and stole dad's Rossi .32 caliber, five-shot revolver. As they drove the country lanes to the store, the designated robber fired the gun out the window to make sure it worked and then reloaded it. Like many sociopaths, he was determined to overcome his victim's resistance and did not mind using deadly force to do so.

The old store owner had considered the danger and made what he thought was adequate preparation. He figured that having thousands of dollars on Friday nights might make him a target, so he had a High Standard .22 caliber two-shot derringer with him.

The robber burst in, announcing a hold up. When he tried to draw the .32, the hammer spur caught on his jeans pocket. As he struggled with it, the old man drew his derringer. He missed the thug with the first shot, but the second struck the robber next to his navel. Hurt but still going, the thug finally pulled his revolver and fired all five rounds. Four struck the old man, three non-fatally; the last round went through this right auricle, killing him. The thug took about $2,100 out of the victim's pockets, but he never touched the cash drawer, which had over $4,000 in it. By the time the robbers sped away, the shopkeeper was dead.

A neighbor found the store owner an hour later. The sheriff determined from blood on the floor that the robber was wounded, and he alerted area hospitals. Sure enough, the thug showed up in the ER, was arrested, and confessed. He was sentenced to life-without-parole. The victim's lucky shot at least insured the capture of his murderer, but if he had sought advice and purchased a more capable gun, he might have lived and left his killer on a morgue slab instead.

The old shopkeeper's first mistake was his choice of handgun. The High Standard derringer holds only two shots. Its trigger pull is a problem, too. It takes about 21 pounds of pressure to pull the trigger on this 16-ounce pistol. This heavy pull on a light gun makes it extremely difficult to keep its small sights and short barrel on target on a range, let alone under the reduced coordination of the adrenaline dump when you are fighting for your life. For about the same price, he could have bought a Beretta .22 auto Model 21A. Because of a much lighter trigger pull, the Beretta is much more accurate than the derringer, has eight shots, and is quickly reloadable with a second seven-shot magazine. With eight accurate rounds, the store owner would have had a much better chance of hitting his attacker multiple times or even making a head shot. Better still, a used five-shot, .38 caliber snub-nose, which has adequate stopping power, would have been about the same price, is more accurate, and is faster to reload with speed loaders than the derringer. Both guns are as concealable as the derringer and both are far more effective. As it turned out, the two-shot .22 derringer was a fatal mistake.

While perfectly capable of killing an adult human, a .22 caliber bullet is a poor stopper. The idea is to *stop* the deadly criminal activity as quickly as possible. Twenty-two hundredths of an inch in diameter and weighing less than a tenth of an ounce, a .22 caliber bullet transfers very little shock (or punch) to the body or to the nervous system. Unless the bullet hits the brain or the spine, a one-shot-stop is very unlikely. If it hits bone in the body, the .22 bullet often shatters, sending shrapnel out to cause bleeding. Hitting bone can also cause it to ricochet inside the body, causing severe tissue damage and more bleeding than from the track of the entry wound. However, it imparts insufficient shock and pain to stop an attacker who could be high on drugs or adrenaline-fueled determination. A person hit with a .22 caliber bullet usually falls down only after his blood pressure drops below that by which the brain can maintain consciousness. By that time, he can do serious harm to others. Any handgun bullet is an iffy bet to stop an opponent instantly, but your chances are much better with calibers larger than .22 or .25. (Jeff Cooper says that if you shoot someone with a .25, he will only get very angry and do you serious harm.) As John Hall, former head of the FBI's Firearms Training Unit once taught me, "When it come to stopping power, big holes are better than little holes; many holes are better than fewer holes."

The lesson is to study, get advice, and get training. Do not rely on "brother-in-law info," or select a security system or gun because a salesman is likeable. The lives of you and your loved ones are at stake: "He who walks with wise men will be wise, but the companion of fools will suffer harm" (Proverbs 13:20). Your future ability to provide and care for them must not be compromised. Give it at least as much study and attention as you would in buying a car. Ask yourself these questions: For what purpose will you use the gun? Will you carry it or keep it in the house or car? What safety measures will you put in place to keep unauthorized hands off it? What is the most powerful caliber of weapon you can proficiently control? What threats do you anticipate, based on your neighborhood, occupation, and lifestyle? To help you answer these questions, find an NRA Certified handgun-safety/personal-protection counselor. Leave your ego at the door and think, read, and listen. Then choose wisely.

Legal and Moral Instruction

Finally, your physical preparedness is woefully and dangerously incomplete without legal and moral instruction. For moral instruction you have started with this book; for legal instruction, you need to find a gun-savvy lawyer. "Where there is no revelation, the people are unrestrained, but happy is he who keeps the law" (Proverbs 29:18). One of the biggest flaws in most people's self-defense preparation is the failure to get legal training. Most people buy a gun, put it in the bedside drawer, and think, "I'm protected!" You might as well put a piano in your parlor, never take a lesson, and claim you are Elton John. Doing the latter will only result in embarrassment. Doing the former could land you in jail or in the morgue or could endanger innocent bystanders. Knowing when to use your gun is at least as important as knowing how. Guess wrong, and you could lose your freedom, your possessions, a loved one, or your life.

For those of you who think you can get away with owning a gun without legal training, you have never been in my shoes. You have never faced the family of a man appealing a manslaughter conviction. He was a good citizen who legally carried a concealed .22 revolver for seven years, but he was totally ignorant of the laws of use-of-force. Drawn into a domestic fight between his brother and the new husband of the brother's ex-wife, he introduced the gun into a totally inappropriate situation for that level of force. The gun went off accidentally, and he got 10 years (the minimum in Alabama for death by firearm) for manslaughter. That man's legal ignorance caused the death of one man, his own imprisonment, and his family to be devastated. They lost him and their financial resources when they had to pay for the cost of the trial and appeals. Legal training, such as in the class I teach, would have saved him all the heartache. As it was, F. Lee Bailey could not have won the trial or appeal.

The smartest start you can make is to take Massad Ayoob's MAG-40 class on judicious use of force and defensive handgun training.[5] Massad Ayoob has thought more extensively, practically, and has written more cogently on self-defense than anyone else for 40 years. He is the best out there on the general law of self-defense, but you still have to consult a good local lawyer for the particulars of your state. Learning your state and local law is imperative, whatever your defensive weapon or martial art of choice, because every state's law makes you liable to innocent bystanders.

Consider a man who I prosecuted for reckless endangerment (a misdemeanor). He had just put his dad in a retirement home. Soon after, his dad's house was burglarized. Knowing burglars often come back, he stayed in the house the next night with an old .32 pistol. The robbers came back, tried to force the front door, and he yelled. They jumped in their van and sped down the street. From the yard, the man fired three rounds after them down the block. A woman taking a walk with her five and eight-year-old kids were in the line of fire. Thankfully no one was hit. Had he hit someone, he could have been charged with a felony because of the legal doctrine of transferred intent. If they had been injured, he could have been sued and probably charged criminally. He was only charged with the misdemeanor. The victim never showed up for court, so the case was dropped, but what the defendant did not know about the law could have left him impoverished or in prison if he had hit someone.

> *23.6 million people (8.9 percent of the U.S. population) use illegal drugs and many of them commit criminal acts to obtain them.[7]*

Being prepared to face predators allows you to respond appropriately and legally to the particular emergency situation. "Those who forsake the law praise the wicked, but those who keep the law strive with [resist] them" (Proverbs 28:4). Consider two real-life situations. I was appointed to defend a young man charged with a robbery. He was one of three young men out cruising one night in a beat-up van about 10 p.m. They spotted a guy and his pregnant wife in their new Mercedes convertible. They followed him several miles through town to his home. The Mercedes man was oblivious to the fact he was being tailed (lack of awareness) and probably had no idea how to confirm it and evade had he noticed (lack of training). The three unarmed robbers blocked him in his driveway and demanded the keys to his car as he and his pregnant wife got out. One of the robbers shoved his wife, and a brief fight ensued in which numbers prevailed. (Neither he nor the wife were seriously injured.) The thugs took the car and drove it around to several parties, showing off for their friends until they got a better deal to trade the car for drugs about 1 a.m. They were arrested within 48 hours and charged with second degree robbery.[6]

The defendant pleaded guilty, and he got 10 years. Rightly so, but do not miss the point. Had the victim seriously considered and prepared for the possibility that he might one day be targeted by criminals, his ability to detect pursuit, confirm it, and direct the cops by cell phone would have thwarted the attempt before it began. Had it come to a confrontation, his gun (fired or not) would have trumped three unarmed crooks, and again, problem solved.

Contrast that guy's lack of preparation to a woman I met soon after I started as city prosecutor. While a student at a state university, she lived in an apartment complex. A serial rapist was terrorizing co-eds who lived off-campus. He had raped seven girls, threatening to kill them if they went to the police. A few victims did go to the cops, but the cases always fell apart when the victims received further threats and refused to testify. The lady I met was his eighth intended victim. Unknown to him, her daddy had taught her to shoot handguns in junior high, and she had kept up her practice. Better still, daddy had given her a .38 revolver and a sense of feisty self-worth that convinced her she would never be a victim.

She was alone in her apartment when the rapist broke in one night. She did not panic, freeze, cower, or plead. She got her gun, shot him, and then called the police. When he called her before the trial to threaten her as he had successfully done before, she replied, "Come ahead, and I'll make sure you don't live to be tried this time!" He never called back. She testified. He went to prison. By refusing to become a victim and by being prepared, she spared herself and future victims from this creep's predation. She exemplified the wisdom of Solomon, who sums up her story this way: "Every prudent man [or woman] acts with knowledge, but a fool displays folly" (Proverbs 13:16), and "The path of life leads upward for the wise to keep him [or her] from going down to the grave" (Proverbs 15:24, NIV).

Criminals make an evaluation of their potential victims. Criminologists call this an "interview" although it is usually careful observation rather than conversation. One of his major considerations when deciding if you will be his victim is whether he thinks you will fight. If so, you might hurt him. Then he wonders, "What if my leg is broken?" But he is not just worrying about the injury itself; he is worrying about the consequences. He thinks, "If I get laid up, someone else will take my corner where I sell drugs, and when I get well, I'll have to fight to get my corner back (and I could get hurt again)." But his biggest concern is, "If I'm hobbling around in a cast in my neighborhood, *I* will become prey on the food chain for my 'friends'." If he perceives that you are prepared, he will turn from you and look for a less capable victim. Annual FBI Uniform Crime Reports show that victims who actively resist criminals with guns are not only hurt less often but are hurt to a lesser extent than those who passively accept the assault.[8] Thus Solomon said, "When justice is done, it brings joy to the righteous but terror to evildoers" (Proverbs 21:15, NIV). Self-defense is justice, and it does bring terror to criminals, deterring them from future crimes.

Karate in a Can

By far, the best form of non-lethal self-defense is pepper spray. I am a certified instructor for its use. Pepper spray has replaced the non-military grade tear gas spray from the 1960s and 1970s. Tear gas formulas were gradually weakened because of eye damage lawsuits until police departments all but abandoned it as useless. As a cop told me in the mid-80s, "It would work on your 80-year-old grandma, but don't try it on a six foot, 200 pound drunk!"

Pepper spray uses the oil of hot peppers, oleoresin capsicum (OC), to produce a burning sensation in the throat, eyes, nose, and lips (mucus membrane areas) as well as any skin that it hits. As your eyes snap shut, they feel as if hot sand were under them. If you are tough and determined, you can open your eyes briefly, but oh it smarts! Pepper spray causes the sinuses to dump mucus down the throat and produces a constricting sensation (although the throat does not actually close). Yet the effects are temporary. The burning sensation ceases after 45 minutes, even without treatment (cold water and dishwashing liquid or baby soap).

Biological heat is measured in Scoville Heat Units (SHUs), a standard developed about 1910. For comparison, Tabasco-based sauces run from 150 to 3,500 SHUs. Pepper sprays run from a quarter-million to 5 million SHUs. Police generally do not use products over 2 million SHUs, since SHU values above that can cause skin blistering and eye damage. I was sprayed with it during instructor training. It feels like bobbing for French fries at McDonald's! Any instructor or officer will be sprayed for three reasons: first, the experience will give officers empathy and compassion for the people they spray; second, so they will not panic under the effects and start blindly spraying pistol rounds; and third, so they will know they can fight through it, concentrate, and still overcome the bad guys. In fights with suspects, cops are often accidentally sprayed by other officers. Using pepper spray on a police officer is a felony in most states. Cops are taught that any person using pepper spray on them intends to follow up with a gun grab to murder the officer. Thus, anyone using pepper spray on a cop will probably be shot.

For several reasons, pure pepper spray is preferable to those products combined with tear gas. As previously stated, tear gas does not work well in its commercial concentrations. Therefore, tear gas simply dilutes something that does work with something that does not. Second, if accidentally released in the home, pepper spray becomes inert in the environment in 45 minutes while tear gas can stay in the furniture or carpet fabrics for up to three weeks! (Tear gas can stay in clothing for up to three washings.) If infants, toddlers, or pets touch the fabrics, you could have an unhappy kid or dog. However, if the combo-spray is all you can find, buy it! Third, unlike tear gas, the pepper spray-based weapons work on any biological organism. On humans and dogs, it works 98 percent of the time. A dog's mucus membrane is on its nose so it is immediately affected. Canine exceptions include some trained attack dogs and of course, rabid dogs.

My dad generally walks twice a day in his Florida neighborhood. Two Rottweilers at one house always barked viciously at him from behind their fence. One day the 100 pound male jumped the fence and challenged him from 8 feet away: head down, ears back, fangs bared, and hackles up. Dad pulled an 8-year-old can of pepper spray ('98 must have been a good year) and fired. The Rottie's eyes slammed shut as he shook his head violently. In his agony, the dog wiped his face on the asphalt, sand, and coquina surface of the beachfront road before abruptly turning and hopping back into his yard. No permanent damage was (or could have been) caused by the pepper spray. The Rotties' owners moved six weeks later. Until they moved, the vicious male never even barked at dad during his twice daily walks. The unsprayed female continued to do so. By the way, the shelf-life of pepper spray is indeterminate, but because the propellant gas might leak, you should not carry it more than four years. My dad was lucky with his old canister.

Biological heat is measured in Scoville Heat Units (SHUs), a standard developed about 1910. For comparison, Tabasco-based sauces run from 150 to 3,500 SHUs. Pepper sprays run from a quarter-million to 5 million SHUs.

As for other animals, pepper spray works on everything from killer bees to bears to alligators. Take snakes for instance. With the exception of coral snakes (on which pepper spray works) all North American poisonous snakes are pit vipers. The pits (located between their nostrils and their eyes) allow them to locate warm-blooded prey by infrared sensing. So what would be the effect on a rattlesnake if you hit him with 2 million SHU's? It would ruin his day, blind his sensor pits, and you would be safe. It would do the same to a water moccasin in the water. Since the early 1980s the U.S. Navy has put OC compounds in the red paint below the waterline on its ships. Barnacles clamp on, the pepper spray burns their mouths, and they let go, thus freeing ships from hydrostatic drag and sailors from the age-old task of bottom scraping. Better still, OC compounds have been in Navy shark repellent since the 1980s. Sharks noses are miraculously keen. They can smell one part of blood in 200 million parts of water. Pepper oil in the repellent turns the water around the swimmer into a hot soup too intense for sharks. That is why I carry a small container in my swim trunks when I go to the beach.

Pepper spray has many attributes that make it ideal for use against humans. Any person responsible enough to drive a car can carry pepper spray and use it properly. The effects are devastating but temporary, stopping 98 percent of humans. The only ones unaffected are those so psychotic or drugged up that they would not feel it if you shot them with a 12 gauge shotgun. Nevertheless, some have died after being sprayed, but only because they already had severe heart or lung conditions complicated by the pepper spray's effects. Often referred to as "karate in a can," the beauty of pepper spray is that no matter how enfeebled by age or disability, if you can point and use hairspray, you can repel a criminal with pepper spray. A second advantage that an 80-year-old has over Chuck Norris is that Chuck must be within touching distance to neutralize his opponent. Armed with pepper spray, the elderly defender does not have to be that close. Pepper sprays have an 8 to 12 foot range. Whether your attacker is a skilled street fighter or armed with an impact or edged weapon, you can strike from beyond his range before he can strike or cut you.

Many uninformed folks are attracted to stun guns, those crackly/ sparkly units that cause electrical interruption of the nervous system when the electrodes touch skin. They look and sound meaner than a striped snake, but appearances can deceive. Only one major Alabama police department has ever tried them and then only for a year and a half. The problem with stun guns is they take 2 to 8 seconds to incapacitate (based on clothing, body fat, and other factors), and the police officer is within reaching distance of the bad guy who (in 2 to 8 seconds) can do a lot of damage at arm's length or closer. The Gadsden, Alabama, Police Department found that injuries to either officer or suspects did not decrease appreciably while using stun guns. They also had a public relations problem. Some citizens expected no injuries to suspects because when they heard "stun gun," they thought the cops had Star Trek® phasers set on "stun." The Gadsden police department finally dropped the stun guns and switched to pepper spray. (I guess they never figured out the Vulcan nerve-pinch either.)

The stun gun's major defect is that you must be within touching distance to use it. Studies have shown that a trained knife-fighter can draw and cut you in several major arteries in less than two seconds! Do you really want to chance that your opponent does not have that skill or does not get in a lucky punch or stab you while you hopefully push your stun gun into him for up to eight seconds? Moreover, are you sure the battery in your stun gun is fully charged? Will your stun gun have the amperage to do the job or just give the bad guy the tingly chuckles? That is another problem. The gun's voltage is always advertised, but it is the amperage that does the work, and amperage is never mentioned. Wouldn't you rather set him afire and temporarily blind him with pepper spray from 10 feet away? If you still want to go electrical, get a Taser instead. A Taser is expensive, but it is a stand-off weapon that really works!

Any person responsible enough to drive a car can carry pepper spray and use it properly. The effects are devastating but temporary, stopping 98 percent of humans.

Another advantage of pepper spray is that it is a multi-shot weapon; some pocket-sized canisters have upwards of 25 shots! Using his pepper spray, Michael Jackson could have taken out every one of those zombies in *Thriller*! Two things to remember when using it: shake it before firing and do not soak down the perpetrators. Oleoresin capsicum is oil that naturally separates from the carrier liquid. You must shake it two or three times before you deploy to mix the pepper spray with the carrier. Walking or jogging will not mix it sufficiently. A few vigorous shakes in the morning may do for the rest of the day, but it is better to make a habit of several shakes as you pull it out of pocket or purse. When you fire, do so in one-quarter to half-second bursts. The pepper spray does not start burning full bore until the carrier evaporates. So do not hose the bad guy down. Just get a squirt to his face while moving off the line of his assault.

You may be thinking, "This will take some practice!" Exactly. Lucky for you, pepper spray is cheap – 8 to 15 dollars per canister (versus stun guns that start at 25 dollars and Tasers that cost the same as a good handgun). You can afford a pepper spray canister for each family member and another one for everyone to practice with.

The final advantage of pepper spray is that it can be easily carried in a pocket. It goes where you go. At the beach, it stays in the pocket of my swim trunks. I never walk outside without it, and it is always with me inside. Even in a home invasion, I have the means to temporarily incapacitate multiple opponents, and if that does not stop them, I have bought time to get to a gun. Nationally known firearms trainer Clint Smith says, "You carry a handgun to fight your way to a rifle or a shotgun to end the fight!" At home you can carry pepper spray so you can fight your way to your handgun. Non-lethal, universally effective, simple to conceal and use, multi-shot, relatively long-ranged, and cheap: that's pepper spray. What's not to like? Especially when you consider that 99 percent of all situations calling for use-of-force in our lifetimes will NOT call for deadly force.

Two things to remember when using it: shake it before firing and do not soak down the perpetrators. Oleoresin capsicum is oil that naturally separates from the carrier liquid. You must shake it two or three times before you deploy to mix the pepper spray with the carrier. Walking or jogging will not mix it sufficiently.

Pepper spray provides a convenient solution to a laundry list of defensive problems and limits your liability because it does not cause permanent damage. Let me illustrate with a personal story. As a city prosecutor, I helped the local police acquire pepper spray, and I had the privilege of trying the first suspect who experienced its effects. The defendant had a raucous party in his downstairs apartment. At 2 a.m., the upstairs couple came down and asked politely if he would mind turning down his stereo. He refused, pulling a small pocket knife. They retreated and called the police. Two officers soon knocked on his door to investigate the call about a "man menacing with a knife." He came out cursing, hands in pockets. Both cops drew their pistols, repeatedly ordering him to "Show us your hands!" They could have justifiably shot him at that point. The stupid drunk yelled back, "Shoot me! Just shoot me, pigs!" It was then that one cop remembered his new pepper spray, so he holstered his gun and hit the drunk with a half-second burst, dropping him like a rock. Game over. Charged with menacing and disorderly conduct, he testified at trial on his own behalf, whining: "They shot me with that pepper spray, Judge, and I have asthma, and I had to go to the emergency room!"

Non-lethal, universally effective, simple to conceal and use, multi-shot, relatively long-ranged, and cheap: that's pepper spray. What's not to like?

"Objection!" I interrupted.

"What grounds? " asked the Judge.

"I'm confused, your Honor. Is the defendant complaining that we didn't *shoot* him too much, or that we only pepper-sprayed him too much? "

"Objection sustained," said the judge with a wry grin.

That is exactly the point of pepper spray. It will stop almost any threat about 98 percent of the time (the same effectiveness as a 12-gauge shotgun) without causing permanent damage to the bad guy. As Obi-Wan said to Luke of the light saber, "It's an elegant weapon." Because it is non-lethal and because its effect is temporary, pepper spray allows us to use non-lethal force to ward off threats even where deadly force would be justified – such as against a knife or nunchuck wielder or a vicious dog. Pepper spray is the "force" that will always be with you!

"If possible, so far as it depends on you be at peace with all men" (Romans 12:18) means not only avoiding conflict, but also seeking the most humane way to ward off damage to ourselves. In former times, alternatives were limited. Abe Lincoln told the story of a farmer who was attacked by a bulldog and who killed it with his pitchfork. When the dog's angry owner asked why the farmer didn't fend off the dog with the pitchfork's blunt end, the farmer replied, "Well I could have, if only he'd come at me with his blunt end." Using pepper spray today, we can produce happier outcomes. Using non-lethal force when possible helps us to "overcome evil with good" (Romans 12:21b).

Do Justly, Love Mercy, Walk Humbly

Holy men like Abraham, Moses, and David used justifiable force against unlawful violence and were blessed by God for it. When asked to specify the greatest commandment of the Law, Jesus replies:

'You shall love the Lord your God with all your heart, and with all your soul, and with all your mind.' This is the great and foremost commandment. The second is like it, 'You shall love your neighbor as yourself.' On these two commandments depend the whole Law and the Prophets (Matthew 22:37-40).

Jesus quotes from Deuteronomy 6:5 and Leviticus 19:18 respectively when answering the question. He combines these two Old Testament scriptures to make a new, greatest commandment. "Loving your neighbor" is not just having warm, fuzzy feelings for him. Loving your neighbor means helping him appropriately when he needs help, including using justifiable force if necessary (Leviticus 19:16).

God teaches us an attitude to govern all human relations: love God and love people, and His lesson applies to our mindset when using self-defense. A good summary verse is Micah 6:8, which says (in the KJV) "He hath shown thee, O man, what is good, and what does the Lord require of thee, but to do justly, and to love mercy, and to walk humbly with thy God?" Rather than making thousands of sacrifices or even offering our firstborn sons, God prefers a humility that leads us to deal with others fairly and legally, treating others as we would like to be treated.

Do Justly

Justice can be an amorphous term in today's world. In the Constitution, "equal justice" means everyone is treated the same before the law, which means all have equal opportunity. In contrast to the Constitution, today's concept of "social justice" argues that everyone should have an equal outcome, regardless of whether they have worked to deserve it or not. This is the philosophy of the criminal. If you have something he wants, he feels privileged to steal it and even harm you in the bargain. When dealing with justice in the Bible, though, we have an objective concept defined by God. Doing justly means living a biblically righteous and loving life while treating everyone according to God's laws and standards.

Doing justly also concerns your conduct in gun ownership. When a civilian justifiably kills or wounds a criminal, many states now shield the civilian from a civil suit by the criminal or his family.[1] However, every state holds a shooter personally liable for every stray bullet and any harm it causes to innocent bystanders or property. Realizing that, you should do everything possible to reduce the chance that you will hit innocent bystanders. To avoid accidental discharges, you must be proficient in all aspects of your chosen weapon. Practice safety, train, and practice your training.

Get Certified

Your first step should be getting certified as an NRA Handgun Safety and Personal Protection Instructor. Not only will it formalize your training, it will also qualify you as an expert witness in your own defense should you ever have to go to court. An expert witness at trial is defined as "a person with special knowledge of a subject, gained by experience and/or education, beyond that of the average person."[2] As a trainer, you can inform others who are not involved in shooting sports and get them to think seriously about self-defense. You can begin to dispel the myths they might have absorbed from TV dramas and the news media, helping them to form a realistic perspective on gun ownership and self-defense. I find I have more fun teaching others than when I am just shooting by myself. Those I teach often find a new, exciting hobby and become an educated friend of the shooting sports. At the very least, if someone hands them a gun, they will know how to check to see if it is loaded.[3]

Next, start studying the subject of gun rights. Learn about the political side of firearms issues. Start by joining the NRA and get active in politics. Politically, the tail wags the dog in this country. Barely over one percent of the voting population actively participates in a political campaign (and that includes stuffing envelopes). Only about 10 percent ever give money to a candidate and only around 15 percent will believe in a candidate enough to put up a yard sign, wear a button, or put a bumper sticker on their car. Nationally, only 48 percent of those eligible will vote in any given election. Four million NRA members (and at least a million more members of several other gun advocacy organizations) preserve the Second Amendment rights of 91 million uninvolved gun owners. You can be part of the tail that wags the dog if you will just get involved.

Study will lead you to some of the fine books and magazines that will teach you about firearms and self-defense issues. You will not lack for information. I read more than 2,000 pages a year (both books and magazines) on these subjects and do not scratch the surface of the information out there. During your study, you will learn from great teachers who can take you from basics to advanced levels of self-defense proficiency. There are many fine instructors and schools that teach firearms skills. However, on the subject of *when* to use force, the Ayoob Group classes by Massad Ayoob are the best. By completing his 40-hour class, you will know more about judicious use of force than 99 percent of judges and lawyers. As you study and train, you will be more useful to your family and fellow citizens, and you will be a more serious, responsible person open to alternatives and less likely to make legal and tactical mistakes. Finally, get training from a lawyer who can give you the legal specifics of your home state. After all, "doing justly" includes being trained to a sufficient level of skill and legal knowledge so that you will pull your gun only at the right time and hit only the right target. "A wise man is strong, and a man of knowledge increases power. For by wise guidance, you will wage war and in an abundance of counselors there is victory" (Proverbs 24:5-6).

God teaches us an attitude to govern all human relations: love God and love people, and His lesson applies to our mindset when using self-defense.

Love Mercy

One of the false stereotypes that anti-gunners like to project is that those who
are serious about self-defense go around looking for a fight. The Karate Kid
learned that proficiency in martial arts would keep him from having to fight. We,
too, can avoid potential danger areas, situations, and people. We can use
de-escalation tactics. We want to live in peace with everyone, but we also
understand the definition of the word *emergency*. As believers, we stand ready to
obey the biblical commands that forbid us to ignore the plight of our fellow man.

That is why many of us carry first aid kits and fire extinguishers in our cars. My
father was also my scoutmaster. Every fourth or fifth meeting, we practiced first
aid. Every patrol in our troop always came home with blue ribbons from every
first aid competition. Dad required such an intensive curriculum because in his 30
years as an electric company right-of-way agent who traveled 12 counties, he was
the first to roll up on three separate accidents with injuries. One time, a man
collapsed with a heart attack right in front of him. The victim had vomited, so Dad
cleared his airway with his handkerchief and then started CPR. Dad and a cop
who had just walked up kept the man alive until EMTs took over. Dad's company
car had a fire extinguisher in it. On two occasions, he drove by houses where
small fires had started. He controlled the flames with the extinguisher, dragged the
smoldering furniture outside, and soaked it with a hose. People lived because dad
had the right training, the right tools, and the will to use them. He not only
exemplified the Scouts' motto, "Be Prepared," but also the "Do unto others"
attitude that all Christians are enjoined to have. Better still, because he loved
mercy Dad passed on his ethics, skills, and will to use them to help others.

When we love mercy, we give others one more chance to fulfill God's promises
and plans for their lives. The sinner has a chance to repent. The believer has the
opportunity to spread God's love. God put it this way through Jeremiah: "'For I
know the plans that I have for you', declares the Lord, 'plans for welfare and not
for calamity, to give you a future and a hope'" (Jeremiah 29:11). Jeremiah says
protecting citizens is a duty of government: "Thus says the Lord [to rulers]:
'Administer justice every morning, and deliver the person who has been robbed
from the power of the oppressor …'" or he warns that God's wrath will come on

those rulers who do not (Jeremiah 20:12b).

As holders of concealed carry permits, we have the means and will to prevent harm to innocents. By saving others, we help God fulfill His good plans for their lives. I interpret Isaiah 54 as a promise of God's favor extended to those Gentiles who would become Christians, but it also applies to the Jewish nation. Among the many blessings God bestows in this chapter, He promises: "If anyone fiercely assails you, it will not be from me. Whoever assails you will fall because of you" (Isaiah 54: 15). From this passage, I surmise that criminal attack is the criminal's idea, and God has given us the authority and means to fight back. Proverbs 11:8 describes the private citizen turning the tables on a criminal: "The righteous is delivered from trouble, but the wicked takes his place."

Next, Isaiah tells us that the technology to defend ourselves is given by God: "Behold, I Myself have created the smith who blows the fire of coals and brings out the weapon for its work, and I have created the destroyer to ruin [bad guys]" (Isaiah 54:16). God says He gives us the ability and the permission to make weapons as well as the guidance to use them so we can bring mercy to the helpless and destruction to criminals. Just as God gives us the brain power to create medical technology to save lives, He gives us the smarts to develop and improve weaponry so the weak can win over bigger, more numerous bad guys. Weapons technology shows us that God loves mercy by giving us the chance to show mercy to others when we use our weapons to stop criminals.

Reliable surveys reveal that 700,000 to 3.6 million times a year private citizens stop crimes with firearms.[4] Gary Kleck, a Florida State University criminologist, says that when private citizens use firearms for self-defense, only two percent actually have to shoot their attackers. In most cases, the attackers run when they see the gun. And it is rare that attackers actually take the gun away from the intended victim.[5] Just as Boy Scouts, lifeguards, EMTs, firefighters, and doctors use their skills and technology to rescue people's futures, so do trained armed citizens, police, and soldiers. It is certainly God's will that we should preserve innocent life and its potential (Jeremiah 29:11).

The following verses from Isaiah make it clear that the prey can and should be taken from evil men:

Can the prey be taken from the [evil] mighty men,

Or the captives of a tyrant be rescued?
Surely, thus says the Lord, even the captives of the [evil]
Mighty man will be taken away, and the prey of the tyrant will be
Rescued. For I will contend with the [evil] one who
Contends with you and I will save your sons.
And I will feed the oppressors their own flesh, and they will
Become drunk on their own blood as with sweet wine. And all
Flesh will know that I, the Lord am your Savior and your Redeemer,
The Mighty One of Jacob. (Isaiah 49:24-26)

How is God going to save crime victims if not by the efforts of godly, trained, armed people? Police are rarely at the scene of the crime as it occurs, but armed citizens are often there. Rescuing victims is certainly God's will and our work. It is doing justly and loving mercy. Remember God's command:

Deliver those who are being taken away to death
And those who are staggering to slaughter.
O hold them back. If you say,
'See we did not know this.' Does He not consider it
Who weighs the hearts? And does He now know it Who
Keeps your soul? And will He not render to man according to
His work? (Proverbs 24:11-12).

These verses are not optional; they are a command from God.

If we believe Jeremiah 29:11, then God has a plan for each person, and He never intends for any person to die before they come to faith in Him (Ezekiel 18:23 and 32). When we step in to prevent the unlawful death of the innocent, God is pleased.

> "Behold, I Myself have created the smith who blows the fire of coals and brings out the weapon for its work, and I have created the destroyer to ruin [bad guys]" (Isaiah 54:16).

Lastly, if we love mercy, we must act from pure motives and within the law. This means eliminating vengeance and malice from our righteous anger. For instance, every police department and responsible self-defense instructor teaches shoot-to-stop, *not* shoot-to-kill. Instructors teach that you continue to shoot *only until* the target falls out of our sight picture. As Massad Ayoob says, "If we were allowed to shoot to kill, then we would be allowed to kill the wounded." Loving mercy means that once a criminal is caught, we wait for God and the law to take their course and punish evil people. It is tempting to watch a TV account of street gangs or the Mafia and say, "We should hunt 'em all down and kill 'em on sight." But that does not agree with God's plan. God does not "wish for any to perish, but for all [to] come to repentance" (2 Peter 3:9, Ezekiel 18:32). God made each person as an eternal being who will spend eternal life in heaven or hell. Gang members have as much right to hear the Gospel and respond to God's love as anyone else. Think of the potential changes in their neighborhoods if many of them were converted! Remove the immediate legal need for self-defense, and our role is not that of avenging angels but as ambassadors of Christ: "Therefore we are ambassadors for Christ, as though God were entreating through us; We beg you on behalf of Christ, be reconciled with God" (2 Corinthians 5:20).

Walk Humbly

If I am an ambassador for the heavenly kingdom, then I am under the orders of the King. I am His servant, and therefore a servant to others a servant to others (2 Corinthians 5:14-15). Few armed citizens train and carry weapons merely to protect their own life and property. Most are ready to protect others and to pass on their life-saving knowledge.

> The fear of the Lord is the beginning of wisdom, and
> The knowledge of the Holy One is understanding. For
> By me [wisdom] your days will be multiplied, and years of life will
> Be added to you. If you are wise, you are wise for
> yourself, and if you scoff, you alone will bear it
> (Proverbs 9:10-12).

When we admit that we do not know everything and therefore rely on God's wisdom, our personal world is safer. "In the fear [reverence] of the Lord there is a strong confidence, and his children will have refuge. The fear of the Lord is a fountain of life that one may avoid the snares of death" (Proverbs 14:26-27). Reliance on God protects our families and us from the wiles of criminals. Walking with God in a life of integrity keeps us out of the orbit of criminals. When W.C. Fields said, "You can't cheat an honest man," he meant that a guy who does not cut corners with others cannot be persuaded to gamble on a shady deal for himself. "The fear of the Lord leads to life so that one may sleep satisfied, untouched by evil" (Proverbs 19:23) and "The fear of the Lord is the instruction for wisdom, and before honor comes humility" (Proverbs 15:33). Many folks flatter themselves that they know how to spot criminals and respond to emergencies, yet they have never gotten formal training or carried the proper equipment to respond.

Likewise, many folks go to church week after week convinced they know it all, but they do not really listen to the preacher and the Sunday school teacher, and they do not study their Bibles. Many are biblically illiterate while professing faith. A friend of mine once attended worship with his cousin. When they arrived at the building, one of the greeters asked why he was carrying a Bible. My friend replied that he always carried his Bible to church. The greeter exclaimed, "What are you, some kind of fanatic?" Some folks either do not want to learn or do not know why they should. Chip Foose, one of the world's finest car customizers, says his daddy taught him that "It's only *after* you become an 'expert' that you begin to learn what you don't know. It's true, I learn more every day."[6] And so should we if we presume to pack arms and use them someday. "Prepare plans by consultation and make war [self-defense] by wise guidance" (Proverbs 20:18).

Humility helps us to learn. We have all heard of the guy who thinks he knows how to handle a car or a gun yet ends up hurting himself or others. "Pride goes before destruction and a haughty spirit before stumbling" (Proverbs 16:18). Going to the range by yourself every six months is no measure of how you will actually do in a fight. Test yourself, and get objective feedback by shooting against a friend. Put lunch on the line so you can simulate a little of the stress experienced in a gunfight. (No, that is not gambling; it is training to shoot under stressful conditions!)

Stress is an amazing factor, and most people do not realize how it will affect their shooting. My first night at a new gun club was great: making new friends, checking out each other's guns, and shooting. The last activity was a bowling pin shoot: at five yards, knock five bowling pins off a three-foot-wide table as fast as you can. The winner is the one who knocks the most pins off the fastest. I had never tried that before (stress), in front of people I had just met (more stress), and in a sport I claim to be good at (even more stress). My gun had 15 shots. The start signal sounded, and my first two shots cleared two pins off the table. My heart leaped at how good I was, and the resulting adrenalin dump caused my heart rate to zoom and my hands to shake. I got "buck fever" and started spraying shots. It took 13 more shots to clear only three more pins off the table, and I finished in the middle of the pack. Real stress with an audience and my pride on the line ruined my aim. I learned two lessons that day: you can't miss fast enough, and stress is a factor you must train to overcome. In a real fight, your stress levels will be significantly higher, but competition will help get you used to the symptoms.

Join a gun club that has IDPA-type combat shoots so you can regularly have the stress of public performance, the practice of different shooting scenarios, and the help of knowledgeable friends who will see and correct your mistakes. These clubs make you use real-world defensive guns and holsters in likely, "real life" simulations. When you hear good advice, listen and then practice it. Do not be arrogant. I can usually outshoot a good friend of mine; yet his sound observations, demonstrations, and advice have always improved my shooting.

Humility keeps us out of fights: "Through presumption [pride] comes nothing but strife, but with those who receive counsel is wisdom" (Proverbs 13:10). A Christian must never act out of annoyance, selfish anger, or to cultivate or preserve a macho self-image. Remember, you will be judged by the standard of "the ordinary, reasonable, prudent person under like or similar circumstances." You do not want a jury to conclude that you are a macho hot head who could not stand to be insulted. *Every* state requires that to claim the legal right of self-defense you must be totally free from fault in bringing on the confrontation. So an insult, a minor push or shove, or getting cut off in traffic should be dealt with by ignoring the act or by responding with proportional force if forced to fight. "A fool shows his ignorance at once, but a prudent man overlooks an insult" (Proverbs 12:16, NIV). You cannot give someone the death penalty because he cursed you, has too many items in the express lane at the grocery store, or jostled you on the street. Instead, the Bible says to walk humbly. Do not take it personally: ignore it.

What about an actual crime though? My rule is, "If it's not going to hurt me, let it go." I was at the beach once with my wife, kids, and one of their friends. As I looked up from the water's edge, I saw a man about 25 yards past our stuff carrying one of our three boogie boards. I said nothing. Could I have stopped him? Yes. Was he bigger than me? No matter, I had pepper spray. Was a beat up, $20 toy worth chancing a fight with a thief? No. Neither my wife nor the kids missed the board. A confrontation could have led to one or both of us getting hurt, involving the police, and causing both hospital and legal expenses 11 hours from home. Worse, it would have introduced stress into our much-needed relaxation. Some verses that support my inaction go like this: "The beginning of strife is like letting out water. So abandon the quarrel before it breaks out" (Proverbs 17:14). "A man's discretion makes him slow to anger, and it is his glory to overlook a transgression" (Proverbs 19:11). "Keeping away from strife is an honor for a man, but any fool will quarrel" (Proverbs 20:3).

I could overlook the theft because I had long ago played out many scenarios and matched them with God's guidelines to decide what I would and would not tolerate and how I would react. That petty thief was not a physical threat to me or mine. To paraphrase Shakespeare, "he who steals my boogie board, steals trash."I let it go and enjoyed my day. "You will keep in perfect peace those whose minds are steadfast, because they trust in you" (Isaiah 26:3 NIV).

Walking humbly means that your martial arts instructor should be a godly person. You do not want to learn dangerous attitudes from an instructor like the aggressive one in The Karate Kid: "Do not associate with a man given to anger or go with a hot-tempered man, lest you learn his ways and find a snare for yourself" (Proverbs 22:24-25). "Blessed are the peacemakers" is not a new idea either. Proverbs 15:18 says, "A hot-tempered man stirs up strife, but the slow to anger pacifies contention [calms the quarrel]." I cannot tell you how many times defense attorneys or defendants told me I should not prosecute because they "had the right to self-defense." That was always nonsense. The facts always showed that the defendants caused the problem by their macho attitude, which legally negated their right to claim self-defense. The Bible encourages us to use our head to live by God's standards. Let Him approve of us instead of us bowing to society's shifting mores (Psalms 118:8).

"He who is slow to anger is better than the mighty, and he who rules his spirit [is better] than he who captures a city" (Proverbs 16:32). Ruling your spirit means that your anger will not cause stupid things to come out of your mouth. Jesus says,

"But I tell you that every careless word that people speak, they shall give an accounting for in the Day of Judgment" (Matthew 13:36). What does that mean for us? Consider "hate crime" laws and the sentencing statutes in both state and federal law that provide for longer sentences. In our culture, the "hilarious" politically incorrect joke you told at the office last year will come back to haunt you. Engage in a physical altercation (or worse) with anyone from a racial, ethnic, national, religious, or sexually-oriented group, and any lawyer worth his contingency fee will find out about your prior biased speech and hang you with it at trial. You might just pay for your careless attitude with a substantial civil judgment. "[A]nd there must be no filthiness and silly talk, or coarse jesting, which are not fitting, but rather giving of thanks" (Ephesians 5:4). "Let no unwholesome word proceed from your mouth, but only such a word as is good for edification [building people up], according to the need of the moment, so it will give grace to those who hear" (Ephesians 4:29). This also applies to "clever" bumper stickers and tee shirts with sayings like: "I don't call 911. I call .357" and "Kill 'em all, let God sort 'em out." I am giving you the hard, legal truth that the stupid things you say can turn a righteous use-of-force into a clear sign of illegal intent by the verbal judo of a skilled opposing lawyer.

I prosecuted a man for DUI once who, at booking, screamed phrases like: "Why aren't you out there arresting these n------ sellin' dope and murdering folks instead of a good white man like me?" He went on like that for 20 minutes on camera while hog-tied. After the jury saw that video, I cross-examined him:

"Sir, do you work with black people?"

"Yeah."

"Do you call any of them 'n------'?"

"Of course not."

"No," I replied. "You'd only say that if you were drunk, right?"

He had no answer. The jury was out 10 minutes and returned with a guilty verdict. By the way, the jurors had chosen a 60-year-old black gentleman as foreman. I do not think that was a coincidence. Careless words will rebound to haunt the speaker: "The lips of the righteous feed many, but fools die for lack of understanding" (Proverbs 10:21).[7] Humility generates genuine concern for others so that we choose our words and actions carefully, and everyone profits thereby.

Furthermore, to "walk humbly" obligates us to respect others. "Do nothing from selfishness or empty conceit, but with humility of mind regard one another as more important than yourselves. Do not merely look after your own personal interests, but also for the interests of others" (Philippians 2:3-4). *Empathy* is the word: seeing things from another's perspective. This is the valuable lesson that lawyer Atticus Finch teaches Scout (and us) in *To Kill a Mockingbird*:

"First of all," he said, "if you can learn a simple trick, Scout, you will get along a lot better with all kinds of folks. You never really understand a person until you consider things from his point of view---"

"Sir?"

"---until you climb into his skin and walk around in it."[8]

In the *Andy Griffith Show* episode when Gomer joins the Marines, Sgt. Carter is exasperated with him. During a break, Andy says, "Gomer, I don't think that Sergeant likes you very much." Gomer's answer exemplifies empathy and humility. "Aw, Andy, he might just be havin' a bad day. Maybe he had a haircut and all them little hairs is ticklin' his neck real bad. That'd make anybody feel out of sorts." My bad days make me realize how fragile contentment can be and remind me to see things from the other guy's side. Just doing that helps me avoid conflict and forge relationships. As a prosecutor, I tried to cultivate a congenial relationship with defense attorneys. I did not see them as my enemies but as colleagues in an adversarial position. Ninety five percent of the time, most would come to me and say, "Look, my guy's guilty, can you cut him any slack?" Then they would tell me the mitigating circumstances, and we would try to work a deal. Some days, though, one would come in and say, "I think my guy really is innocent, can you give this an extra look?" You bet I would. We played it straight, never let it get personal, and gave each other mutual respect and a fair hearing. It worked well for the guilty, the innocent, the victims, the lawyers, and society.

Our humility lifts others when we show respect for them. Being polite, having manners, and showing kindness, understanding, and patience *never* go out of style. Social climbers only use those traits with those they think can help them climb the ladder: "He who hates disguises it with his lips, but he lays up deceit in his heart. When he speaks graciously, do not believe him for these are seven abominations in his heart ...a flattering mouth works ruin (Proverbs 26:24-25,

28b). Those same "superior" people treat as "inferior" waitresses, secretaries, clerks, public servants, kids, old folks, and service people – anyone who they think cannot advance them. Someone said that our character is revealed by how we treat those who can do nothing for us. A waitress in my Sunday school class once related how her worst customers were the "Christian" Sunday lunch crowd. She said they were regularly the least polite, the most demanding, and gave the worst (or no) tips. That is poor performance from a group who claims to follow a man who described His own mission in these words, "[T]he Son of Man did not come to be served, but to serve, and to give His life as a ransom for many" (Matthew 20:28). If we practice Jesus' servant attitude, how will our lives, marriages, neighborhoods, culture, and world change? I guarantee that everyone would be a little happier and a little nicer to each other. "He who restrains his words has knowledge, and he who has a cool spirit is a man of understanding" (Proverbs 17:27).

Finally, humility reminds me that I do not know it all. So I need to be on the lookout for anyone and any experience that can teach me something new. One morning, I walked my two-year-old daughter up an icy sidewalk to daycare.

"You don't have to hold my hand daddy," she said. "I can walk by myself."

"No sweetie," I replied. "It's slippery."

"What's slippery?" she asked.

I immediately realized that when it comes to life's slippery road I often think, like my toddler, that I can handle it without God, though I am as ignorant of the dangers as she was. I thanked God then and there for His guidance, care, and His ability to teach a 40-year-old through a toddler. "He whose ear listens to the life-giving reproof will dwell among the wise" (Proverbs 15:31). "But everyone must be quick to hear, slow to speak and slow to anger" (James 1:19b).

Micah 6:8 is the best place to sum up self-defense. Before anything else, we should be sure that we are doing justly, loving mercy, and walking humbly with God. As Jeremiah 29:11 tells us, He has plans for every person's life "for good not harm," even felons. But when a felon's deliberate action leaves us with no safe retreat and at most a few seconds to react and save innocent lives, Scripture encourages, yes, even commands us to save lives with reasonable force.

Am I my Brother's Keeper?

The defense of self and others is the most basic of human instincts. When danger threatens, every animal will flee or fight, depending on the circumstances. Even the smallest mouse will fight to protect her young. Survival is a God-given instinct. Some may argue that because self-defense is natural it is not spiritual, so Christians should not engage in it. This is not true. God has given us many instincts that can be used for good or bad, and He has told us how to use each for good.

Sheeple

There are people who, for various reasons, chant the mantra, "Call the police … call the police." Some are politicians who love controlling others to the point of denying weapons to the public. Perhaps they are busybodies who do not care about unintended consequences or the moral and practical effects of their laws just as long as the laws are mandatory (but often with exceptions for themselves). Others say "call the cops" because helping others in need interrupts their cocooning. Air conditioning and automatic garage doors make it easy to ignore neighbors. Most call-the-cops folks have never considered the facts of violent crime and criminals; they simply take it on faith that the government has a token presence in their community and will unerringly follow through and protect them.

People in the self-defense community have a name for the entire call-the-cops crowd: *Sheeple* are those who trust government as an omnipresent, unerring, benevolent shepherd. Thus sheeple do unquestioningly what they are told. Yet in every state and federal jurisdiction, the law says that the police have no duty to protect specific individuals, just society at large.[1] If you could sue the fire department for not arriving before your house burned down or if you could sue the cops for not arriving before your rapist left, very soon there would not be any fire and police departments.

Sheeple look at Bible verses with the command to help others, and they object. They say, "Times are different today. Now we have organized police forces, which did not exist in ancient times." True, but to believe that this relieves us of the obligation to protect innocent life is to ignore God's moral imperative based on a societal convenience. Ignoring a rapist in the act because police might arrive in time to stop him is as morally bankrupt as refusing to turn your garden hose on your neighbor's burning house because firemen ought to be on the way. Under the Mosaic Law, women were told to expect help if someone attempted to rape them.

> If a man happens to meet in a town a virgin pledged to be married and he sleeps with her, you shall take them both to the gate of that town and stone them to death – the girl because she was in a town and did not scream for help, and the man because he violated another man's wife. You must purge the evil from among you. But if out in the country a man happens to meet a girl pledged to be married and rapes her, only the man who has done this shall die. Do nothing to the girl; she has committed no sin deserving death. This case is like that of someone who attacks and murders his neighbor, for the man found the girl out in the country, and though the betrothed girl screamed, there was no one to rescue her (Deuteronomy 22:23-27).

If the victim did not cry for help in town where her screams would likely be heard, she was considered complicit in the sex and was to be punished as a consensual fornicator. However, the girl who was attacked in the country had no duty to cry for help because it was unlikely that a rescuer would be within earshot. The point is, however, that women had the right to expect help if they were attacked. The Mosaic Law encouraged aid to those threatened by criminals.

"The cops will protect me" is the first article of faith among sheeple, and it leads to disaster. Police are indeed our official safety shepherds, but those who make up "the thin, blue line" are too few to provide personal security to everyone, everywhere, all the time. Response times to 911 calls vary according to the actual number of officers on duty, distance to the scene, priority of the emergency, and numbers of competing emergencies. Effective intervention may have to wait until cops get a clear picture of what's going on inside and sufficient numbers of officers arrive to intervene (as happened at Columbine). In seven and a half years as City Prosecutor, I tried only one case where the cops arrived while an assault was in progress. When seconds count, the police are just minutes away.

The second article of faith among sheeple is the expectation that certain dire emergencies will *never* happen, along with a constant anticipation that life will remain routine, and this leads to tragedy. Sheeple need to understand the definition of the word *emergency*. Any Red Cross lifesaving instructor will tell you that 40 percent of yearly drowning victims never intended to be in the water. Yet many people fail to teach their children how to swim, which is a basic survival skill. Although the Boy Scout motto "Be Prepared" is taught as a basis for self-reliance, most people never think carefully, procedurally, or creatively about possible emergencies until one arises. I carry fire extinguishers in all of my cars, but only after having a car fire without one. Unfortunately, the first and last thought of most victims of violent crime is, "I can't believe this is happening to me!"

The third article of faith among sheeple is the misconception that all laws are logical and rational: "for our own good." Some sheeple have an almost religious faith in government. They ignore the fact that laws are often written to promote a special interest, to enhance the control of politicians over the citizenry, to reward campaign donors, or to increase revenue. Laws, when introduced, can be crafted by fine construction and good intent; however, by the time the deals and compromises of the legislative process are over, the law may have morphed into a totally different animal. As Otto von Bismarck said, "He who loves the law and sausage should never watch either being made."

The Luby's Cafeteria tragedy of October 16, 1991, combined all these sheeple presumptions into a deadly perfect storm. That Wednesday, Dr. Susanna Gratia-Hupp went to Luby's in Killeen, Texas, for lunch with her parents. Shortly after, George Jo Hennard drove his pickup through the front window and killed a doctor who came up to see if he needed help. Armed with two high-capacity 9 millimeter semi-auto pistols, Hennard began methodically to kill the patrons. Susanna's father turned over their table for cover and then heroically tried to rush Hennard. He was shot dead. Tommy Vaughn, a patron turned hero, smashed through a window to allow Susanna and others to escape. Her mother refused to leave her father, and she was also killed. It took 22 minutes for the first officers to arrive (both were off-duty but armed). By then, Hennard had killed 23 people. After being wounded by the cops, Hennard killed himself. Until the Virginia Tech massacre, this was the deadliest firearms-related crime in U.S. history.[2]

Let us analyze how the sheeple articles of faith contributed to this tragedy. The first deadly false truism is, "The cops will protect me." The first sheriff's deputy arrived 22 minutes after Hennard drove his pickup through the front window. Hennard had a 17-shot Glock pistol and a 15-shot Ruger P89 with spare magazines of ammo. As a former auxiliary cop, city judge, city prosecutor, and nationally certified legal use-of-force trainer, I can tell you that cops admit they are almost never present when the crime is committed. Their role is *reactive*. The vast majority of the time the police only arrive in time to clean up the mess and draw chalk lines around victims' bodies. Unless you have a bodyguard, you had better find a way to keep you and yours alive until the cavalry arrives.

The second deadly false truism of sheeple is, "That kind of stuff never happens." No one in that restaurant was mentally prepared for what happened that day. They had simply never spent five minutes playing "What if ___?" and thinking of a response. Al Gratia, Susanna's father, and Tommy Vaughn were the only two present who recovered from their shocked disbelief to take action. Gratia died heroically, creating a diversion that allowed Vaughn to smash the window and lead others to safety. "But nobody could have done anything," cry the sheeple. "He had guns!" This sort of hopeless ignorance caused many to die that day. The investigation showed that except for the two heroes and those who escaped with Susanna, the victims froze. Hennard killed slowly, deliberately, often addressing his prey before carefully aiming; he killed at a rate of about one murder per minute. His frozen, amazed prey simply waited to die. His modern weapons did not kill them as much as their own inaction. Given their inert surrender, had Hennard used a muzzle-loading civil war musket, firing a maximum three rounds a minute, the death count would have been the same after 22 minutes.

Had his victims not assumed a sheeple mentality, they might have known that only 25 percent of people shot by handguns actually die; however, the statistics change if you lie still so that deadly aim can be taken on your brain. Had they known that fact, they might have run. As the distance from a gun's muzzle increases, the chance of a miss increases exponentially. Even screaming and running in all directions would have considerably reduced Hennard's ability to draw a bead on any single person. In fact, the dynamics of shooting state that moving to the *outside* of a shooter's gun hand keeps him from tracking his target as effectively. Al Gratia had the right idea: if all those people (or at least all the adult males) had rushed Hennard from all directions and dog-piled him, casualties would have been far fewer. Finally, remember what I said about pre-thinking emergencies and the tools that may be at hand? Everyone in that cafeteria had an excellent weapon right in front of him: a heavy dinner plate! What person does not know how to hum a Frisbee at someone? Imagine if Hennard had been pummeled from all directions by these whirling, rock-hard missiles? What if his prey had immediately followed their throw with a mass charge and dog-pile? What if instead of duck-and-cover the students and the teachers at Virginia Tech had been taught to volley textbooks, purses, and shoes while charging the gunman? What if we all decided to spend five minutes a week anticipating different emergencies? What if we made a few basic preparations for those events? If we did, we probably would act instead of freeze in an emergency. In other words, we would no longer be sheeple. In these examples, I am not trying to denigrate the victims. However, they illustrate the unfortunate fact that relying on cops and failing to realize, prepare, and react can be a fatal error because bad things do happen to good people.

The last article of faith among sheeple is the false belief that all laws are good and must be obeyed, even when doing so might mean the death of you and your loved ones. That is exactly what happened to Dr. Gratia-Hupp on that terrible day. You see, in 1991, Texas had no concealed carry law but did allow loaded handguns to be carried in vehicles. As a chiropractor, Dr. Gratia-Hupp feared that a gun law violation might put her license in jeopardy, so she left her revolver in her car instead of taking it into the restaurant. She is certain that she could have saved her parents and most of the others that day had her revolver been in her purse. The Texas legislature, who had hitherto refused to pass concealed carry, had never been confronted with a horror like that day in Killeen. So like good sheeple, they assumed that such an atrocity would never happen. Susanna, with no sheeple blood in her veins, won a seat in the Texas legislature and launched a crusade that resulted in a sound concealed carry law for Texas. She is a hero who has given a fighting chance to millions of Texans who were previously denied that right by shortsighted, bad laws. She is the kind of person Proverbs speaks of: "… [S]he who refreshes others will [herself] be refreshed" (Proverbs 11:25).

There is one final lesson to learn from Killeen and horrible events like it: that objective evil exists in this world, and it must be confronted and defeated, sometimes on the scene. Loving God and your neighbor as yourself (Leviticus 19:18) includes fighting in defense of your neighbor. "[B]ehold now is the acceptable time, behold now is the day of salvation ..." (2 Corinthians 6:2b). "Do not withhold good from those to whom it due, when it is in your power to do it. Do not say to your neighbor, 'Go, and come back, and tomorrow I will give it'" (Proverbs 3:27-28).

Both God and society have set limits on our behavior that we can choose to observe. Besides telling us how we should behave, God gives us the information, ability, and help (through the Holy Spirit) to live out His will. Among this information, God has addressed self-defense and has given us His principles for it in His word.

These principles are exemplified in the Ten Commandments. When God instructs us to do or not to do something, He instructs for our good. For instance, God's two reasons for saying "You shall not" are to protect us and to save us for something better. When He says, "You shall," as in "honor your father and mother," He wants to prevent all the bad things that can happen to a society or to its people when they disregard, disobey, and mistreat their parents. Crime is, after all, an attack on authority. If children do not respect parental authority, they will not respect other people or society's laws when they become adults. In each command that God gives us, we must consider both the reasons to comply and the possible result if we choose not to comply. Just as words mean things, acts of omission and commission have results as well, especially in the realm of self-defense.

The first four commandments deal with our relationship to God. He is the Creator, Sustainer, and Savior. To conduct our lives properly, we must recognize and worship Him as such. The last five commandments are framed as negatives and deal with our relationship to others. "You shall not covet" forbids envying another's possessions, situations, or relationships so that you want to take them away. God does not forbid us from wanting things, but He does forbid such a strong desire to have things that it supersedes the rights of others and our own logical needs. The implied opposite of covetousness, then, is to celebrate and be joyful for what another has and to help build a society and relationships that will help him earn and enjoy it. Such altruism benefits everyone.

The commandment, "You shall not murder," raises the question of what its opposite action should be. Does it mean that if I see someone being murdered, I should just stand by? After all, as long as I do not participate, I have not broken the command, have I?

Cain, the first murderer, gives the answer. When God asked him, "Where is Abel your brother?" Cain answered, "I do not know. Am I my brother's keeper?" (Genesis 4:9). What Cain meant as a rhetorical question supplies its own answer: I am indeed my brother's keeper. God has placed on all of us a moral imperative to care for others when they are in need. Therefore, "You shall not murder" tells us that we have the duty to save life in any legal way possible.

God consistently sets forth an imperative to do good. The Masoretic Text of Leviticus 19:16-18 reads like this: "Thou shalt not go up and down as a tale bearer among thy people; neither shalt thou stand idly by the blood of thy neighbor: I am the Lord … thou shalt love thy neighbor as thyself: I am the Lord."[3] Jewish scholars who comment on the meaning of Leviticus 19:16 state that if I see my neighbor's son drowning, I should try to save him. If I find his donkey in a hole, I should pull it out. If I see someone unlawfully trying to harm him, I must intervene. "Do unto others" did not begin with Jesus. This command was God's principle from the start. If I love my neighbor as myself, then I will aid him in any way I can.

Here is Solomon's take on giving aid; he recommended God's command to help those in danger.

> If you are slack in the day of distress, Your strength is limited
> Deliver those who are being taken away to death,
> And those who are staggering to slaughter,
> O hold them back.
> If you say "See we did not know this,"
> Does He not consider it who weighs the hearts?
> And does He not know who keeps your soul?
> And will He not render to a man according to his work?
> Proverbs 24:10-12

This is a command from God to rescue people from death. In verse 10, God tells us that if we are indifferent when danger threatens others, our moral indecision will even keep us from protecting ourselves when threatened.

Verses 11 and 12 conjure visions of Solomon's descendants being herded onto trains and whipped into gas chambers while the residents of towns only a mile away deny knowledge of the camp and claim the stench is from a glue factory. Does anyone with a heart and a brain disagree that such evil acts should be prevented? God tells us here that He will not tolerate moral cowardice and inaction when the lives of innocents are threatened. He will sometimes deliver justice in this life and always in the next. He will not accept lame excuses either, such as "That's a job for the police."

6

God's Warrior – David and Self-Defense

Have you ever thought what you would do if you were in a convenience store or bank when an armed robbery occurred? At what point would you intervene and under what conditions? Would you react differently if your spouse or kids were with you? Have you taught loved ones a code word by which they know to flee or find cover because you are about to engage the bad guy?

Here are my answers to those questions (for which I am indebted to Evan Marshall: cop, author, college professor, and survivor of three shootouts). If an armed robbery goes down while I am in the snack aisle, I will pay attention, memorize details of the robbers, their car and tags, take cell phone photos if possible and generally act like I am from out-of-town. I will have already scoped out concealment and cover when I came in. I will slowly and quietly move to cover or to an exit, unless one or more of the following four scenarios occurs:

1. A firearm is discharged (not necessarily at anyone). Just the chance of harmful ricochet is enough to force me to preclude their recklessness as quickly as I can.

2. Actual violence (with or without weapons) is used against staff or patrons.

3. They start searching the patrons. If they find my gun or concealed carry permit, they are likely to disarm and hurt me.

4. They order everyone to lie down or start herding them into a cooler or storage room. Ask any robbery/homicide investigator, and he will tell you that if robbers do either of those two things, there is more than a 90 percent chance that they are about to execute the witnesses.

If loved ones are with me, then my first act will be to sneak us out, but if one of the scenarios listed above occur, I am going to move fast and decisively as they go for cover or an exit. Yes, we have signals. No, I will not tell you what they are. Get your own that fit your family. By the way, I have taught my family the difference between cover (something that stops a bullet) and concealment (that merely keeps the bad guys from seeing you). You should, too.

As Edmund Burke said, "All that is necessary for the triumph of evil is that good men do nothing."[4]

My lawyer buddy was on an out-of-state trip getting breakfast with his family at a fast-food joint. After getting mom and the two kids settled with their food, he went up front to find something. He noticed a tattooed skinhead-looking guy in line with the pearl grip of a snubby .38 revolver peeking out of his front pants pocket. My buddy instantly did a 180, walked to his table, and quietly ordered the family to drop everything and head for the exit. Once in the car, he drove a few hundred yards to a gas station and called 911 on his cell phone. Did my buddy have a gun? Yes. Could he possibly have been over-reacting to nothing besides an honest citizen who did not understand the concept of carrying concealed? Yes. Did he do the right thing by getting himself and his beloved non-combatants out as soon as he saw a potential danger? Absolutely. Does he regret the 12 bucks worth of food left on the table? Not at all.

Like my friend, armed Christians do not go looking for fights, and they avoid fights if they can: "If possible, so far as it depends on you, be at peace with all men" (Romans 12:18). However, if felons force us into defensive action, our training, tactics, and forethought are necessary to get us through.

Learning from David Today

We can learn several lessons from David's victory over Goliath. First, practice and skill with your weapon of choice gives you the confidence and ability you will need in an emergency. Next, thinking tactically beforehand about hypothetical situations will help you approach emergencies with a plan.

David is one of the most fascinating men of the Bible. The Bible portrays him as a man like any of us, with all the human virtues and faults. Here we are concerned with David the warrior. Several incidents in his life are relevant to our understanding of the biblical view of self-defense.

David's first act of self-defense was his duel with Goliath. It began as a reflection of his character. Jesse told David to take some food to his brothers and their captain. So David got up early in the morning and set off (1 Samuel 17:12-20). Now that is a miracle of God! At his dad's behest and without griping, a teenager got up at the crack of dawn and did his chores! The rest of 1 Samuel 17 tells the story. Goliath (9 ½ feet tall) challenged Saul to settle the war between Israel and Philistia by trial by combat between two champions. It was common in ancient warfare for nations to avoid general bloodshed by having duels between champions or between whole units as late as the 4th century B.C.[1] Since David's battle was one-on-one combat, the situation is relevant to self-defense. The duel was sanctioned as part of a national war effort. However, today all modern statutes forbid dueling, and a self-defense claim is not available to either combatant in court.[2] In any case, David was still in a kill-or-be-killed situation. It required situational awareness, proficiency with his own weapon, and knowledge of the capability of his opponent's weapons and tactics. Above all, it required absolute conviction of the rightness of his cause and his own actions in killing his enemy.

David was not a 21st century man who lived in a post-Christian, post-modern society where many hold that there are no absolutes of right and wrong. He saw the duel as a reflection of the cosmic eternal war between God and Satan (1 Samuel 17:26(b), 31-37, 45-47). Paul explains this in Ephesians 6:10-12:

> Finally, be strong in the Lord, and in the strength of His might. Put on the full armor of God, that you may be able to stand firm against the schemes of the devil. For our struggle is not against flesh and blood, but against the rulers, against the powers, against the world forces of this darkness, against the spiritual forces of wickedness in the heavenly places.

David understood that Israel was to be God's example to the world of His love, justice, and mercy. The Philistines had to be stopped from extinguishing that light in the world. In any episode of our life, we must always remember that our conflict with another person is never just between the two of us. God has a holy intent for both of us and our futures from that moment on. At a minimum, it is God's will that evil acts must be prevented and good acts must be encouraged. Someone is always watching to see how we, as Christians, will respond. Beyond that, there are consequences for our own lives and others that we will not realize for years down the road. As Christians, we know that our lives, words, and deeds have eternal significance.

The history of Israel's wars since they left Egypt shows that though they fought the battles, God had given the victory.[3] Before Saul, David showed he understood the significance of someone facing up to and defeating Goliath. He said, "Let no man's heart fail on account of him; your servant will go and fight this Philistine" (1 Samuel 17:31-37).

We should understand deterrence as David did. The armed, trained defender of the innocent is a terror not only to the present predator, but to all those who would be tempted to follow in the predator's footsteps. That is why violent crime rates are lower in states that have concealed carry laws (as studies by John Lott and Wright and Rossi have shown).

David understood the goodness and godliness of saving innocent life. By preserving the lives of innocent victims and protecting survivors from dealing with life-altering trauma, we allow them to fulfill all their potential with which they might bless the world. Failing to stand up is fatal. As Edmund Burke said, "All that is necessary for the triumph of evil is that good men do nothing."[4]

David understood that ultimately, true Evil cannot be waited out, compromised with, or appeased. Evil must be defeated. Pacifists with bumper stickers proclaiming, "War is NOT the Answer" ignore the fact that people like Goliath have bumper stickers on their chariots that say, "War is ALWAYS the Answer!" Pacifists fail to recognize that over the past two centuries, war gave America its independence, freed the slaves and made them citizens, destroyed Nazism, and destroyed the equally militarist/racist Japanese Empire. Finally, the readiness and resolve to go to war, if needed, eventually collapsed Soviet communism, the greatest threat to freedom in history.

Verses 33-37 of 1 Samuel 17 show that David knew the battle was God's, not his. Saul objected that Goliath (apart from his size and apparent weapon advantage) had far more battle experience than David. David responded that God had empowered him to kill a lion and a bear barehanded on separate occasions. David was convinced that God would defeat Goliath through him in a like manner. The citizen who exercises lawful self-defense can have the same confidence. "Do not be afraid of sudden fear; or the onslaught of the wicked when it comes; for the Lord will be your confidence, and will keep your foot from being caught" (Proverbs 3:25-26). When David said, "The Lord who delivered me from paw of the lion and the paw of the bear, He will deliver me from the hand of this Philistine" (verse 37), he was actually saying, "Look king, that's a 9 ½ foot tall dead man over there. I'm just going down there to convince him of it." By faith, David believed that Goliath was defeated before he even started into the Valley of Elah. Here David teaches a lesson constantly repeated in Scripture: the God who helped me then is able to help me now.

In his selfless heroism and faith in God, David models Jesus, the Good Shepherd, who laid down His life for His sheep (John 10:1-8). That is why I have chosen the term *shepherd* to describe armed citizens, police, and soldiers who stand ready to defend others. The shepherd recognizes the enemy, knows his own capabilities and practices to preserve and improve his skills. He is constantly alert for danger to his flock. Just like Jesus and David, the shepherd does not care about the odds, because preserving the sheep is worth his life. David had God's promise that He would be with him and would never leave him (Deuteronomy 31:6; Joshua 1:5). We have the same promise (Hebrews 13:5b-6). If we truly love others, then we will equip and train for and then act to save them in emergencies. Jesus has set the example for us: God plus one is greater than any opposition.

As David walked to the valley floor, he stopped at a brook and gathered five smooth stones. I have always wondered, "Why five? If David had all this confidence, why not just get one rock?" The first answer is that Goliath had four sons, or possibly brothers (2 Samuel 21:15-22). David had probably heard this and wanted backup ammo in case Goliath's family was there, got mad at the outcome, and tried to avenge him on the spot. Second, five stones meant David was prepared for a miss or the necessity for subsequent blows to kill Goliath. Just as modern bullets can miss or fail to stop the bad guy with the first hit, so could a stone. David's faith and sling training made him sure of the outcome, but God had not been explicit as to how David would kill Goliath. So like a modern cop, soldier, or licensed gun owner who trains in failure drills and carries spare magazines and/or a backup gun, David was ready to finish the job if Plan A went wrong. Third, he got creek stones because they are rounded and therefore aerodynamic. Manufactured sling stones from antiquity were fashioned like tiny footballs to fly true.[5]

When Goliath saw that an unarmed shepherd boy (instead of a "worthy opponent") had been sent against him, he was insulted. He then tried to terrify David, cursing him by the Philistine gods and threatening to leave his corpse unburied, perhaps a more terrifying threat than death itself to ancient people (1 Samuel 17:41-44). Undaunted, David let Goliath know his perspective with this reply:

> You come to me with a sword, a spear, and a javelin, but I come to you in the name of the Lord of Hosts, the God of the armies of Israel, whom you have taunted. This day the Lord will deliver you up into my hands, and I will strike you down and remove your head from you. And I will give the dead bodies of the army of the Philistines this day to the birds of the air and the wild beasts of the earth, that all the earth may know that there is a God in Israel, and that all this assembly may know that the Lord does not deliver by sword or by spear; for the battle is the Lord's and He will give you into our hands (verses 45-47).

Incensed, Goliath strode toward David, who ran at him, simultaneously loading his sling. Firing, David hit Goliath dead center of the forehead. As my dad would say, "Right between the running lights." Instantly, Goliath crashed face down. David ran up, drew the dead man's sword, and beheaded him, displaying his massive head to both armies and proving that Goliath was not just stunned. The amazed Philistine army panicked and routed. The Israelites pursued and killed tens of thousands (1 Samuel 18:7) until the survivors reached refuge in Gath and Ekron (verses 48-52).

The most important lesson that David teaches with Goliath is that a deep conviction about the rightness of defending innocent life is vital to an effective response. It gives us the assurance that self-defense is God's work, and that He is using us to do it (Ephesians 2:10). Criminals usually initiate the action, so self-defense is reactive. The last thing you need when you have two to three seconds to meet an assault is to decide whether your response is justified before God. This is no time to start tackling major theological questions. Indecision and hesitation on your part will mean catastrophic failure. Beforehand, you need to be as certain of your righteous actions down to your core as David was that day with Goliath. Then you will be free to use your training, skills, and weapons to maximum effect. Finally, to survive mentally and spiritually, join David and make the Lord your Shepherd (Psalm 23). As Isaiah puts it:

For the Lord God helps me, therefore, I am not disgraced; therefore, I have set my face like flint, and I know that I shall not be ashamed. He who vindicates me is near; who will contend with me? Let us stand up to each other; who has a case against me? Let him draw near to me. Behold the Lord God helps me; who is he who condemns me? Behold, they will all wear out like a garment; the moth will eat them. Who is it among you that fears the Lord, that obeys the voice of His servant, that walks in darkness and has no light? Let him trust in the name of the Lord and rely on his God (Isaiah 50:7-10).

With this attitude, you can defeat any giant in your life.

The Law and Mercy

Alabama's self-defense statute defines when physical force can be used in self-defense: "A person is justified in using physical force upon another person in order to defend himself or a third person from what he reasonably believes to be the use or imminent use of unlawful physical force by that other person."[1] *Imminent* is the key word here. As stated earlier, the threat must actually be happening or just about to happen. Latter parts of the statute use the terms "using or about to use," "committing or about to commit," and "in the process of unlawfully and forcefully."[2]

What is the difference? *Committing* or *using* occurs when the criminal strides up to you in a dark parking lot and says, "This is a stick-up!" with a gun in his hand, aimed at you. "About to commit (or use)" is the same scenario, but he is pulling up his shirt tail as one hand reaches inside his waistband for what appears to be a pistol grip, or his pointed finger in his pocket makes you think he is pointing a gun at you. In either case, the law describes this threat as clear and present danger and allows you to react with force.

"Does this mean the bad guy must actually swing a ball bat at my head before I can pull my gun?" No. In court, you will be judged by the standard of "the ordinary, reasonable, prudent person (ORPP) under like or similar circumstances." The law says the jury will be asked to decide whether the average person – under the same circumstances and knowing what you knew at the time – would have been justified in using deadly force (or any degree of force less than that) under the particular facts of your case. If he says he is going to hurt you with the bat and is within range to do so (police standard is 21 feet), you can draw your weapon before he strikes.

What does "knowing what you knew at the time" mean? Let's say that as a teenager you saw a karate demonstration. The presenter showed you his prowess with nunchucks (foot-long wooden sticks attached by a chain or leather thong, a weapon made famous by Bruce Lee). During the presentation, he broke concrete blocks with them and warned everyone not to try them without professional training (pointing out that he had broken three of his own ribs while perfecting his technique). He further explained that they are deadly weapons banned in several states, and you should run if anyone ever pulled these on you unless you had a firearm.

Ten years later, a driver runs a red light and hits your car. He exits his vehicle, screaming profanity. You ask him to calm down, tell him you are on your cell phone to the cops, and they will come straighten things out (so you are acting in an ordinary, reasonable, and prudent manner). From less than 20 feet away, he yells, "I'll straighten you out." Reaching into his back seat, you see him pulling out a set of nunchucks in each hand. You remember what the karate demonstrator said about them 10 years ago (therefore, anyone who knows what you do would recognize them as deadly weapons). Just as he straightens up and starts to twirl them, his eyes bulge as he sees your 9mm pointed at his chest. (Drawing your gun is prudent to prevent him from closing to within striking distance.) You stay on the phone with 911. He throws his weapons back into his car and backs up saying, "Hey man, it's cool." You reasonably decide not to shoot him because he has stopped his threat. You holster your gun as the cops arrive. They detect alcohol on his breath, confirm from witnesses that you had the light, and take the guy into custody for DUI, reckless driving, and misdemeanor menacing.

The cops check your concealed carry license and let you go once the accident report is written. Why didn't they arrest you? Because both you and the police knew these facts:

1. Nunchucks are a deadly weapon.

2. An average person can cross seven yards in less than two seconds and hit you (faster than most people can pull a concealed gun and fire one round).

3. The attacker could have pulled a firearm (instead of the nunchucks) from the car and shot you instantly, so you were justified in drawing your weapon as he reached into the car.

4. His out-of-control demeanor, profanity, and specific threat would tell any

reasonable person that he intended harm. When he reached into his car, it was logical to assume that he was not going to pull out a Bible and ask you to pray with him.

Therefore, your response was ordinary, reasonable, prudent, and lawful under these particular facts.

Your knowledge and training regarding such threats, demeanor, and his proximity justified your pulling your gun as he reached into his car; your anticipation that he would offer violence was reasonable. Your knowledge and training is a factor the jury must consider: what you knew under the "like or similar circumstances." Had his weapon been a firearm, there is little chance you could have drawn fast enough after you realized what he had in his hand. Consequently, the law allows a reasonable person to react by anticipating a deadly assault. In addition, the more you have learned and the more you have been trained explain the "reasonableness" of your actions at the time. Be able to document your training and study. All the self-defense books, videos, articles, experiences, and training you have studied and experienced comprise the totality of your reasonable, conscientious action in the matter. In other words, the law recognizes that the Israeli Air Force is not the only outfit that can conduct a preemptive strike. As Supreme Court Justice Oliver Wendell Holmes put it, "Detached reflection is not required in the presence of an upraised knife."[3]

Ability, Opportunity, and Jeopardy

How do we know when we can use force? Competent police and civilian self-defense instructors teach three critical factors that must coincide to justify use-of-force: ability, opportunity, and jeopardy.

Ability

Ability means your opponent has the power to kill or cripple by armed or unarmed attack. You must be able to show a jury that you knew his weapon was readily capable of causing death or permanent injury. That is fairly easy to determine. But what if he was unarmed? Then you must show that even though he was unarmed the attacker had the power to kill or cripple because of greater size, ferocity of attack, or martial arts training, for example. Next, you can show that one of several factors was present that triggers the "unequal force" or "disparity of force" doctrine. These factors give the unarmed attacker such an overwhelming advantage in the fight that it is highly likely you could have been killed or maimed for life had you not used the equalizing force of a weapon. You will find this concept in any good criminal law textbook.[4]

The first unequal force factor is force of numbers. The U.S. Supreme Court case of *Beard v. United States* addressed a man threatened by three attackers in a feud over a stolen cow.[5] The court said the lone defender was justified in pulling a shotgun, first because of their stated threats to kill him and because of their superior numbers. A second factor arises when a healthy attacker assaults an incapacitated victim. In *Beard,* the defendant/victim was nearly blind as well as outnumbered. Whereas a healthy adult male would normally not be justified in pulling a gun in a fair fight with another healthy adult male, Mr. Beard, outnumbered and handicapped, could do so.

A third factor is male versus female. The average female has about 80 percent of the upper body strength of the average male. Consequently, in a stand-up fight, women are at a disadvantage. I once testified on disparity-of-force in a case where a female slapped a male co-worker who had grabbed her by the upper arm. She slapped his face once, and he let go. There was an administrative review to see if she would keep her job. Her defense team brought out two relevant facts: she was further handicapped by Crohn's disease, and the male co-worker had a history of harassing her through verbal taunts and practical jokes. As I explained to the review board, even without factoring in Crohn's disease, her status as "the weaker sex" under the disparity-of-force doctrine allowed her to respond to his offensive touch (which is Physical Harassment, the lowest level of assault in Alabama) by escalating one level above his violence (a grab or shove) to a slap or hit. She would have exceeded the allowable force had she continued slapping him after he let go, or had she hit him with a mop (or any higher level of force). As it was, however, her one slap escalation was completely justifiable under the law.

Great size versus a significantly smaller opponent is a fourth factor that would allow a "munchkin" victim to raise the force level. As the 19th century saying goes, "God created men, Sam Colt made them equal." In *Defensive Tactics with Flashlights*, Jon Peters, a nationally known police impact weapons instructor, computes the chances of survival of an unarmed person of a particular size (of the same sex) against an unarmed person of murderous intent of the same or larger size.[6] It is interesting reading that clearly illustrates the disparity-of-force concept.

A fifth factor considers an elderly or handicapped person against a younger and/or physically superior attacker. Obviously, this scenario would allow the wheelchair-bound or an 80-year-old person to escalate his response to a younger, healthy attacker. Pepper spray is an excellent equalizer for the elderly. Unlike martial arts, pepper spray does not require months and years of strenuous physical training and can be carried concealed in any pocket. All you do is shake, point, flick off the safety, and fire a short burst. Since it works against any biological organism, pepper spray is perfect for dogs and any feral critters that may cross your path.

If you know your attacker is a martial artist, then you would be allowed to escalate your force level under this doctrine as well. If you suddenly find yourself in a fender-bender with Mike Tyson and he comes at you screaming threats, you should definitely pull an equalizer fast because you know about his boxing prowess, size and age advantage, lack of self-control, and criminal record. Otherwise, he could kill you with one punch. What if some guy starts kata moves and announces he is a black belt (but is not), and you respond in a way that seriously injures him? You are allowed to escalate based on reasonable appearances under the ordinary, reasonable, prudent person standard. As long as you escalate to the appropriate level, you are legally okay, but it will be regrettable for him. Since he voluntarily caused your reasonable escalation, he has "assumed the risk," and in many states, if no criminal liability is found in your act of self-defense, he is absolutely barred from filing a civil suit.[7]

The sixth factor that allows you to escalate force is personal knowledge (not second-hand) of the vicious nature of your attacker, combined with the savagery of his attack. This is another way the "knowing what you knew at the time" part of ordinary, reasonable, and prudent person comes in. I consulted on a case that illustrates this perfectly. In that case was a man who would attack people without provocation. Let's call him Bob. His two best friends said that he could be a very good friend at times, but both also stated, "He needed killing!" The defendant in the case was a pool player with a generally inoffensive demeanor. Let's call him Fred. I consulted with his defense team. Bob and Fred knew each other from the local pool hall.

Two weeks before the shooting, Bob and Fred had a conversation. Bob told Fred that he had just bailed out of jail on a first degree felony assault. Bob said to Fred, "See this blood on my boots? I had fun gettin' this blood on my boots. Know how I got it on them?" Then Bob proceeded to tell Fred how he had pulled his pickup into the parking lot of an auto parts store. As he walked past his truck bed, he saw a stranger coming out of the store. "I didn't like his looks. So I reached into the bed of the truck and got a log chain with a big lock on it and beat him with it till he didn't move no more." Bob's savagery sent the man to the hospital, and Bob was arrested. Fred heard this story from Bob's own mouth and grimly watched how he laughed as he told his story. Thus Fred had personal knowledge from Bob himself that proved Bob's violent reputation in the community.

Two weeks later, Bob and Fred were back at the pool hall. Bob was in a bad mood because the guy who was supposed to buy dope from him had not shown up, and Bob needed money. Fred was playing pool across the room with one of Bob's friends. He and Bob's friend got into an argument about the original bet and payment on the outcome. Bob heard the disagreement and suddenly stormed across the hall, getting in Fred's face. When Fred backed up and pointed out that this was not Bob's business, Bob started screaming profanities and swinging. Yelling he would kill Fred with his bare hands (despite the fact that he was 2 inches shorter and 20 pounds lighter), Bob attacked, backing Fred up until Fred fell backwards onto a pool table.

Bob leaped onto the table, straddling the supine Fred, raining blows on Fred's face while repeatedly screaming that he would kill him. We must understand Fred's predicament here. Bob had the ability to cause serious injury or to kill Fred at that moment. In a standing situation, a punch's power is reduced by the fact that the head and body can give, or "roll with the punch" when struck. With a slate table beneath him, Fred took the full mechanical force of the blows to his face and skull. Ask any orthopedist, chiropractor, or martial artist; they will tell you that broken facial bones, spinal and brain damage, or other permanent injury is highly likely in such a situation.

Under Alabama law, assault first degree constitutes using fists as a deadly weapon in a case of brutal beating[8] where the attacker intends to cause serious physical injury.[9] Serious physical injury, under the law, is an injury that creates a substantial risk of death, serious or protracted disfigurement or impairment of health, or protracted impairment or loss of any bodily organ (case law includes broken bones under this).[10] Under Alabama's self-defense statute, the victim can use deadly force to stop a first degree assault, which justifies what Fred did next.[11]

With Bob attacking and threatening to kill him, Fred reasonably believed he had one chance. He pulled a .38 revolver, but he did not fire immediately. Instead he jammed the muzzle twice into the side of Bob's neck. Now the neck is a "pain compliance area." Police officers are taught that pressing a knuckle into the side of a resisting suspect's neck will cause such nerve pain that most suspects will immediately cease resisting and comply. Despite being poked so hard that his neck had two bruises in a perfect profile of the gun's muzzle, Bob's murderous frenzy kept him from noticing that Fred had a gun.

Desperate, Fred decided he had no choice but to fire. Yet instead of pressing the muzzle to Bob's head and firing, assuring his death, Fred fired downward into Bob's chest. I think he was shooting to stop, not to kill, but the bullet hit the heart and ended Bob's life. Under the laws of God and man, it was a clear case of justifiable homicide: self-defense. Fred's escalation of force was justified (despite the fact that Bob was unarmed) based on four reasons from the disparity of force doctrine: Bob's repeated threats to kill Fred, the savagery of the attack, the immediate likelihood of serious injury, and his personal knowledge of Bob's savage nature. These are the various criteria that you would use to determine an attacker's ability to do harm and your right to use appropriate force. The attacker's ability to do harm is the first criterion of a legal use-of-force response. Fred acted as an ordinary, reasonable, and prudent person.

Opportunity

Opportunity is the second part of determining whether an opponent can harm you and whether you must respond with force. Opportunity means that your attacker can immediately use his power to kill or cripple you like the unarmed attacker in my previous example. Straddling Fred on the pool table, Bob clearly had opportunity. The factors to be considered in opportunity are the type of weapon and whether an attacker is within striking distance to harm you with it. Is he at seven yards with a ball bat? He has opportunity. Is he 50 yards away? No opportunity exists. He cannot immediately hurt you. At seven yards, you can legally shoot him; at 50 yards, no go.

Jeopardy

The final criterion is *jeopardy*. You are in jeopardy if your opponent has ability and opportunity while using words, body language, facial expressions and vocal tones, gestures (both gross and fine motor), and other movements that indicate an impending attack or intent to harm you. In other words, he is demonstrating to the whole world that his intent is to harm you, just as Bob did in my example. When ability, opportunity, and jeopardy coincide, the *preclusion* of his illegal attack is justified. Preclusion is the police training term for whatever means will effectively stop the assault. Fred's knowledge of Bob's vicious nature plus Bob's brutal assault and stated intent to kill all put Fred in jeopardy and justified his deadly response.

A Venn diagram illustrates this concept perfectly.

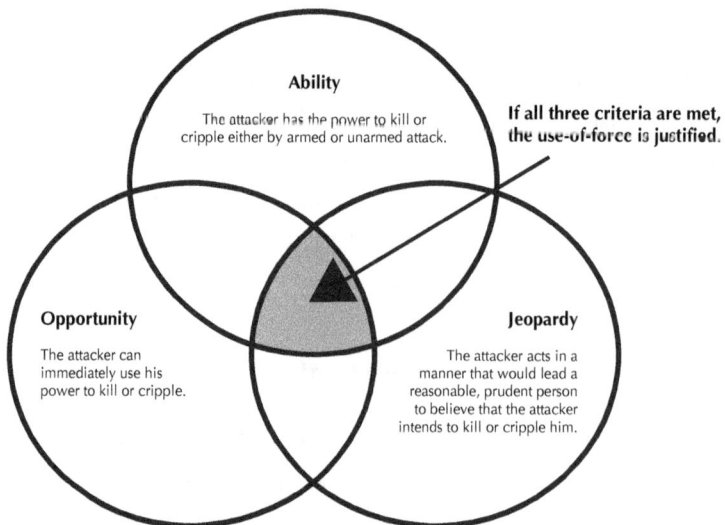

Ability
The attacker has the power to kill or cripple either by armed or unarmed attack.

If all three criteria are met, the use-of-force is justified.

Opportunity
The attacker can immediately use his power to kill or cripple.

Jeopardy
The attacker acts in a manner that would lead a reasonable, prudent person to believe that the attacker intends to kill or cripple him.

When ability, opportunity, and jeopardy coincide, an innocent victim can legally use appropriate defensive force. The more you learn about the law, weapons, and martial arts, the better you will be able to apply this concept as an ordinary, reasonable, prudent person.

David, Mercy, and Self-Defense

One of the basic rules of self-defense is that we can only defend ourselves when actually in danger, not because we think we might be attacked. To be legally and morally eligible to use self-defense, the danger to you or to a third party must be immediate. The danger cannot have happened 30 seconds ago. It has got to be now.

Three incidents in David's life illustrate this basic component of self-defense: First when he refused to kill King Saul in the cave (1 Samuel 24), second when he prevented Abishai from killing Saul in the desert near Ziph (1 Samuel 26), and third when David "cooled off" and spared the life of a very rude man named Nabal. In these three incidents, David demonstrates his refusal to take revenge or to kill based on ambition. David lived a life of forgiveness, even for those who hated him and repeatedly tried to kill him.

Though Saul made numerous attempts to end David's life, at no time did David retaliate or plot to overthrow Saul, despite the fact that David was God's chosen king. Instead, he reacted with mercy, forgiveness, and avoided war with Saul.

Between the two episodes with Saul, for several months, David's men had voluntarily guarded the herds and flocks of a rich man, Nabal. At harvest time, David asked for some food as a reward for his men. Nabal sent back an insulting reply, stating that he was not going to pay attention to a runaway outlaw chief. David became furious! He ordered his men to arm themselves and swore he would not leave one male alive on Nabal's land.

Abigail, Nabal's wife, met David on the way. She apologized to David for her husband's idiotic rudeness ("Nabal" in Hebrew means "fool") and begged him to forgive. David cooled down and led his men back to camp. We should learn from his character and self-control in this story. Though momentarily exasperated, David listened to reason and reconsidered. We are to be the "ordinary, reasonable, prudent person" and not "fly off the handle." As James says, "But everyone must be quick to hear, slow to speak, and slow to anger; for the anger of man does not achieve the righteousness of God" (James 1:19b, 20).

David exercised mercy because he realized God had a plan. In his Psalms, David asked God to execute justice on his enemies in His time, not in David's time. David refused to preemptively strike those who did not immediately threaten him or his people. He realized that his job was to preserve, protect, and defend – not to punish. In the same way, modern statutes require that both police and civilians use only the amount of force "reasonably necessary" to effect an arrest or to defend life. Once the attack stops or control is gained, our force must de-escalate proportionately.[11] One more kick or punch "for good measure" or "to show who's boss" does not follow the law nor does it comply with "love thy neighbor as thyself" (Leviticus 19:18). David's relationship with God gave him the moral standards to avoid unnecessary violence and to have a relationship with God that spiritually saved him.

If you are going to defend yourself based on Biblical morals, you have got to have a relationship with God, not just knowledge of the rules. Like David, it is best when we develop a lifelong relationship of trust in God's mercy, love and grace. When, like David, we can look back on how God has intervened, guided, and protected us, we can regard our future difficulties with the right attitude. David models both the moral and the modern legal standard for us: that force should only be used when there is a direct, immediate threat against us or an innocent third party, and that mercy should always be foremost in our thoughts.

Trusting in God will help you, like David, to meet that standard. David's faith can be summed up by Psalm 27:1, "The Lord is my light and my salvation, whom shall I fear? The Lord is the defense of my life, whom shall I dread?" Study this psalm. It teaches us that God is in control. If you truly believe that, then no matter what job you work, what disabilities you endure, no matter which political party controls the White House and Congress, you can know that God has a purpose and a plan for your life. As David said, "When evildoers came upon me to devour my flesh, my adversaries and my enemies, they stumbled and fell. Though a host encamp against me, my heart will not fear; though war rise against me, in spite of this I will be confident" (Psalm 27:2-3). Because you know the righteousness of defending innocent life, you can defend it with a clear conscience. And as a consequence, you will not hesitate when the situation requires an immediate response. Self-defense allows us to secure God's protection in the here and now as well as the sweet by-and-by.

David shows us the necessity for decisiveness in emergencies. Yet his actions also teach that we must never use force unless the threat is immediate. Rather, in those circumstances, we must leave our adversaries to the wisdom and justice of God. "Trust in the Lord with all your heart, and do not lean on your own understanding. In all your ways acknowledge Him, and He will make your paths straight" (Proverbs 3:5-6).

Vengeance is Thine, Lord, Not Mine

God forbids vengeance. Paul starts his directions for mercy, forgiveness, and witness in dealing with others with Romans 12:9-16. Then he continues with warnings against revenge and how to replace it with love (verses 17-21). Not returning evil for evil means refusing to "fight fire with fire." This does not mean we cannot use a gun if the bad guys do; it means the *motives* for our actions cannot be sinful. Only responses based in Scripture are legitimate. We must never assume that self-defense is "the lesser of two evils." It most certainly is *not* evil. If you have read this far, you know that self-defense is a righteous and holy remedy for evil, not merely a regrettable option. Our motives and actions are (and must be) 180 degrees from those of the felons we are trying to stop. Therefore, legal self-defense can never be described as "meeting evil with evil" (Romans 12:19-21). Our act may end with the injury or death of the criminal, but he created that danger and suffered for it. He forced us to preserve what is innocent and good. In fact, the felon's injuries are self-inflicted, and we have overcome evil with good (Romans 12:21).

Let's say you come home unexpectedly and find a burglar in your home. He dashes out another door and runs down the street, so you pull your revolver and fire after him. Wrong! This is vengeance, legally, morally and biblically. You are getting even for the outrage of his violating your home. If your shots miss, you are criminally and civilly liable for any damage to property or any injury to innocent people. In fact, since the burglary is over and he poses no threat, you are criminally and civilly liable to him if you hit him! If he is not an immediate threat or refusing to leave your house, his crime is a matter for the cops and your insurance company. When I speak on self-defense, outraged citizens often exclaim, "You mean if a guy is stealing my car, I can't shoot him!?"

"Nope," I reply. "Not unless he tries to run you over with it."

"What if I catch someone raping my daughter?" they will ask.

The law says that if he ceases the attempt to rape, you cannot fire as long as he does not try to resume the rape or to disarm you. To do otherwise is vengeance. However, if he rushes you, even unarmed, you can fire. I am aware of no state law that requires you to fight for possession of your gun with a criminal. Romans 12 teaches us that we must not act out of rage or frustration. Rather, we must let the Holy Spirit guide us into being "the ordinary, reasonable, prudent person under like or similar circumstances;" that is the standard by which we will be judged. Use of legal defensive force is like being a husband or a church elder: it is not so much a position of authority as one of responsibility.

Beware of the all-too-common (and all-too-prevalent in popular thinking) macho mentality about self-defense. To see this bold ignorance on display, check out the comments section of any internet story about self-defense or victimization. You will see the full panoply of the crowd that thinks: "My gun makes me a man, and I can solve any problem with it." Nearly all of the comments are short on education and long on myths. If someone with legal training and experience tries to introduce facts, these commandos simply redouble their ignorance parade.

Unfortunately, when members of this group actually find themselves in bad situations, their legal fantasies and moral ignorance guarantee legal disaster. They will spend upwards of a thousand dollars on a new gun, ammo, and accessories but will balk at spending less than half of that for legal counsel and firearms training. I do not know why some people are so resistant to instruction. Instead of spending five hours in class with me and walking out of that class legally prepared to judiciously apply any level of force, they will wait until their media-infused "information" gets them criminally charged and civilly sued. Apparently, they would rather spend 50 to 100 thousand dollars on their defense lawyer than pay a fraction of that to learn self-defense law and tactics. And the cost is more than monetary. Think of the effect negative publicity will have on their home life, business, and reputation. Please get trained and educated. Do not give yourself and other gun owners a black eye and ruin your life because you shirk the responsibility of gun ownership. Which do you think will stand up in court: acting according to the law or acting according to your personal sense of outrage and justice? You know the answer.

The law requires that any justifiable level of force must be *only* the level reasonably necessary to stop the required criminal threat or act – and no more. The U.S. Supreme Court standard for police officers allows deadly force to be used on a fleeing felon only if the felon is an immediate threat to you or other innocents,[1] and this is a good standard for civilians to follow as well. Romans 12:17-21 emphasizes the moral aspects of state laws by urging us to examine our motives and methods:

> Never pay back evil for evil to anyone. Respect what is right in the sight of all men. Never take your own vengeance, beloved, but leave room for the wrath of God, for it is written, 'Vengeance is mine, I will repay,' says the Lord. 'But if your enemy is hungry, feed him, and if he is thirsty, give him a drink, for in so doing you will heap coals of fire on his head.' Do not be overcome by evil, but overcome evil with good.[2]

One reason for the Mosaic Law was to short circuit vengeful acts. We all know what vengeance is, whether it is called *payback, vendetta,* or perversely, *justice.* Vengeance is a premeditated act intended to return hurt for hurt (and usually to deal a greater hurt than we received). When we shoot a rapist in the act, we do not act from vengeance but from the simple, decent desire to defend and preserve innocent life. That act is right in the sight of all mankind (Romans 12:17b). There is no Bible verse or sane person who would dream it legally correct or biblically moral for us to sit by and watch while our family or other innocents are slaughtered. "But the attacker is a fellow human being," cries the pacifist. True, but his intent and felonious acts have separated us from him *in that moment* as far as your pet kitty is from a Bengal tiger. His morals and goals are alien to those of typical humans, and we must meet his violence with God's morality until he is no longer a threat. "When justice is done, it brings joy to the righteous but terror to evildoers" (Proverbs 21:15, NIV). Recall the verses already presented that command us to defend the innocent (such as Proverbs 3:27-28; 24:11-12). Everyone with moral sense would applaud us for saving victims from an undeserved fate. So does God. Remember Leviticus 19:16(b): "neither shall thou stand idly by the blood of thy neighbor."[3]

However, we should not run around looking for trouble. Self-defense cannot be claimed by one who deliberately places himself in a position where he has reason to believe his presence will provoke trouble. Paul tells us that "[I]f possible, so far as it depends on you, be at peace with all men" (Romans 12:18). That is easy if we are walking in Christ: "let everyone be quick to hear, slow to speak and slow to anger" (James 1:19b). We will learn to listen to people, giving them consideration and respect. We will train to ignore slights, insults, and arguments with strangers. We will develop strategies to stay out of trouble. I long ago adopted one of Massad Ayoob's suggestions to diffuse trouble. When I am out of my hometown, I carry a 10 or 20 dollar bill in a money clip so I can "buy off" potential attackers on the street. The clip gives weight to the cash and allows me to toss it from a safe distance. As a lawyer, I know how costly defending a criminal or civil use-of-force charge can be. If I can buy off a thug or two without having to hurt them or without having to use force when my wife and children are present, I will certainly do so. But if the attacker persists in assaulting me, the situation no longer depends on me being at peace with them. They have forced my response.

If I can silently intimidate to prevent muggers from focusing on me, I will do it. When I had a job on the road and frequently had to enter dangerous areas, I carried a large, aluminum, two-pound police flashlight outside my hotel room night or day. Bad guys know what cops use those for: to strike with bone-breaking force or to blind temporarily with bright light. Through two years and six states, no one ever bothered me. These flashlights are highly effective. When I was an auxiliary officer in my hometown, another part-time officer related his flashlight episode when he was a New Mexico sheriff's deputy. He and his partner were questioning a man at a domestic violence scene. My friend had his light resting on his shoulder when the suspect suddenly pulled a .25 automatic. My friend crashed the barrel of the flashlight into the suspect's forehead, dropping him immediately. The suspect sued for "excessive use of force." At trial, his lawyer asked him to identify the cop who hit him. He gazed over the courtroom and then replied, "I can't remember." Case dismissed.

Injuring the felon is legal because his felony has literally deprived him of law-abiding citizen status.[4] Lawyers are taught this concept as the Doctrine of Competing Harms. To preserve innocent life, lesser laws can be temporarily ignored. If your son has a compound fracture or your daughter has a severe allergic reaction that makes it difficult for her to breathe, then you have good reason to run 90 MPH up the road to the ER (with your emergency flashers on). If a cop stops you (or you stop for him), he will either see or hear what is wrong and probably escort you to the ER. However, he may also give you a ticket (or two) once the kid is safely in the ER. In court, you can state the emergency and the Doctrine of Competing Harms. If the judge is worth her robes, she should dismiss the case.

The Doctrine of Competing Harms especially applies in self-defense cases. Whereas we are not normally allowed to harm others, the felon's assault has rendered his life less valuable to society than that of his innocent victim, who can justifiably use appropriate force under the law. Therefore, legal self-defense is not vengeance. It is the logical, rational response to a dire emergency created by a criminal predator. The ordinary reasonable prudent person (ORPP) will use force only to the extent of the law and only for the duration of the threat. The kind of felony or misdemeanor committed statutorily determines the level of force the ORPP can use. The Christian ordinary reasonable prudent person will educate himself legally and spiritually so as not to go one punch or bullet beyond that which is necessary to stop the threat. In the end, the felon has only himself to blame for injuries, but the armed citizen gets credit for a now-safer community. As Jeff Cooper, the father of modern gun fighting said, "If violent crime is to be curbed, it is only the intended victim who can do it. The felon does not fear the police, and he fears neither the judge nor jury. Therefore, he must be taught to fear his victim."[5]

9

Bringing the Criminal Under Control

Ruthless and depraved people have existed throughout time. The world in our day is no kinder or gentler than in Joshua or Paul's day. Despite the wishful thinking of many, some people deliberately choose to do evil to others. I know this. I practiced criminal law for 17 years. (Trust me, I'm a lawyer.) Once they have picked a victim, human predators can rarely be diverted from their course by reason or kindness. When on the hunt and attack, a criminal cannot understand grace, especially when high on drugs. In surveys, violent predators have admitted that 70-75 percent of the time they have committed violent crimes under the influence of drugs or alcohol.[1] You cannot reason with such a person, especially when he has the advantage. However, criminologists have determined that between one and three million times a year felons become *reasonable* (run away, stay for the police, are wounded or killed) when confronted by armed citizens who have the determination and weaponry to resist them.[2]

Pacifists generally take Matthew 5:39-42 out of context, summarizing thusly, "Don't resist a criminal. If he wants to take your jacket, let him have your shirt too; and if he wants anything from you, go the extra mile." Let's examine this scripture using the following example. You are a bank teller who is handed a note that says, "This is a hold up. Put all the money in the bag." So you give him the contents of your cash drawer, thoughtfully not including the explosive dye pack. After all, it is not in the spirit of giving to get him caught, is it? Then you say, "Certainly, brother, Jesus loves you and so do I. Here's the bank's money and my wallet. You can get my home address from there. Oh, and take my car keys, too. My teenage daughter is home alone, and I'm sure she'll gladly cater to your every whim in the Spirit of Jesus. Remember, God loves you!" Do you really imagine your actions would be an effective witness? Is your action what Jesus intended? Would He handle it that way? How would your daughter feel about that? Let's be real here. We all knew it

was a joke when comedian Henny Youngman said, "But take my wife – please!"
But if pacifist Christians are sincere about turning the other cheek and giving to
those who ask in this manner, they must concede its logical conclusion in this
scenario and carry it through. Did Jesus really mean to put us in this position?

Do you really think the bank robber will be so overwhelmed by your
generosity that he will drop his knife, fall to his knees, and beg you to lead him
to Christ? It is possible (such things have happened), but it is highly unlikely.
Instead, he will reason that your abject fear of harm is all that motivates you to
"go the second mile." He will take what he wants, just as he would have done
whether you complied or were forced. Moreover, this "witnessing method" will
not prompt him to think about Jesus any more than with a victim who silently
complies. Statistically, it is almost certain that he is high at the time, so he will
not understand your "witness," nor will he remember it later. In my law practice,
I found it was common that clients were so high when they committed their
crimes that they could not remember the details of their offense just a month later.
Sometimes, they could not recall the date or even the month of their arrest, but
that could have been because they had been arrested so many times.

Even if a robber is not high, he will not recognize any witness you try to make
because he is *in control* of the situation at that moment! Paul makes this very
point in 1 Timothy 1:12-16. He states that he (Saul) was the criminal who *refused*
to understand Jesus as Messiah. Saul was convinced he was doing right and
serving God. He heard Stephen preach and watched him die. Yet the eloquence
of Stephen's words, his exemplary life, the miracles he performed, and his bravery
and forgiveness in death toward his murderers all bypassed Saul's understanding
until Jesus forcibly took control of him on the Damascus Road (Acts 9). Saul
spent the next three days blind, fasting, and praying. Only after Jesus rendered
him helpless and forced him to reexamine his life did Saul acknowledge Jesus as
the promised Messiah. When Ananias came to lead him to Christ, Saul/Paul was
ready. He believed, repented, and was baptized (Acts 22:3-16). Paul, the apostle,
says he would have remained Saul, the fanatic religious murderer, had Jesus not
stopped him by miraculous force. Moreover, he would have continued to think he
was doing right!

When a criminal commits a crime, he too thinks he is doing the right thing for himself. And, like Paul, he will not change his mind until first brought under control. Criminals are people who have accepted an anti-social, selfish attitude as their lifestyle. They do not think they make mistakes, and all their problems come from the mistakes made by others. They view each of their victims as a resource, and harvesting that resource is their job. Organized crime types will gain power and cash through drug sales, corrupting unions and politicians, protection rackets, gambling, and prostitution. Street criminals satisfy their need for cash through theft, burglary, and robbery; they satisfy their lust for sex, control, and power through beatings and rape; and they relieve their frustrations with others through assault and murder. Most street criminals do not set out to hurt you to get what they want. However, they are determined to have their way, so if you are hurt in the bargain, your pain is not their problem. Your pain is how they make their living and how they ease *their* pain. A criminal's feelings are far more important to him than your incidental injury or your loss in the transaction, so he will hurt you if he has to and walk away completely unconcerned for your injury and distress. These individuals are what criminologists call sociopaths.

Psychopaths, such as serial killers and home invaders, seek to inflict and enjoy their victim's pain. For psychopaths, controlling victims and causing them to suffer is the point of the exercise. Fortunately, these guys are a tiny part of the total criminal population, but they are dangerous beyond their numbers because many of them are very smart. Ted Bundy is an example. In 1993, I learned about him at a Department of Justice school for police advisors at the FBI Academy. The chief FBI profiler, Bill Hagemire, spoke to us for two hours about Bundy. He debriefed Bundy during the last two years of Bundy's life, and Bundy called him his best friend. He said Bundy (who had an I.Q. of 135) once made this chilling comment:

"You cops don't understand us serial killers. The world of crime is like a lake. The criminals are fish and you cops are the fishermen. Most of the little fish are stupid. They swim around near the surface and bite on any bait you throw in, so you can catch them anytime. Then there's the bigger fish. They usually stay in the middle depths and they last longer. Once in a while though, you'll lure them to the top with the right bait and catch them. Then there's the big fish like me. We lie on the bottom, constantly looking up and we learn from everything you do – and you *never* catch us!"

Bundy studied his victims, sometimes for weeks, and would break into their houses to learn personal information. When he finally met them, he enjoyed getting them to violate the "Don't talk to strangers" rule before he kidnapped them. As he studied them, he scouted safe locations up to 100 miles away so his plan would not be interrupted. He wanted to make sure he could relish their pain and fear as he raped and murdered them. You do not want to come across his kind. Yet, after being convicted and brought under control, Bundy was brought to Christ on death row by a Florida district attorney and his wife. Would Bundy have repented and come to Christ if he had not been caught and imprisoned? Most who knew him would likely say, "No!" Like Paul, psychopath Bundy would have continued to pollute the earth unless caught or killed. Likewise, both Jeffrey Dahmer and Manuel Noreiga came to Christ after they were arrested and convicted.

Sharing the Gospel with Your Attacker

To respond to the Gospel, a person must first be ready to surrender his will. Armed robbers at large are highly unlikely to do so. However, if you wound or apprehend a criminal, he is under control, and you have choices to make. Ananias was not too sure about going to see Saul because he knew Saul's history, but God reassured Ananias, and he met with Saul (Acts 9:10-19; 22:11-16). This example makes your duty clear: if you bring a criminal under control, you must visit with him in the hospital or jail and share the Gospel with him. You should also see to his needs (insofar as the authorities allow) and learn about him and his family; in other words, you must try to befriend him. That will leave an enduring impression on him! He knows you have no obligation to do any of these things, and none of his other victims ever acted in such a positive manner. He will wonder why you are doing it. You are to treat him as taught in the Sermon on the Mount and Romans 12.

> Abhor what is evil, cling to what is good … rejoicing in hope, persevering in tribulation, devoted to prayer … Bless those who persecute you, bless and curse not … do not be haughty in mind, but associate with the lowly… Never pay back evil for evil to anyone … If possible, so far as it depends on you, be at peace with all men … Never take your own revenge, beloved, but leave

room for the wrath of God, for it is written, 'Vengeance is mine, I will repay' says the Lord. 'But if your enemy is hungry, feed him, ... and if he is thirsty, give him a drink, for in so doing you will heap burning coals on his head'. Do not be overcome by evil, but overcome evil with good (Romans 12:9-21).

Let's break down these verses. "Abhor [hate] what is evil, cling to what is good." The old saying is still biblically true: hate the sin; love the sinner. Even though you despise his deed, you must fight through the justifiable anger. The anger was right and good when he attacked, helping you to focus the adrenaline rush and apply your defensive skills effectively. But when he has been neutralized and/ or wounded, you must refocus, call 911, and begin first aid. Remember, if he is capable of survival, he is capable of redemption! God has to knock some people flat on their backs to make them look up. In the aftermath, God can use the mercy we show to reform him. "Rejoicing in hope, persevering in tribulation, devoted to prayer" (verse 12).

Paul said we need empathy to have a relationship with others:

"For though I am free from all men, I have made myself a slave to all, that I might win the more ... to the Jews I became as a Jew, that I might win Jews; to those under the Law as under the Law, ... that I might win some ... To the weak I became weak ... I have become all things to all men, that I may by all means save some" (I Corinthians 9:19-22).

The criminal might ultimately reject us. His first sociopathic impulse might be to blame us. Almost every criminal client I had whose probation was revoked blamed someone else, despite the fact that he had only four rules to follow: do not commit another crime, do not use drugs, pay your fines and court costs, and keep your appointments with your probation officer. Creatures of habit, they went right back to their criminal haunts, friends, and lifestyle. They lasted an average of six months on probation. Like clockwork, they would commit another crime, have a dirty drug test, or just decide that nobody would notice if they quit seeing their probation officer. I cannot tell you how many times I heard, "It's my girlfriend's fault!" or "I didn't have the dope! The other three guys in the car had the dope!" (Eye roll is appropriate here.) So do not be surprised if he replies to your first aid and hospital or jail visit by blaming you for his injuries and incarceration. That is why Paul tells us "to persevere in tribulation" and "be devoted to prayer" (verse 12).

I once had a jailed client with two separate felony charges. He asked me to get a highly advantageous deal from the D.A. I replied that such terms would be very difficult, but that I would do my best. He then asked me to pray with him and I did. He appeared calm and even spiritual throughout our discussion. That was on Thursday. The following Monday, the more serious of the two charges came up for trial. I negotiated both cases with the D.A. (the lesser charge was on a later docket) on the exact terms my client had requested. The deal was so good that when the second case came up two months later, the D.A. (a nuke-'em-til-they-glow-and-then-shoot-'em-in-the-dark kind of guy) could not believe he had made such a deal until I retrieved the first case file and showed him the agreement. When my client came in that morning, I told him that his prayers had been answered. Instead of thanking me (or God), he added several more demands he had thought up over the weekend. He declared he would not take the deal unless his new demands were also met. When I replied that asking for more would cause the D.A. to revoke the offer, he started cursing me loudly, right there in court. He finally pleaded to the original deal.

"Bless those who persecute you. Bless and curse not. Do not be haughty in mind, but associate with the lowly ... " (Romans 12:14,16b). Criminals are experts at telling you what you want to hear if they think it will help them. Jail-house conversions are common, and some are genuine, but do not count on it. One of the reasons criminals are criminals is their ability to manipulate others and their refusal to accept responsibility for their actions or for the effect their deeds have on others. They must learn that from Genesis to Revelation, the Bible says our thoughts, words, and actions have consequences. If my client treated his lawyer this way, imagine how he might react to you from his hospital bed. If he blames you for his injuries, you must "speak the truth in love" (Ephesians 4:15), firmly reminding him that he *forced* you to cripple or maim him, but that he can be born again from his wheelchair to a new life both here and in eternity.

There may be a time where his continued rejection tells us we need to quit trying. Jesus does not expect us to beat our own heads against a wall. Right after telling us not to judge by our subjective measures but rather by the objective Word of God (Matthew 7:1-5), Jesus illustrates objective judgment by saying not to give holy things to dogs or throw pearls to pigs (Matthew 7:6). When Jesus sent His disciples on their first mission trip, He told them not to waste their time with those who refused to listen but to shake the dust off their feet (Mark 6:11). There comes a time when we know we are wasting our time and we should back off. Yet, we still devote our attacker to prayer because the Holy Spirit can use the foundation we have laid to bear fruit. Down the road, some other Christian (in or out of prison) or various experiences might be what God uses to turn on the light bulb in our attacker's head.

Forgiving Our Attacker

Personal forgiveness of our attacker means dumping our resentment, outrage, and vengeful feelings toward him. We make a conscious decision to put aside our feelings. The punishments and restitution provided by the justice system exist, in part, to allow victims to put the injury behind them. However, personal forgiveness does *not* include dropping the charges. Since the government's criminal code is God's method to control crime, we must let the system work: "leave room for the wrath of God" (Romans 12:16a). We are all responsible for our actions, and by accepting the consequences of our actions, we learn right behavior. Our attacker must do the same. As egocentric as they are, sociopaths will rarely change based on mercy and breaks. Dropping charges just convinces them that they have beaten the system again. They share a common human prayer: "God, if you'll just get me out of this, I promise I'll be good from now on – until I feel better!" As soon as the prosecutor/incarceration/probation pressure is off, they often return to the same neighborhood, friends, temptations, and dead-end choices – unless they are convinced there is a better way.

Nor should their apparent conversion negate or reduce their sentence. Let the law take its course. You may recall the Texas murderer who became a Christian on Death Row. Several prominent Christian leaders lobbied for commuting her sentence to life without parole because of her conversion. I disagree. Any convicted felon who becomes a Christian must be content to endure his sentence. We reap what we sow. If it is prison, then he must learn to live a godly life there as preparation for his new way of life when he is released. If it is the death penalty, then he can take comfort in God's promises for eternal life. We will encourage him as we do dying believers in any terminal situation. Jesus makes clear that our life here is temporary and is not the point of our earthly existence. Moreover, the tribulations of this life will be wiped away by the glories of Heaven. "For I consider that the sufferings of this present time are not worthy to be compared with the glory that is to be revealed to us" (Romans 8:18). "[B]ut just as it is written, 'Things which eye has not seen and ear has not heard, and which have not entered the heart of man, all that God has prepared for those who love Him'" (1 Corinthians 2:9).

Consider working with a prison/jail ministry. By doing so, you will gain a post-graduate education in evangelism and in understanding the criminal mind and method. If that is not your calling, you can support those who are engaged in such a ministry. Another idea is to encourage your congregation to work in and with crime-ridden communities. Children who live there generally lack positive parental models. Many never see any successful adults except pimps and pushers. Most of the folks who reach the middle class in these neighborhoods immediately move out, so kids have little chance to see legitimate role models. Christian volunteers, scout masters, tutors, and organizations like Big Brothers/Big Sisters can all make a huge difference. You cannot save the whole world, but perhaps with God's help you can save one person. Then the whole world becomes a better, safer place.

Government, Armed Citizens, and Pacifism

In Romans 13, Paul follows the theme of defeating evil in our personal lives through love with his discourse on government defeating evil by force. In Romans 12, he speaks of our dealings person to person, while Romans 13 starts out with a Christian citizen's obligation to government and government's obligation to keep peace between citizens. But Romans 12 ends by saying in verse 21, "Do not be overcome by evil, but overcome evil with good." Then chapter 13 begins by describing government as a God-ordained good for overcoming evil. One chapter speaks of personal responsibility for peace and the other of government's responsibility to impose peace in a civil society. Romans 13:1 says we should obey the law because God establishes governments on earth and delegates His authority to them to enforce civil order among us.[1] If, as some argue, man is inherently good, then we do not need government. On the other hand, if man is inherently good, where in history do we find that perfect, peaceful utopia founded by inherently good people?

The Role of Government

Romans 13:1 also says that God authorizes government to enforce rules to prevent chaos. Verse two tells us that by rejecting the law, men reject God, and for that they deserve punishment. Deuteronomy 1:17 explains that the judgment belongs to God, and He orders that the punishment fit the crime (Exodus 21:12-36). Romans 13:3 says only those who commit evil acts need fear the authorities, whereas government is set up to reward good behavior (1 Peter 2:13-17). In verse four, Paul calls government "a minister of God to you for good. "But," he continues, "if you do what is evil, be afraid; for it does not bear the sword for nothing, for it is a minister of God, an avenger who brings wrath upon the one who practices evil" (Romans 13:4). "A minister for good" means that God intends for government to promote a civil society where honest citizens can pursue their lives in peace.

Paul can speak first-hand about the role of government to bring peace because he lived during the age of the "Pax Romana" (Roman Peace). This period began in 30 B.C. after Caesar Augustus defeated Anthony and Cleopatra, ending nearly 80 years of intermittent Roman civil wars, slave revolts, and conquest. Rome's conquests during the second and first centuries B.C. saw the defeat of any serious outside enemies of the Empire for the next 200 years. Piracy was rare. The main pirate strongholds had been wiped out by Pompey in 67 B.C.[2] Nearly 51,000 miles of Roman roads crisscrossed the Empire, making trade and communication among the Empire's 75 million subjects easier than ever before.[3] Roman law insured reliable and uniform standards of justice throughout the Empire, while allowing the various provinces to practice a measure of self government and free trade so long as it did not conflict with Rome's rule.[4]

Thanks to Alexander the Great, common Greek (Koinonia) had been the universal language of the Eastern Empire since 323 B.C., with Latin dominating the west.[5] Consequently, if you knew both languages, you could travel from Britain to the Euphrates and communicate effectively. Peace, ease of travel, and simple communication made the spread of the Gospel far less difficult than it would have been in any other age to that point. These facts are partly why Paul says in Galatians 4:4 that Jesus was born "in the fullness of the time" – it was the ideal time and situation for the spread of the Gospel from Palestine.

Yes, the Roman government was pagan. Yes, it had many bad features and evil leaders. When Paul wrote the book of Romans, Nero, one of history's most wicked men, was emperor. Yet God used the "Roman Peace" as the ideal environment for the Gospel to spread throughout and even beyond the Empire in the first century A.D. God's sovereign will made even a pagan empire "a minister of God … for good" (Romans 13:4a).

Now back to the book of Romans. After telling us that the peaceful and godly have nothing to fear from government, Paul issues this dire warning to criminals: "But if you do what is evil, be afraid; for it [government] does not bear the sword [the death penalty] for nothing; it is a minister of God, an avenger who brings wrath upon the one who practices evil" (Romans 13:4). Paul is explaining that government's role replaces the "avenger of blood" in Numbers 35. Secular government is now God's agent to "bring wrath" on criminals. Therefore, government appoints law enforcement agents who have the power of the "sword" and gives them the training, equipment, and legal means to use it. Throughout Anglo-American history, those agents have historically been able to deputize citizens as needed to aid in their efforts to catch criminals. Duration of service and qualifications required vary. For example, as a volunteer auxiliary officer in Ohio, I had to take a 40-hour mini-basic police academy on the law, along with 16 hours of firearms instruction. Once sworn in, I had full arrest powers as long as I was with and under supervision of a fully-qualified officer, although a regular officer once told me I was "totally unqualified" to be a cop because I did not eat doughnuts or drink coffee! In Alabama (as in most states), deputizing can be instantaneous if an officer directs a citizen to help him apprehend a felon.[6] "Raising a posse" is not done only in cowboy movies.

Self-defense is the difference between having a chance to tell the police what happened and the police guessing as they draw a chalk line around your body.

Armed Citizens

So what about the holder of a concealed carry permit? He too has been deputized. Government gives him permission to carry a "sword" (concealed handgun) "for defense of himself and others … if it appears that the applicant has good reason to fear injury to his person or property or has any other proper reason for carrying a pistol."[7] In Alabama, permits are granted by Sheriffs. As of this writing, all but one state (Illinois) and the District of Columbia have deemed it right and proper for their citizens to bear concealed arms. Most states require several hours of legal training and firearms qualification. Handguns are emergency tools, like a fire extinguisher. They are rarely needed, but if needed they are the *only* thing that will solve the immediate problem: violent criminal attack. Any cop will tell you that 99 percent of the time, they are not on the scene during the commission of a violent crime, but the victim always is. By giving you the choice and authority to carry, the government gives you a chance to tell the police what happened instead of a police officer drawing a chalk outline around your body. By authorizing us to arm and defend ourselves and others, government has deputized private citizens to resist crime at its outset. Most of the time, criminals consent to be held for the police, which prevents them from committing other crimes until the cops can catch them. If they press their attack and die, problem solved. If they are wounded and run, they are usually arrested at the ER soon after. Thus, the government authorizes the concealed weapon permit holder to be part of the "sword" that God intends criminals to fear in Romans 13:4. And it is truly "not borne in vain" (KJV).

In all three editions of his book, *More Guns, Less Crime*, John Lott affirms that concealed carry reduces violent crime. Since the late 1980s when Florida started the surge for right-to-carry that swept the nation, no state has re-imposed restrictions on the right to carry.[8] And in those states that allow concealed carry, not only has violent crime gone down but legal concealed-carry holders are extraordinarily law abiding, with even fewer law violations than off duty cops![9] Moreover, Lott's research shows that those carriers who resist criminals are hurt less often and to a lesser extent than those non-carriers who do not resist (pacifists, take note):

> During the 1990s, for example, assault victims who used a gun for self protection were injured 3.6 percent of the time. This contrasts with 5.4 percent of those who ran or drove away, 12.6 percent of those who screamed, and 13.6 percent of those who threatened the attacker without a weapon. Those who took no self protective action at all fared the worst – 55.2 percent of them were injured.[10]

Lott also notes that criminals tend to move out of counties that adopt concealed carry. As criminals flee those counties, the bordering counties without concealed carry see a simultaneous rise in violent crime. The bordering "carry" counties see violent crime drop 400 percent below the neighboring "non-carry" counties.[11] Evidently, concealed carry laws are a terror to evildoers and make everyone safer by increasing the number of "sword bearers" on the street. Yet Lott says that in concealed carry states, only two to seven percent of the population will choose to obtain a permit.[12] Evidently, even a small minority of these "deputized" citizens are sufficient to make everyone safer since violent felons never know who is and is not armed.

Criminals themselves testify that armed citizens are a deterrent. In *Armed and Considered Dangerous, A Survey of Felons and Their Firearms*, James Wright and Peter Rossi surveyed almost 2000 "gun-predators" and non-gun using felons serving time in 11 state prisons and chronicled their views on their use of guns and gun use by their intended victims.[13] When asked by Wright and Rossi to agree/disagree with the statement, "A criminal is not going to mess around with a victim he knows is armed with a gun," 56 percent of criminals agreed. To the statement, "A smart criminal always tries to find out if his potential victim is armed," 81 percent agreed. They also said they would avoid armed citizens. As to whether criminals are more worried about meeting an armed citizen than a cop, 57 percent said citizens would shoot them more readily than cops. Seventy-four percent said burglars avoid occupied homes for fear of being shot, while 58 percent said a gun-armed store owner would not be robbed often. Wright and Rossi point out that the felon's fears are justified. In any given year, more felons are shot to death by armed citizens than by cops.[14] Thirty-nine percent admitted they were deterred from committing a crime because "they knew or believed the victim was carrying a gun." Thirty-seven percent had run into a victim with a gun, and 34 percent had been "scared off, shot at, wounded, or captured by an armed victim." Sixty-nine percent knew someone who had experienced those same outcomes.[15]

During the 1990s, for example, assault victims who used a gun for self protection were injured 3.6 percent of the time. This contrasts with 5.4 percent of those who ran or drove away, 12.6 percent of those who screamed, and 13.6 percent of those who threatened the attacker without a weapon. Those who took no self protective action at all fared the worst – 55.2 percent of them were injured.

Beware! Although the deterrence rate is roughly two thirds, one quarter of these predators were *not* scared off by meeting armed victims.[16] Just as police officers know they can face criminals who have nothing to lose, we must be determined to carry the fight to the end if necessary.

Significantly, Wright and Rossi found that criminals were most concerned about running into armed citizens in states with the highest per capita density of gun ownership. All these facts support Proverbs 28:1(a): "The wicked flee when no one is pursuing." The logical conclusion from this data is that felons are less likely to carry guns in states with high gun ownership (because of fear of being shot by victims) and are more likely to carry guns in states that restrict gun ownership.[17]

Jeremiah says protecting citizens is a duty of government: "Thus says the Lord [to rulers]: 'Administer justice every morning, and deliver the person who has been robbed from the power of the oppressor ...'" or he warns that God's wrath will come on those rulers who do not (Jeremiah 20:12b). What does God say about politicians who would deny citizens the right to defend themselves? Isaiah 10:1-2 tells us:

Woe to those who enact evil statutes
And to those who constantly record unjust decisions,
So as to deprive the needy of justice
And rob the poor of My people of their rights,
So that widows may be their spoil
And that they may plunder the orphans.

Politicians who deny us our rights to self-defense condemn us all to victimization. The old saying is true: "When guns are outlawed, only outlaws will have guns." These politicians are condemned by God: "Woe to those who call evil good and good evil; who substitute darkness for light and light for darkness ... Woe to those who are wise in their own eyes and clever in their own sight! ... and take away the rights of the ones who are in the right"! (Isaiah 5:20-21; 23b).

The research of Lott and Wright and Rossi demonstrates empirically what Romans 13:1-4 says: the government's sword – whether wielded by the death penalty, cops, or armed citizens – is clearly a deterrent that saves lives and make everyone safer. We are part of the "sword not borne in vain." Scriptures tell us we have a duty to help others in need.[18] Secular government has wisely delegated its authority to allow free citizens to do just that with our carry permits. To accept that duty to respond as a trained, armed citizen is to be prepared to do God's will.

In his conclusion to his story of the Good Samaritan, Jesus asked, "Which of these three do you think proved to be a neighbor to the man who fell into the robber's hands?"

And he replied, "The one who showed mercy toward him."

And Jesus said to him, "Go and do the same" (Luke 10: 36-37).

Just as Jesus "went about doing good" (Acts 10:38), Christians are commanded to do the same: "while we have opportunity, let us do good to all men" (Galatians

6:10). Paul adds that there will be "glory and honor and peace to every man who does good, to the Jew and also to the Greek" (Romans 12:21). "For we are His workmanship, created in Christ Jesus for good works, which God prepared beforehand that we should walk in them" (Ephesians 2:10). "All Scripture is inspired by God and profitable for teaching, for reproof, for correction, for training in righteousness, that the man of God may be adequate, equipped for every good work" (2 Timothy 3:17). Saving others from physical harm is one of the good works God means for us to do.

However, some may ask, "Will all these people toting guns cause more problems and crimes?" That is a fair question. The answer is no. Consider these facts: "There are about eight million currently issued concealed carry permits in the USA. In 2012, we had the lowest rate of violent crime in 40 years."[19] Permit holders commit murder at a rate of 1/182 of the rate of the general public. In Lott's survey, 14 states revoked carry permits as an aggregate average of just over one-tenth of one percent. Most of the revocations are for minor state violations such as failure to maintain auto insurance or carrying guns into legally restricted areas. Concealed carry permit holders almost never commit violent crimes.[20] We may be the most law abiding and peaceful segment of the entire U.S. population!

Pacifist Christians

So where is the pacifist Christian who is ready to waive a white flag when the latest incarnation of Charles Manson enters his home? Does he truly believe that as Manson's "family" disemboweled Sharon Tate and threw her unborn child across the room, her last thought was "Thank God I don't own a handgun!"? Ask yourself whether a person who would give up his family to such depravity is worthy of the love, trust, and faith of his wife and children. But do not take my word for it. Speaking to Timothy on how church and nuclear families should care for each other, Paul commands: "But if anyone does not provide for his own, and especially for those of his household, he has *denied* the faith and is *worse* than an unbeliever" (1 Timothy 5:8, emphasis mine). Does "providing for your own" include making sure your family is safe? Does it mean your responsibility ends if you provide food, shelter, and clothing? Does it also mean teaching your kids how to cross the street, to swim, not to talk to strangers, to be careful drivers, to administer first aid, and to practice fire safety? Does it mean teaching them about locks, alarms, dogs, non-lethal weapons, and finally guns? Or does it mean that once the felon defeats your lock and alarms, you are going to say, "Okay, you win! Go ahead, take what you want, and murder my family"? On the other hand, if failing to provide for your family means that you have denied your faith, then Paul is saying that preserving your life and the lives of your loved ones is a *basic tenet* of the Christian faith.

Consider these facts: "There are about eight million currently issued concealed carry permits in the USA. In 2012, we had the lowest rate of violent crime in 40 years."[19]

I was on the phone last night with a lady from my Sunday school class whose husband was on his way to Texas in his 18-wheeler. Deputies had been chasing several felons through her neighborhood for an hour. She called to get a legal recap on protecting herself and her two daughters with her .357 magnum should one of the bad guys break in. She personifies the meaning 1 Timothy 5:8. She was determined to protect them and to justify the love and trust of her husband, her children, and God who gave them to her. She fulfilled her Christian duty as a wife and mother, according to 1 Timothy 5:8 and the rest of Scripture.

To sum up, Paul says that if you refuse to provide for your family (food, shelter, clothes, and safety), your moral and spiritual standing before God is *worse* than that of an unbeliever. Is it time for you to prayerfully consider whether the words "pacifist" and "Christian" really go together?

Military and Police

The Faith of a Centurion

You might say this chapter is the reason for this book. When I wrote the 28 page precursor to this book in 1999, I asked some of my police officer friends to review the material. One said, "This is good, but could you please write something about how to serve as a Christian police officer and soldier?" (He also served in the National Guard.) As the War on Terror progressed, I became alarmed at the high per-capita occurrence of Post Traumatic Stress Disorder (PTSD) among our troops. One cause of this affliction is guilt that comes naturally after having to kill justifiably. Because of my training in the causes and effects of PTSD, I know that religious people recover faster from it since they have an objective base that tells them that God not only forgives but also commands them to rescue those in peril with deadly force if necessary.[1]

In other chapters, I have described how God's heroes often used deadly force in righteous causes and were blessed by God for doing so. Yet Satan, our accuser (Revelation 12:10), constantly tries to fill us with false guilt for something we did or failed to do, though there is no condemnation for our action or inaction in Scripture! False guilt is certainly the basis for many cases of PTSD. If God has not called something a sin, then we should not either. Satan uses society's legal, moral, and cultural misapprehension, our scriptural ignorance, and our own insecurity to grind us into mental and physical helplessness. But consider Satan's fate and our victory in Revelation 12:10-11.

> Then I heard a loud voice in heaven saying, "Now the salvation, and the power and the kingdom of our God and the authority of His Christ have come, for the accuser of our brethren [Satan] has been thrown down, he who accuses them before our God day and night. And they overcame him because of the blood of the Lamb and because of the word of their testimony, and they did not love their life even when faced with death."

Satan tries to convince us that we are guilty of countless sins we have never committed. Yet Satan's end is certain, and so is our victory. Verse 11 describes those who overcame Satan through the forgiveness of Jesus' blood and their own testimony of God's Word, including their self-sacrificing lives. This sounds like Christian soldiers and police officers.

Jesus warns us not to listen to Satan's accusations. He gives us the Holy Spirit to guide us into all truth (John 16:13a) and to convict us about sin, righteousness, and the judgment to come (John 16:8). The Holy Spirit's job is to convict us when we have actually sinned, urge us to repent, and let us know that God forgives completely: "if we confess our sins, He is faithful and just to forgive us our sins and to cleanse us from all unrighteousness" (1 John 1:9). In other words, we can know that there is such a thing as righteous self-defense that does not need forgiving, but when we do sin, we can repent, get forgiveness, and move on.

A biblical perspective on use-of-force will help anyone suffering from the guilt that is a part of PTSD by allowing him not only to recover but also to return to duty, whole and confident. As Peter tell us: "Therefore, prepare your minds for action, keep sober in spirit, fix your hope completely on the grace to be brought to you at the revelation of Jesus Christ" (1 Peter 1:13).

In the United States, most police and military are likely Christians or Jews who would appreciate biblical guidance on how to do their jobs. Some civilian pacifists, however, tell them their job is incompatible with their faith, yet neither the Old Testament, Jesus, nor His New Testament followers endorsed pacifism. Pacifism was a corruption of Christ's message that likely started in the late first century as heresies began to creep in, and then began to be taught in the mid-to-late second century A.D.

Does God Love Soldiers and Police?

So how did Jesus and His followers deal with the police and the military in the Bible? They dealt with soldiers as police officers because in ancient times soldiers filled the office of law enforcement. As John the Baptist preached repentance to prepare the way for the Messiah, many converts asked advice about their lifestyle changes (Luke 3:7-14). John told the general public to share, and he told the tax gatherers to collect only what the law allowed. When converted soldiers asked him what to do, he told them not to extort money from anyone, never to make false accusations, and to be content with their wages. The Bible identifies John as the forerunner of the Messiah, foretold by Isaiah 40:3-5 (as quoted in Luke 3:4-6):

> The voice of one crying in the wilderness, make ready the way of the Lord, make His paths straight. Every ravine shall be filled up and every mountain and hill shall be brought low; and the crooked shall become straight, and the rough roads smooth. And all flesh shall see the salvation of God.

John's job was to prepare men's hearts to receive the Messiah through repentance of sin (Luke 3:3, 7-9). Yet, when soldiers (acting in their role as police) asked what they needed to do to show they had turned to God, John told them to conduct themselves honestly (Luke 3:14). Notice that John *did not* say, "Quit the army!" He told them how to please God *without* stating or implying that their profession of arms was either a sin or a hindrance to living a holy life. Therefore, you can prepare the way of the Lord, straighten up lives, serve as a good example, and fix a corrupt world while serving in the police or the military! If God had said otherwise and John did not tell them so, he failed his mission to "prepare the way of the Lord." Jesus, however, said John fulfilled his role magnificently. Jesus called him "more than a prophet," saying no one born to that point was greater than John (Matthew 11:9b, 11a). He endorsed everything John said without contradiction. Had there been anything negative to say about a military career or a career in law enforcement, John, inspired by the Holy Spirit, would certainly have said so. Instead of condemning armies or the profession of arms, John was only concerned with making warriors godly men.

How did Jesus deal with and instruct soldiers? In Matthew 8:5-13, Jesus encounters a Roman centurion. A centurion was the equivalent of a military officer (from lieutenant to major), who commanded from 100 to 600 men or who led all the centurions in a legion as the "First Spear." This centurion sought Jesus because his servant was seriously ill. Luke tells us that local Jewish leaders endorsed this man to Jesus, stating, "He loves our people, and built our synagogue" (Luke 7:4-5). This Roman, an officer in a pagan army of occupation, had developed a love for God and His people. (Loving God teaches us to love others of every nationality, race, and faith.) Today, when our soldiers build schools and hospitals in the countries they are helping to become free nations, they are acting just like this faithful centurion. So from the Centurion's example, we can first conclude that you can be a career soldier or cop and love God. Second, this man also spent money and time ministering to the Jews, which shows that his profession did not interfere with living his life in a godly fashion. Finally, we see that soldiers and cops (including this Roman occupier) can be a positive, godly witness among people (subject Jews) who are initially hostile to them and even win them over!

When Jesus replied that He would come immediately to heal the servant, the centurion begged Him not to come because the centurion said he was not worthy to have Jesus under his roof (Matthew 8:8a). Now this might mean he respected the Jewish aversion to visiting a Gentile's house, but that was not the case. Rather, the centurion realized that Jesus was God incarnate. In verse 8b he says, "[J]ust say the word and my servant will be healed." He recognized that God the Father had given Jesus all power at His command, unlimited by time or space. Then in verse 9, the centurion gave this insightful analogy to Jesus: "For I also am a man under authority, with soldiers under me; and I say to this one 'Go!' and he goes, and to another, 'Come!' and he comes, and to my slave, 'Do this!' and he does it. Now when Jesus heard this, He marveled, and said to those who were following, 'Truly I say to you, I have not found such great faith with anyone in Israel'" (Matthew 8:10).

Jesus was taken aback and not merely by the fact that this Gentile believed He had the power to heal at a distance. More surprising was his understanding of Jesus' position with God, revealed by the centurion's analogy. The centurion said he and Jesus were *both* under authority. The centurion was under his chain of command, starting with military tribunes (colonels), up to the Senate, and ultimately to the Emperor Tiberius himself. The centurion realized that Jesus likewise was delegated power under His Father's authority. The centurion stated that he derived his authority over those below him from the authority that descended from the Emperor while Jesus got His from God. Nor did the centurion have to be face-to-face with a subordinate to pass orders. He could simply send the order, knowing it would be obeyed. Likewise, he knew Jesus could heal remotely as well. Just as he expected instant obedience from his troops, he knew Jesus had instantaneous command over the physical and spiritual universe. By describing Jesus as under Jehovah's authority and therefore having all power over the world, he confessed that he recognized Jesus as the Messiah! A Gentile soldier, probably taught the Old Testament by his Jewish friends, realized who Jesus was *before* most Jews. By contrast, it was not until over a year into Jesus' ministry that His own disciples recognized Him as Messiah (Matthew 16:13-20).

Jesus told those with Him that the centurion was the first of multitudes of Gentiles who would become children of God by faith in Him (verses 11-12). Jesus then told the centurion, "'Go; it shall be done for you as you have believed.' And the servant was healed that *very* moment" (verse 13). Because he left as soon as Jesus said this, we know the centurion believed in total faith that Jesus could do, and in fact had already done, what He said.

If soldiering or policing is an occupation condemned by God, how is it that this centurion was not only uncorrupted by his profession, but that he was more spiritually perceptive than most of God's chosen people? Jesus had made Capernaum His base of operations during the first year of His ministry, so it is fair to speculate that the centurion had been watching and listening and had become convinced of Jesus' true identity during that time. Notice this important point: Jesus did not require or even imply that this believing centurion should quit the army before or after receiving his miracle. Jesus' only comment was that he was a Gentile. He had nothing to say about the soldier's profession. The obvious conclusion from this account is that military and police service does not hinder a relationship with Jesus Christ. In fact, a relationship with Christ can flourish while practicing these professions.

However, this centurion was not the only perceptive Roman soldier. The centurion who headed the crucifixion detail also realized Jesus' divinity. When he saw Jesus' uncomplaining submission to the torture, His forgiveness of the thief and His accusers, His refusal to rail back at those mocking Him, the uncanny darkness at noon, and the earthquake when Jesus died, he concluded: "Truly this was the Son of God" (Matthew 27:57).

A third example comes in Acts 10, where we meet the centurion Cornelius, a cohort commander in the seaport of Caesarea (verse 1). Like the Roman centurion with the sick servant, Cornelius was a believer in Jehovah. Not only he but his entire household (family, servants, and military staff) believed (verse 2a). He too

God knows the difference between murder and killing in battle or in law enforcement situations.

gave alms to the Jews and sought God in prayer on a regular basis (verse 2b). While praying, he was visited by an angel who told him to send men about 30 miles down the coast to Joppa to summon the apostle Peter. The angel said that God wished to reward his good works and faith, and that Peter would tell him what he needed to do (verse 4b-8). Cornelius sent for Peter the same afternoon.

Peter was praying the next day when he saw a vision of unclean animals being lowered from heaven, animals that the Jews were forbidden to eat (Leviticus 11; Deuteronomy 14:1-21). Then a voice from heaven told him to kill and eat these animals. He replied, "No way! I have never eaten anything that is not kosher!" But the voice replied, "What God has declared clean, you must no longer consider unholy." This happened three times (Acts 10:9-16, paraphrased). While Peter considered what this vision might mean, Cornelius' men arrived downstairs. The Holy Spirit told Peter that He had sent these men and to accompany them to Caesarea (Acts 10:17-20).

The next day, Peter set out with the men, along with some fellow Christians. At this point, all Christians were either former Jews or Samaritans. Before He ascended to heaven, Jesus told the disciples that they would be His witnesses in Jerusalem, then Judea, then Samaria, and then to the most remote parts of the globe (Acts 1:1-8). About one or two years after the birth of the Church at Pentecost (Acts 2), the Jewish leaders began to persecute the Church, starting with the stoning of Stephen (Acts 6:8-8:3). As a result, the believers scattered. Phillip the deacon fled to Samaria, (home of the "black-sheep cousins" of the Jews) and began to convert them to the Gospel. Peter and John joined him in the mission (Acts 8:4-25). A short time thereafter, Peter's mission to Cornelius fulfilled the last part of Jesus' prophecy about taking the Gospel to the ends of the earth (to non-Jews).

Peter met Cornelius and realized the vision meant that God had declared Gentiles "kosher" and ready to hear the Gospel so they could enter the church on the same basis as Jews and Samaritans (Acts 10:24-29). Cornelius had gathered his relatives and close friends, all Gentiles, who were excited to hear Peter's message (verses 24 and 33). Peter proclaimed the Gospel to them. While he spoke, the

Holy Spirit fell on the Gentiles as it had on Peter and the Apostles at Pentecost
(Acts 2:1-12). In other words, they were able to speak in the native tongues of
their listeners. (On Pentecost, the apostles spoke the Gospel to at least 15 different
nationalities/language groups without ever having studied those languages (Acts
2). So these Romans were able to speak in Hebrew/Aramaic, which was the native
tongue of the Jewish Christians with Peter (Acts 10:44-46). Peter then realized that
the visitation of the Holy Spirit had empowered the Gentiles in the same manner
as it had the apostles at Pentecost. Therefore, this was God's signal that Gentiles
were as worthy as Jews to be Christians. So Peter baptized them into Christ (verses
47 and 48) and defended his actions to the elders and other apostles in Jerusalem,
who acknowledged that it was God's will that the Gospel should be shared with
all people from then on (Acts 11:1-18).

Once again, a professional warrior was chosen to demonstrate true faith in
God. Out of all the professions in the Empire, the Holy Spirit chose a soldier to set
the example as the first Gentile convert to Christianity. Cornelius rejected the vast
menu of pagan gods and philosophies to seek the one true God. "How blessed are
those who observe His testimonies, who seek Him with their whole heart" (Psalms
119:2). A soldier in an army of occupation charged with keeping the peace
(a police captain), he pacified the Jews with kindness and empathy. The Jews
responded to him with love, taught him about God, and God rewarded his sincere
search for truth. Cornelius brought his family, servants, and some other soldiers
into the faith with him. He fulfilled many prophecies from the Old Testament,
for example, "I will also make You [Israel and Jesus] a light of the nations so that
My salvation will reach the end of the earth" (Isaiah 49:6).[2] Peter told him about
Christ's death, burial, and resurrection, and Cornelius placed his faith in Jesus.
Peter told Cornelius to be baptized (as he did the Jews on Pentecost, Acts 2:38),
and Peter defended Cornelius' conversion to the leading Jewish Christians. But
Peter *never* told Cornelius to quit the army. Peter obviously had not learned to
preach pacifism nor an anti-military message from Jesus. When ordered by the
Sanhedrin not to preach any more in Jesus' name, Peter and John replied that they
could not "stop speaking what they had seen and heard [from Jesus]" (Acts 4:19-
20). Had Jesus taught anti-military pacifism, His disciples would have also done
so. They did not because Jesus did not. They had never seen or heard any such

thing from Him. Before Cornelius became a Christian, his life honored God and caused him to be favored as the first Gentile convert. We can trust that he kept his military career after his conversion. Before or after, his profession of arms did not hinder his witness or status before God.

The fact is that neither John the Prophet of Christ, Jesus Himself, nor the Apostle Peter ever told soldiers and police officers that their chosen profession was opposed to living for God. If you have read to this point, you know that simply because our job requires us to kill in lawful situations does not separate us from a relationship with Jesus. Only those who ignorantly or doggedly cling to the discredited mistranslation, "Thou shall not kill," correctly translated, "Thou shall not murder," believe such. Just as Abraham, Moses, and David could lawfully kill and still have an intimate relationship with God, so can today's soldier or police officer. David never got in trouble for his warfare, only for his murder of Uriah. God knows the difference between murder and killing in battle or in law enforcement situations.

Think of all the good work that our police and our military do. Would Jesus require them to stop protecting the weak and to stop arresting the guilty? Would He ask them to suspend their vigilance because they might be called upon to kill? And what of those who manned the front lines in the Cold War? We never had to fight a land war in Europe or launch an ICBM because our armed soldiers' willingness to fight was enough to keep the Soviets from taking that gamble. Had our warriors not been there with weapons and prepared to protect us, we would have shared the same fate that Poland, Czechoslovakia, and others did in post-WWII. The question is: "Should evil be allowed free rein?" Should society's chaos reflect one of the saddest verses in the Bible: "In those days there was no king in Israel; everyone did what was right in his own eyes" (Judges 21:25)? Jesus never intended such a thing, nor does any honest reading of the Bible support such an anarchistic idea as to do without police and military.

Paul was under house arrest while waiting for his hearing before Nero. He was guarded by members of Caesar's bodyguard (who also acted as Rome's police force), the Praetorian Guard. Can you imagine being stuck with Paul eight hours a day (Acts 28:16; 30-31). He apparently converted many because Paul comments that the Gospel had become well-known throughout the Praetorian Guard

(Philippians 1:13). Through Paul, many of them were won to Christ, yet he makes no mention of requiring them to quit their military/police service. Even after the conversions among the Praetorians (Philippians 1:13), we hear of no desertions or resignations because of their new allegiance to Jesus. Apparently, pacifism and anti-militarism was not part of Paul's teaching on the Christian life.

Instead of condemning armies or the profession of arms, John was only concerned with making warriors godly men.

When about 40 Jews took an oath to assassinate Paul at his trial before the Sanhedrin, the Roman commander in Jerusalem sent him under escort to Governor Felix in Caesarea (Acts 23). Paul was protected by 400 infantry and 70 cavalry under two centurions (verses 23-32). Paul accepted this escort without reservation or criticism at having to be protected by soldiers. The soldiers suppressed a riot and prevented murder by escorting an accused man to a safe venue for a fair trial (Acts 22-23). The Roman commander Claudius Lysis and his men acted as a force for good and order in the world and he acted to do God's will. Had Paul's life ended in Jerusalem, we would not have several of his letters (the "Prison Epistles," written from Rome), which make up much of the New Testament. We must also note from this example that God does not provide supernatural protection for all Christians from all threats at all times. Civil order and protection is primarily the responsibility of the police, the military, and when necessary, the armed citizen.

Paul has other things to say about soldiers, and *none* of it is bad. He says a soldier is worthy of his pay (1 Corinthians 9:7a), implying that he must be doing something worthwhile to earn it. He asks Timothy to share hardships with him as a good soldier of Jesus Christ (2 Timothy 2:3-4). In other words, Christians are God's soldiers in spiritual battle. He says good soldiers pay close attention to their duties and avoid outside jobs and distractions in order to please their commander. Notice he does not say their duty is to desert in the name of pacifism. He calls dear friends in Christ "fellow soldiers" (Philippians 2:25, Philemon 2). If being a soldier was a sign of disgrace to a Christian, why did Paul use the term as an obvious compliment and frequent metaphor for the faithful Christian life?

We have already heard Paul say the government's police powers are a good thing for all (Romans 13:1-7). Police are "peace officers" first and foremost. He tells us citizens to obey the police and the authority they represent. He instructed Titus to teach Christians on Crete thusly: "Remind them to be subject to rulers, to authorities, to be obedient, *to be ready for evey good deed*" (Titus 3:1, emphasis mine). Concealed carry makes us ready for at least one good deed: the defense of others. Peter agrees with Paul on a Christian citizen's duty:

> Submit yourselves for the Lords' sake to every human institution, whether to a king as the one in authority, or to governors as sent by him for the punishment of evildoers and the praise of those who do right. For such is the will of God that by doing right you may silence the ignorance of evil men. Act as free men, and do not use your freedom as a covering for evil, but use it as bondslaves of God (1 Peter 2:13-16).

Submitting "to every human institution" surely includes serving in the armed forces or as a police officer.

This passage reminds me of a case I saw in city court. The charge was failure to obey a lawful order by a police officer and obstructing traffic.[3] Police were directing traffic at the end of a huge church convention that included delegates from all over the U.S. At one exit, officers directed traffic to turn right only to speed things up and avoid a snarl with traffic on the next street to the left. Temporary signs said, "Right Turn Only." Nevertheless, one church lady was determined to go left because her son wanted a soft drink and there was a convenience store to the left about a block down. The officer blew her whistle and pointed right when Church Lady started left, but Church Lady shook her head "no" and pointed left. The officer repeated her command as Church Lady continued slowly left – toward the officer. The officer stood her ground until Church Lady nudged her with the car's fender, whereupon the officer stopped and arrested her. Throughout the trial, Church Lady could not be budged from the opinion that she had the *right* to go left despite the officer's orders. The judge found her guilty and sighed, "Ma'am, if you had just obeyed the officer, we wouldn't be here at all." Romans 13:1-2 says, "Let every person be subject to the governing authorities … he who resists authority has opposed the ordinance of God and …will receive condemnation on themselves." And they make other Christians look bad, too.

Both Paul and Peter call the army and the police, as representatives of government, servants for good and for God. Jesus and all the Gospel writers knew the world is a tough neighborhood, and that force can and should be legitimately used against evil men and nations so that *all* might live in peace. "But," some might say, "didn't Paul say our weapons aren't physical, and that we don't fight physically?" Yes, but the context of that comment is 2 Corinthians chapters 7 and 10 through 12 where Paul is correcting the Corinthians for their pride and foolishness that caused them to fight with each other and split the church, listen to false teachers, and question Paul's authority. What he is saying in 2 Corinthians 10:1-11 is that he will not use worldly arguments ("our weapons are not of the flesh ..."), standards of behavior, or philosophy when dealing with spiritual matters. Rather, he uses only the reasoning of God's Word, godly examples, and the wisdom of the Holy Spirit to win over or discipline those who oppose him.[4] These verses have nothing to do with renouncing the use of physical weapons against worldly evil.

Similarly, Paul is not renouncing the use of weapons in Ephesians 6:10-20 when he says in verse 12 that "our struggle is not against flesh and blood, but against the powers, against the world forces of darkness, against the spiritual forces of wickedness in high places." He is reminding us instead that the source of all evil is spiritual. Paul reminds us that in every interpersonal, police, or national defense dispute there are larger issues of good and evil that have cosmic, historical, and spiritual significance. In verse 13, Paul starts his brilliant analogy of likening truth, righteousness, the Gospel of peace, faith, salvation, the Word of God, and prayer with the specific arms and armor of a Roman soldier. If arms and armor were forbidden to Christians, why would Paul liken them to some of the best attributes of the Christian life? Look at how he compares the Roman military sandal with the "Gospel of Peace" (Ephesians 6:15), calls the Bible itself an offensive weapon "The Sword of Spirit" (verse 17b), and in Hebrews he refers to the Word as a "two-edged sword" (Hebrews 4:12). He clearly implies that arms and armor were appropriate for physical warfare, and he likens the function of each to aspects of successful spiritual warfare. I have searched the New Testament and nowhere do I find a single condemnation of the profession of arms or any reference to it being against Christian ethics. Instead, Scripture deals with and alludes to this profession in only the most positive light.

The Christian as Soldier

I have loved military history as far back as I can recall. Part of it is because of the heroes I have known or have heard about from my family. My mother's five uncles all served in WWII (four in the Army and one in the Navy). One spent six months as a POW in Italy. My dad spent four years in the Navy before and during Korea. His brother-in-law landed in Normandy on D plus 17. My father-in-law volunteered for the Army in WWII despite the fact that as a farmer and an only son he was doubly deferred from the draft. He spent 14 months in a German POW camp. Another uncle served in the Army in Europe in WWII, while my wife lost an uncle in a B-24 over the Mediterranean. My doctor is an Army Reserve Colonel who spent six months in Baghdad riding on patrol with troops. He is also the combat medic for our city's SWAT team. My first boss (judge) at the Alabama Court of Criminal Appeals fought from Africa to Germany in WWII. The sacrifices and patriotism of these brave men have been a lifelong inspiration to me. Soldiers are a special breed and are national treasures. When I say soldiers, I include infantry, airmen, sailors, and marines.

While many points addressed in this book apply to police officers and soldiers, several issues are different for the military. Unlike cops, who usually go home after a shift, soldiers are deployed for months and years before going home. Often they are subsequently redeployed to combat theaters. That situation produces unique stresses, and just because you knew about it going in does not make it any easier.

Another difference is the rules for use-of-force. A Marine Gunny friend once asked me to teach civilian use-of-force rules to some of the Marines under his command. These men worked as bouncers in town during their off-duty hours. Some had a hard time with certain facts, such as Alabama does not allow the use of deadly force to protect mere property.[1] Another fact is that the law only allows private citizens the use of equal force to meet force unless the attacker escalates first.[2] These men were warriors, taught a combat ethic of destroying the enemy or compelling his surrender under threat of death. Because of this training, several believed that a drunk who resists when asked to leave a bar was to be met with any force short of the deadly level. Their misconceptions had to be corrected, their warrior ethic translated into the citizen-applicable law.

Another difference between police and military is the duration of the mission. Street patrol officers get a call, make an arrest, and, except for court, their case is over, which enables them to move on to their next call. Military actions are rarely over quickly, although there are exceptions (Grenada, Panama, and Desert Storm). A soldier might not live to see the end of a war, or he might be wounded or reassigned to another theater. A war can last for a decade or more and be lost like Vietnam. But remember, the sacrifices soldiers make are not in vain. Vietnam taught us valuable lessons about having clear goals before committing troops, which resulted in the Reagan/Bush doctrines. Our military is more likely to learn from mistakes and to implement improvements than any other military in history.[3] Civilian and military review produces new strategies, tactics, weapons, logistics, and safety equipment. Flak vests have given way to Kevlar armor with ceramic or steel ballistic plates. Cobra gunships are replaced by Apache "flying tanks," and communications are integrated like never before. As a result, thousands of lives are saved and enemies decisively defeated in record time. The lessons of Vietnam gave us the lopsided victories of Desert Storm and Iraqi Freedom. Never forget that you are a link in a long chain stretching into the future. As Paul said regarding credit for winning souls: "I planted, Apollos watered, but God was causing the growth ... For we are God's fellow workers; you are God's field, God's building" (1 Corinthians 3:6 and 9). A soldier's life work is not the end. God is in all outcomes, never fear.

The biggest difference, though, is the mission itself. A police officer, by law, can use deadly force only as a last resort. The military's mission is to compel the enemy's compliance with national political goals by threat of or by actually killing people and destroying their military equipment and economic infrastructures. In general, deadly force is the soldier's only appropriate force level until the enemy surrenders. In fact, it is their God-given mission. As the psalmist tells us in Psalms 149:5-9:

Let the godly ones exult in glory;
Let them sing for joy on their beds.
Let the high praises of God be in their mouth,
And a two-edged sword in their hand,
To execute vengeance on the nations
And punishment on the peoples,
To bind their kings with chains
And their nobles with fetters of iron,
To execute on them the judgment written;
This is an honor for all His godly ones!
Praise the Lord!

This scripture reminds us of what we did to Saddam in the Iraq War and the Nazi leadership at the Nuremburg trials, doesn't it? In any case, this Scripture says that the profession of soldier is a godly, honorable one that fulfills God's will in human history.

Ancient Israel did not rely solely on arms for its freedom but on God to bless their use.

You are my King, O God;
Command victories for Jacob.
Through You we will push back our adversaries;
Through Your name we will trample down those who rise up against us.
For I will not trust in my bow,
Nor will my sword save me.
But You have saved us from our adversaries,
And You have put to shame those who hate us.
In God we have boasted all day long,
And we will give thanks to Your name forever.
(Psalm 44:4-8)

Sometimes God miraculously saved Israel in war, but He did not tell them to throw their weapons away. God usually acted through Israel's use of arms.[4] In Isaiah, God says He will be "[a] spirit of justice for him who sits in judgment, a strength to those who repel the onslaught at the gate [soldiers]" (Isaiah 28:6). God will help godly soldiers just as He did David in his just causes.

A soldier's use of force is triggered by two standards: the rules of engagement and fire discipline. The rules of engagement are set at national command levels according to what policy ends are wanted. They set out the general parameters for weapons use. Once those conditions are met, fire discipline (when to start and stop shooting) controls the exact duration of the force. This decision is made by commanders on the scene, depending on the tactical situation.

Fire discipline is ingrained in every soldier because it is vital to the survival of him and his unit. Fire too soon and you give away your position. The enemy you meant to ambush escapes and can call in artillery or airstrikes on your position. Firing too soon can mean engaging at too long a range (missing the bad guys), allowing the enemy to find cover and retaliate. Just as vital, ceasing fire immediately on command allows escape from counterfire, not revealing position by gun flash or sound, and preventing "friendly fire" mistakes and civilian causalities. In every event, the command structure covers the soldier with general rules and tactical orders on when to fire.

As discussed in Romans 13:1-7, every citizen is subject to the lawful commands of government. God establishes government to bring order to the world. Titus 3:1 says we are to obey government so as to be ready for every good deed. 1 Peter 2:13-17 says that we are to obey authority, as its purpose is "punishment of evildoers and the praise of those who do right" (verse 14). Therefore, soldiers are bound to follow all lawful commands. Naturally, atrocities and crimes against the defenseless are never excusable, even under orders. They clearly violate "love thy neighbor" and "do unto others." After all, the hallmark of the American military (with a few exceptions) has been one of basic humanity to foes, especially in victory. That is why Germany and Japan are now our friends. However, as long as the enemy is under arms, we should always fight to win as quickly and decisively as possible (mindful of the fact that democratic societies like ours do not tolerate wars of attrition very well). The fight should continue vigorously until the enemy is convinced that quitting is the only logical decision left.

Victor Davis Hanson, one of America's most perceptive historians, says Patton was right to reject the conservative approach of Eisenhower and Bradley:

> Patton, the blustering big mouth, was not merely a realist but a real humanitarian, for he sensed that in contrast to his superiors he could wage a war so mobile, flexible, and lethal – aiming always for vast encirclements – that the Americans would never need to draw on their human reserves and in fact would lose fewer causalities than the Germans. Again, the obscenity in Patton's mind was a complacent war of static fronts, huge numbers of men engaged in rear-echelon tasks, commanders ensconced hundreds of miles to the rear, dreary communiqués – war as a daily grind that would inevitably

grind the Germans up first. His diary entry on May 17, 1944 notes, "Made a talk ... As in all my talks, I stressed fighting and killing." In sum, Patton knew, as Macaulay once wrote, that "the essence of war is violence, and that moderation in war is imbecility."[5]

Patton's wisdom was proven by the fact that from August 1944 to May 1945, his 3rd Army inflicted casualties on the Germans at a ten-to-one ratio over its own losses.[6]

We must concede that America has not always engaged in just wars, or perhaps it is better to say that America's engagements have not always proceeded from entirely pure motives. The War of 1812 was started in part to wrest Canada from England. The Mexican War was aggressive as well (though Mexico was planning to retake Texas). Likewise, the Spanish-American war was a war of conquest excused as "liberating" the Cubans and the Philippinos (but we did give them their freedom later). The real reason was America wanted to get in on Europe's and Japan's 19th century race for commerce, colonies, and seapower. Certainly, the destruction of American Indians and the conquest of their lands is a dismal episode of our nation's expansion. However, soldiers are not the policy makers. They do not judge policy, they implement it. American soldiers leave it to history to judge the policies of their civilian leaders. They follow and are protected by the U.S. Uniform Code of Military Justice. Never forget, though, that the majority of the time the U.S. has fought wars to set men free: The Revolution, the Civil War, WWII, the Cold War, Korea, Vietnam, Desert Storm, Bosnia, and the Iraq and Afghanistan fronts in the war against radical Islamists.

No one should ever forget that the U.S. military is responsible for freeing millions of people from death and slavery in the last 150 years. The Civil War freed four million slaves. New democracies were formed from the destroyed Russian, German, and Austro-Hungarian and Ottoman empires after WWI. All of Europe and Asia in WWII were saved from Nazi tyranny and Japanese imperialism (no less cruel and racist than the Nazis). We preserved freedom for South Korea.

Our military freed several hundred million from Soviet Communism in Eastern Europe and in the U.S.S.R. at the end of the Cold War. In the past decade, fifty million were freed from tyrannical dictators (Saddam Hussein and the Taliban) in Iraq and Afghanistan. Though there was no direct conflict between the U.S. and the U.S.S.R, the fact that our military and NATO stood ready with a credible defense/retaliation against Soviet aggression finally collapsed the Soviet system from within. Those who stood ready to fight during that 45-year-long watch along the Iron Curtain are no less heroes than those who have braved actual battle. The cold warriors' eventual victory was as significant as any war ever won. What we must never forget is that the Bible allows and blesses self-defense against objectively evil men and nations who would harm others. In the last hundred years, American troops have been employed to free people from various tyrannies without aggrandizing ourselves. We freed their victims and defeated their aggressors, and then we gave them back their countries. As Colin Powell once told the French, "The only foreign territory we've ever demanded is enough ground to bury our dead." The American military's record of giving freedom to oppressed people is unmatched in the annals of all history.

The first "Army of God" was Abram's posse in Genesis 14. God blessed them for rescuing innocent people from aggression. God ordered Moses to form the second Army of God from the freed Israelites (Numbers 1:1-19). It totaled 603,550 men (verse 46). Numbers Chapter 2 tells us that the army camped each night with God's Tabernacle in the center (verse 2) with three tribes each to the north, south, east, and west. Therefore, the primary job of the first Jewish army was to protect the House of God. The "profane" (as the pacifist point of view perceives) actually performed the holy service of protecting the sacred. This sets the precedent that the godly purpose of a righteous army is to protect good from evil by being the barrier between the two. Thus, God supports righteous soldiers. "In that day the Lord of hosts will become a beautiful crown and a glorious diadem to the remnant of His people; a spirit of justice for him who sits in judgment, a strength to those who repel the onslaught at the gate [soldiers] (Isaiah 28:5-6).

Solomon reinforces his prior points about not allowing the righteous to be victimized in Proverbs 25:26, "Like a trampled spring and a polluted well is a righteous man who gives way before the wicked."[7] This simile demonstrates the despair of the desert traveler who, upon arriving at a well or oasis expecting life-giving clean water, finds instead that it has been ruined. In the same way, citizens have a right to expect police and military protection (failing that, the armed citizen can step in). It is the height of cowardice and callousness to hang back when we have the means to rescue others, especially when they are expecting us to help. When leaders retreat before and appease tyrants (like Chamberlain and Daladier before Hitler and Mussolini at Munich), it is the common man who falls under tyranny. While leaders should not be prone to violence (Titus 1:7 and 9), they should always be ready to stand firm for what is right (verse 9). 1 Corinthians 16:13 says, "Be on the alert, stand firm in the faith, act like men, be strong." Failing to stand up to evil eventually causes more lives to be lost. Even after Hitler attacked Poland, the British and French simply camped behind the Maginot Line, despite the fact that Germany was virtually defenseless in the West. Germany's Siegfried Line was an empty shell, and 90 percent of their army was in Poland. Had the Allies surged into Germany in 1939, they could have stopped Hitler there and saved millions of lives.

God requires that warriors be ready to defend others (Proverbs 25:26). God seeks such armed, trained, prepared people to protect, preserve, and defend the innocents.

> The people of the land have practiced oppression and committed robbery, and they have wronged the poor and needy and have oppressed the sojourner without justice. I searched for a man among them who should build up the wall and stand in the gap before me for the land ... (Ezekiel 22:29-30).

Our military and police make up this wall and stand in the gap to protect civil society and the nation's interests. God says that when a watchman warns of war and danger and the citizen ignores him, the citizen is responsible for his own death. But if the watchman fails to sound the warning and his fellow citizens die because they cannot prepare, God holds the watchman guilty (Ezekiel 33:1-6). Since WWII, the United States cannot afford to ignore the world's conflicts in a world with ICBM's, so our military stands vigilant for any threat.

Conduct of War

We have already noted our obligation to protect innocent life in criminal and civil matters (Leviticus 19:6). Mosaic Law required the life of the person who ignored or allowed obvious dangers to others.[8] Loving our neighbor includes providing for his safety. Psalm 82:3-4 orders us to "Vindicate the weak and fatherless, do justice to the afflicted and destitute. Rescue the weak and needy; deliver them out of the hand of the wicked." In short, no one in the military should doubt that he or she is literally doing God's work.

Some will argue that shedding blood disqualifies us for holy service. They cite David, whom God forbade to build His Temple because he was "a man who had shed much blood in war" (1 Chronicles 22:8; 28:3).[9] This is another example of verses taken out of context. God told David that He used him to defeat Israel's enemies: "And I ... have cut off all your enemies from before you ..." (2 Samuel 7:9). So God directed and blessed David's wars. However, this does not establish a rule that anyone who kills in war cannot be used by God for anything holy.

Solomon killed to secure his kingdom yet was appointed by God to build His Temple. The difference between David's and Solomon's bloodshed was one of volume, not the deeds of state themselves. Remember too, Moses killed both in self-defense and in wars for God, but he was not forbidden to build and dedicate the Tabernacle. Therefore, killing people for reasons of state does not disqualify us from being used by God to do His work. David's entire relationship with God was singular. God, for His own reasons, forbade him the honor of doing one specific, holy work for Him. David was not rejected by God in any other sense. For example, God did not keep him from writing most of the Psalms or from bringing the Ark to Jerusalem (2 Samuel 6:12-19). Likewise, God will not reject the modern Christian warrior from spiritual fellowship.

Hebrews 11 is often called "God's Honor Role of the Faithful." Along with Abraham and Moses, several warriors who defended Israel are included.[10] They were all blessed by God for what they did and held up as spiritual examples for us to follow. They helped bring about God's eventual victory in Christ by preserving Israel by force of arms. After all, if no Israel, then no Messiah (Hebrews 11:39-40). Likewise, had Washington and the Continental Army not outlasted the British, all the subsequent good that America has done for the world would never have happened. These soldiers fought in faith, knowing that defending God's people in war was a righteous act, trusting God to give them victory.

In the Old Testament, all God's warriors knew that He had brought them to war, and their skills and weapons allowed God to use them for His glory. Knowing their cause was just, they trusted God for the outcome. David summed it up this way:

> Blessed be the Lord, my rock,
> Who trains my hands for war,
> And my fingers for battle;
> My lovingkindness and my fortress,
> My stronghold and my deliverer,
> My shield and He in whom I take refuge,
> Who subdues peoples under me
> (Psalm 144:1-2).

God's warriors made their weapons and skills available to God, who gave them the ability and the victory. Today, America deploys our soldiers not to expand territory but to stop terrorism, atrocities, genocide, and naked aggression of other countries or groups.

The Bible also makes clear that readiness for war with weapons is good. We have seen that God is the One who gives mankind the ability to make weapons (Isaiah 54:16-17). Samuel told the Israelites that kings would require standing armies where previously they only maintained a militia (1 Samuel 8:11). Occupiers had refused to allow the Jews to have weapons in order to prevent revolt.[11] It reminds me of the bumper sticker, "A man with a gun is a citizen. A man without a gun is a subject." David praised God for training him to wield weapons and to wage war in a wise and just manner (Psalms 144:1; 18:34). He said godly people are well-armed people (Psalms 149:4-9). Psalm 149 declares that the godly should have arms to defeat tyrants and bring them to justice.

The Old Testament soldiers recognized that the Lord is the one who saves, not the warrior or the weapon. In Psalm 44:4-8, the writer affirms God's control of a war's outcome:

> You are my King, O God;
> Command victories for Jacob.
> Through You we will push back our adversaries;
> Through Your name we will trample down those who rise up against us.
> For I will not trust in my bow,
> Nor will my sword save me.
> But You have saved us from our adversaries,
> And You have put to shame those who hate us.

In God we have boasted all day long,
And we will give thanks to Your name forever.

The Israelites believed they and their weapons were tools that God used for His holy purposes. Psalm 46:1 agrees: "God is our refuge and our strength, a very present help in trouble." Generally, God expects us to defend ourselves, while looking to the righteousness of our cause in His eyes and relying on Him for the outcome. So, just as we must arm ourselves as individuals, nations must have armies. God blesses both as long as the cause and actions are just. "Do not fear, for I am with you; do not anxiously look about you, for I am your God. I will strengthen you, surely I will help you, surely I will uphold you with My righteous right hand" (Isaiah 41:10).

13

The Aftermath

Once you (cop or soldier) are convinced that you can righteously use force and even kill with God's blessing, you have vastly improved your likelihood for surviving violence. Not only can you fight without doubt, you can also deal successfully with the psychological aftermath. Furthermore, you can also help those who have been traumatized by combat and those who have become victims to regain their emotional, psychological, and spiritual stability. Yes, there is a time to *kill*, but there is also a time to *heal* (Ecclesiastes 3:3). Debriefing and mutual support are critical to a warrior's endurance, helping him to receive and process objective feedback and to gain a positive perspective regarding events about which he sees only a small part of the whole picture. To understand this and many other vital concepts, I highly recommend Lt. Col. Dave Grossman's book *On Combat*. He is a professor of psychology who trains the police and military to prepare for and deal with the before, during, and aftermath of combat. *On Combat* and his other work *On Killing* are must reads for the armed citizen, cop, and soldier.

Once you have been forced to kill justifiably, you will have to deal with the personal consequences. One consequence is the legal aftermath. If you are a police officer, the Shooting Review Board determines whether you followed department policy and the law. After that, a criminal charge or civil suit could result, depending on the laws of your state. If you are a soldier, you might be subject to investigation by the Judge Advocate General (JAG). To defend your actions in court, you must educate yourself about perceptual distortions caused by the brain's reaction to life-threatening events; among many of these reactions, time seems to move in slow motion, sound diminishes, and visual distortions cause opponents to appear larger and closer. Your mind needs at least 48 hours after the incident to get everything straight before you can file an accurate report. The

immediate effects of post-shooting adrenaline can cause nausea, crying,
confusion, or a lack of emotion and a slow response to others.[1]

The immediate physical effects are another consequence. Have you ever been
in a low-speed, non-injury, fender-bender car wreck? The following day, did you
notice that your entire body was sore? That soreness was caused by your body's
flight-or-fight-reflex, which shot adrenaline into every muscle cell of your body.
The instantaneous muscle contraction burned sugar and created lactic acid,
resulting in your muscle soreness. Additionally, sleep disturbances will last a week
or two until the adrenaline flushes out of your body. Plus, the survival instinct will
cause your brain to remain hyper-vigilant, making it hard to accept the vulnerable
state of sleep for a couple of weeks. You must also deal with the reaction of
friends, family, co-workers, and strangers. For a description of these effects and
their treatments, read Dr. Alexis Artwohl and Loren W. Christensen's book *Deadly
Force Encounters,* which will help you understand what you are going through
and suggest other resources.[2]

Another consequence is long-term mental effects. In his book *On Killing,*
Grossman points out that we are hardwired *not* to kill other humans.[3] Studies after
WWII revealed that even under enemy attack, only 15-20 percent of American
G.I.s actually fired their weapons at the enemy.[4] Even when killing is morally and
legally justifiable, about half of the people forced to kill will have psychological
disturbances afterward. Long term effects include exhilaration, remorse and regret,
rationalization, and finally acceptance.[5]

Post combat trauma symptoms can include many kinds of reactions. These
occur in about 50 percent of people who experience combat, but virtually no
one will experience all of them. The recent threat to your life can cause anxiety
problems: nervousness, difficulty concentrating, irritability, angry outbursts,
higher sensitivity to danger, and fear of future fights. Physical reactions to stress
are common: head/body aches, insomnia, indigestion, diarrhea, and constipation.
The reaction may show in nightmares, social withdrawal, failure to perform
sexually, hyper sexuality, guilt, and depression.[6]

If you suffer any of these post-combat symptoms, reaffirm the moral correctness
of your actions through the Bible and with a professional counselor. Religious
people tend to recover from any of these symptoms faster than non-religious

people because they have a framework of faith that helps them put it all in perspective. The best way to beat these long-term effects is to treat the deadly force incident and its results as a learning experience. Your dear friends, comrades, and counselors will help you sort out and analyze the situation. Do not learn the wrong lesson: that the experience was so horrible you will do anything rather than go through it again. That will get you a desk job or removed from the police force or the military. Worse, if you return to civilian life having decided that your life and the lives of others are not worth defending, what will happen to you and your loved ones when you are challenged with a situation that calls for using your defensive skills? You must accept the responsibility to learn what can make you a stronger person and a more effective warrior, both physically and spiritually.

Remember, a spiritual battle exists behind any physical battle. Understand that both spiritual and physical battles are first fought in the mind, and your survival and victory depend on your deeply held convictions before, during, and after combat.

The Battle in Your Mind

Whether you are a soldier or a cop, the key to surviving combat with a healthy outlook on life is to understand that you are a God-ordained shepherd (Romans 13:1-7) who is lawfully and morally using force to protect the innocent. Whatever killing you had to do to defend the defenseless is based on holy, lawful commands by God Himself through His Word. Your actions follow in the footsteps of Bible heroes who slew to protect innocents. Remember Abraham, Moses, Gideon, David, Nehemiah, and hosts of others who fought for their kin and country and were blessed by God for doing so. Remember, being a soldier did not keep the centurion from being praised by Jesus as the most faithful person He had ever met. Realize that Cornelius' profession was no impediment to faith that caused God to honor him as the first Gentile convert to Christianity. Never forget that you fight for a country which for more than 200 years has used its armed forces across the globe to provide more freedom to more people more consistently than any other society in history.

Never let the nay-sayers, the pacifists, the armchair quarterbacks, the media, or the dishonest politicians give you the slightest doubt about the righteousness of what you do and the benefits to your fellow man that flow from your actions. Never pay attention to those who do not even know which end of the barrel the rounds exit. When dealing with the physical/psychological effects, cling to God's Word first, and then seek help. Debrief with wise, godly supervisors and comrades. Seek out good ministers, chaplains, and mental health professionals who can help you through the pain. Teach yourself, your family, and your friends the principles in this book and the books I have recommended; that will prepare you to act appropriately if and when the time comes. Teach these principles to your co-workers, and then you will have a supportive team in place if you ever have to enter a combat situation. "Therefore humble yourselves under the mighty hand of God, that He may exalt you at the proper time, casting all your anxiety on Him, because He cares for you" (1 Peter 5:6-7). Remember, a spiritual battle exists behind any physical battle. Understand that both spiritual and physical battles are first fought in the mind, and your survival and victory depend on your deeply held convictions before, during, and after combat.

Consider Eugene Peterson's paraphrase of Ephesians 6:10-18 in *The Message*:

And that about wraps it up. God is strong, and He wants you strong. So take everything the Master has set out for you, well-made weapons of the best materials. And put them to use so you will be able to stand up to everything the Devil throws your way. This is no afternoon athletic contest that we'll walk away from and forget about in a couple of hours. This is for keeps, a life-or-death fight to the finish against the Devil and all his angels. Be prepared. You're up against far more than you can handle on your own. Take all the help you can get, every weapon God has issued, so that when it's all over but the shouting you'll still be on your feet. Truth, righteousness, peace, faith, and salvation are more than words. Learn how to apply them. You'll need them throughout your life. God's Word is an indispensable weapon. In the same way, prayer is essential in this ongoing warfare. Pray hard and long. Pray for your brothers and sisters. Keep your eyes open. Keep each other's spirits up so no one falls behind or drops out.[7]

In the final analysis, being a cop or soldier is an act of love. In 1 Corinthians 13:7a, Paul says Love "bears all things." In the Greek, the word *bears* means *to cover* or *to protect* (as in covering-fire or the protection a shield provides). In verse 5b, Paul says Love is unselfish and "does not seek its own." Love does not act solely for its own benefit, even to sacrificing one's life for another. Love also "endures all things" (verse 7d). It hangs in there for the long haul, no matter what the odds or how tough the challenges. Protecting, unselfish, enduring Love: that is the blessing the U.S. military and police officers bestow on America and the world. Remember that.

Intermission

Abram – Father of Faith and Self-Defense

This is a fictional account from Genesis 14 of Abram's rescue of his nephew Lot and many other families who had been taken hostage.

How it might have happened ….

Abram ignored the spectacular sunset. Concern creased his brow as he gazed south toward the desert and the cities beyond. For months now, word of the four kings advancing from the Lands-Between-the-Rivers had come across Jordan with breathless refugees. Moving south from Damascus since the early spring, they had smashed every city and people east of Jordan down to Hazazon-tamar at the top of the gulf leading down to the Red Sea. From there, they had headed northwest to Kadesh, defeating the Amalekites, then turned east toward Sodom, Gomorrah, and three minor cities at the south end of the Dead Sea. "The five kings of those cities," Abram thought, "would surely turn out and fight them."

Abram feared for his nephew, Lot, a man of wealth and influence, who would naturally join the battle. Never a deep thinker, Lot had chosen the opportunities for trade, culture, and excitement in the Five Cities over the pastoral life.

"Uncle," Lot had said, "There's a great future to be had by settling there. Besides, the Lord has not yet told me where I'm to settle in Canaan."

"There is much evil and worship of false gods there," answered Abram, "two major reasons why God told me to leave Ur to come here. I like the country life here in the hills around Hebron – more elbow room for my flocks and herds."

"But Uncle Abram," Lot had countered, "a man of your wisdom would prosper politically as well as financially. You could become a King among Kings in the Five Cities, a great man!"

Abram smiled, "Then when greater men become jealous and come to take those cities, I would be their target – and you too." Abram placed a fatherly hand on Lot's shoulder and looked earnestly into his eyes. "Lot, I love you as my son; please don't go where your body and soul will be targets. Stay here in the hill country and let the great temptations and affairs of the plainsmen pass you by. After all," he said with a wry smile, "the lion never bothers to chase the mouse. Stay near me and let the dangers of the wide world overlook our happiness."

They had parted in friendship, but Abram had not seen Lot since he settled in Sodom. His heart ached for news of his nephew. "Help him Lord," he prayed, "and if he needs me, let me come to his aid."

Twilight came. Abram gazed upward to count the first three stars in the sky. It was the start of a new day by his people's reasoning.

"My Lord!" The call jerked Abram from his reverie. Over the lip of the hill came Peleg, the faithful scout who served as Abram's eyes and ears roundabout Hebron. Another, unknown to Abram, leaned on his arm. Dark, large, days-old scabs marred the left side of his face and shoulder. "He must come from the battle" thought Abram.

"My Lord," said Peleg, "this is Sered. He was captured in the battle but escaped during the sack of the cities."

"Sit, my son," said Abram gently "and tell me of my nephew Lot, if you know."

"Truly my lord, he lives," sighed Sered through parched lips.

"Praise God!" cried Abram. "Quickly, tell me what happened!"

After a long pull on Peleg's water skin, Sered continued raspily: "Three days ago, the armies of the five cities formed southwest of Zoar. The four kings outnumbered us, but our flanks anchored on the Salt Sea on our right and the pitch marshes on our left. Lot counseled this so they couldn't outflank us. But Chedorlaomer outflanked us anyway. He sent chariot troops around the marshes days before. When we were fully engaged, they attacked us from the rear. Bera, king of Sodom, panicked and broke for the marshes. He bogged down, and they finished him with arrows. Birsha, king of Gomorrah, fled with him and fell too, but most men broke and ran north. Lot led a group of archers and slingers, including me, trying to cover the retreat. We came to Gomorrah at sundown, but a second enemy-flanking force had already reached the unmanned cities behind us and had taken them. At Lot's command, I slipped away and came the 40 miles here to tell you."

"Bless you, my child!" exclaimed Abram. "But how do you know Lot lives?"

"It was clear, my lord, that they were herding, not butchering us. Their goal is plunder, slaves, and tribute, not slaughter."

"Enough. Thank you dear boy! You shall have rest and reward. Peleg, take Sered to camp. Arrange for food, water, and someone to dress his wounds; then return with my Chief Steward, Amram. Send word to my Amorite allies to meet me at my tent as well. Summon Joktan and Kemuel too."

As the two left, Abram trotted off to select a ram to sacrifice. He would thank God for sparing Lot and ask His wisdom and blessing on what he must now do.

An hour later his men and friends assembled in his tent. None could help being impressed by Abram. Though 78, he looked no more than 45. In an age when average life expectancy was 120 years, he was still impressive. Nine years his junior, Abram's wife Sarai looked even younger and was spectacularly beautiful. Her beauty and his own foolish lie had nearly brought disaster in Egypt, but he was wiser now, having since learned complete trust in his God. Abram's wealth, wisdom, character, faith, and humility were legendary. In every way, none could doubt that his faith in his nameless, invisible God was justified – save only the fact that he and Sarai had no heir.

"My friends," he began, "by now you've heard Sered's tale, and the urgent need upon me."

"You have but to name the request," said Mamre, "and my brothers and I shall fulfill it! We are already gathering our forces. Just tell us when we leave!"

"Thank you, dear friend," said Abram, "but I don't need all your men for fighting. Will you, Eschol and Aner, please tally off enough men to protect and mind my flocks, herds, and people until I return?"

"It shall be done my brother. Let us add our strength to your army!"

Abram smiled, "Thank you Mamre. I thank God constantly for such true neighbors as you."

"What is your plan?" asked Eschol.

"We can't fight a pitched battle. What good has numbers done any kingdom against these four kings? We will go quietly, fast and far. Stealth and surprise will achieve what I seek; the return of my own and justice for the helpless."

Mamre, Eschol, and Aner bowed slightly, touching their brows and lips in gesture of shalom. "It shall be as you say, my wise friend."

"Many thanks," replied Abram, "your loyalty and sacrifice will not be forgotten."

"Now to our plan, Amram. How many trained fighters have we in our three companies?"

"Three hundred eighteen," he replied, "archers, javelineers, and slingers. For close combat, they have throw sticks and thrusting spears, and they're well practiced with all of them. All can move fast and light, living off the land."

"Excellent!" said Abram. "We will go in three companies of combined arms under you, Joktan, and Kemuel, as we have practiced. Mamre, Eschol, and Aner will lead their own men. The enemy is moving back north on the east side of Jordan. These kings are surely going to Damascus, 120 miles from the battlefield at Zoar. They will move slowly, encumbered by livestock, loot, and captives. Their greatest hindrance, though, is their own pride. They left no kingdom to oppose their return, and they rest assured that none would dare attack them now. That overconfidence is now our greatest strength. We move at first light. See to it friends!"

Then Abram said, "Amram, Peleg, Sered, stay a moment please. Sered, my son, how do you feel?"

"Better, my lord. Peleg's wife bound my wounds, and I've been well-fed and watered. This foundling lamb needs only a night's rest, a new sling, and I'll be ready to fight again!" Sered's eyes flashed eagerness, belying his battered face.

"Excellent! I need your help on this expedition," said Abram. "Only you can identify Lot and the other captives from the five cities for us. We must find them among the horde, and pluck them out as jackals snatch a lost lamb."

"Peleg?"

"My lord?"

"Sered will go with you and your scouts. We will move north, keeping the Jordan and its ridges between us and the foe. Take your team across Jordan at Jericho, when the enemy catches up, shadow them. Learn all you can. Find Lot and his wife. The marauders will likely stop at Dan on their way to Damascus.

Once you're sure they're headed there, break away and meet us on Mount Hermon. From there we'll plan our assault." "Very good, my lord. May God bless us and grant us success!" Peleg and Sered left.

"And what are your orders for me lord?" asked Amram.

"Most trusted one, I have a battle plan requiring special supplies. Add enough cargo donkeys to carry small oil lamps, rams' horns, and drinking pitchers. One set each per man. If there aren't enough in Hebron, we'll buy them on the way. Have everything ready by the morning sacrifice."

"It will be done lord," affirmed Amram.

After Amram left, Sarai appeared from the bedroom of the tent and hugged Abram. "Husband," she asked, "*must* you risk yourself to rescue your foolish, reckless nephew? After all, you warned him."

He put his arm around her and sighed. "God wants us to love with deeds, not just words. The only truly just world exists when we do for others what we wish they'd do for us in the same situation."

"I know," she agreed, "but it's hard, sometimes, not to just want to be undisturbed by those who've made their own bed."

"But remember, Sarai, that no one in Canaan invited these marauding kings to come stealing and killing as they wished. No matter how inoffensive we are, there are always evil men who won't let others alone."

"You're right," she sighed.

"Think what an awful world this would be if it were ruled solely by the strongest and only to serve their whims. No one could then live quietly." Abram began to pace as he talked. "God *hates* evil! To be angry with evil *is* godly, and a godly man *must* oppose it. Violence is ugly, but it's not the ugliest thing. The ugliest thing is to care about nothing more than my own peace and safety." He was now gesturing energetically, releasing the previous few days' tension as he paced. "If I have nothing for which I am willing to fight, then I have little chance of remaining free … unless I'm protected by better men than myself! Lot needs me, and the kidnappers who took him need a lesson!"

Sarai came to him, cupping his face in her hands. "You've gotten yourself quite worked up, my lord," she purred, her eyes flashing admiration and love. "Come to bed now, you've a big day tomorrow."

"Just one more thing," he said as he stooped over an ivory-inlaid, ebony trunk. Opening it, he withdrew a razor-sharp Egyptian sickle sword, bright bronze with an ivory grip with gold inlay, a parting gift from Pharaoh.

Before his assembled household, Abram performed the morning sacrifice. As the firstling roasted on the altar, Abram's prayer rose with the pungent smoke. "Lord God, King of the Universe, the One, the Only, look upon us in Your love. You have brought us safely from Ur to Haran, exchanging false gods and a bad society for Your promises. You kept us safe through famine and protected us to Egypt and back. You settled us here in Hebron with faithful and dear friends. We praise You for leading us, for giving us Your mercy and wisdom. Thank You for teaching us right from wrong and that right thought must result in right living. Never let us become complacent when our neighbor is in need, as he is now. Our brother Lot and his family have been violently taken, along with their neighbors, by men who acknowledge no law but themselves. We ask Your blessing as we go the rescue. Protect us. Protect Lot's family and fellow captives. Strengthen our arms to punish the evildoers. May it be Your will that we return successfully and safely. May You accomplish it in such a way that all who hear cannot help but see Your hand has done it. May the outcome change the hearts of all the people in Sodom, Gomorrah, and the other cities of the plain when they realize You alone have saved them. May they turn their hearts from their vain beliefs and cultures and live in Your light. Make us strong for battle. Teach our hands to war. Confuse our enemies' minds. Break their bow and spear. Guard, O Lord, our going and our returning. For our success we look to You, and we will give You all the glory. Amen."

Goodbyes said, they were on the march within the hour. Abram and his leaders marched at the head of the column. "Brothers, we can make 25 miles a day. The pack mule team can catch up when we stop at the north end of the Sea of Kinnereth. We'll be ahead of the four kings by then, so we can move north together. The enemy will head for Damascus to sell the captives and divide the loot before they split up to go to their own kingdoms. They'll be lucky to make 10 miles a day, encumbered as they are with their prizes. They've 170 miles to Damascus from Zoar, and they're four days along now. It's high summer, two months until autumn rains. The only reliable water sources across their line of march are the Arnon, Jabbok, and Yarmuck rivers; and they'll be small creeks by now. They can't go far east of the Jordan if they mean to keep the flocks and herds they've stolen, their captives and themselves watered. That country is too rough to move fast."

"We'll stay out of sight and ahead on the west side of Jordan. Peleg, this is where your team and Sered come in. Track them on the east side. Note their speed, route, routines, numbers, and how they're doing for water. Your prime mission is to find the captives. How are they guarded, and how well? Meet me every sixth day and report."

"Yes Lord," replied Peleg. "I'll keep a close eye on stragglers, too. We'll need information near the ambush point."

"Exactly," agreed Abram. "But no killing, we don't want them on their guard until we spring the trap."

Six days later, Peleg and his scouts came in. During supper, he reported to Abram and the leaders.

"You were right, lord. Their water problem is critical, and it's to our advantage. The four kings took most of the fighting men and are hot footing it for Damascus. They're making 15 miles or more a day. But the captives and herds are straggling far behind, guarded by only a couple of thousand troops. From their lack of discipline, you can tell they believe they've eliminated any danger. They're not sending out scouts. We were able to mix with the shepherds and the flocks. The guards assumed we were captive shepherds, too. They talked freely. They are supremely confident that the war is over and they'll enjoy the pickings when they get home."

"Glory to God!" said Abram. "The Almighty confounds their counsels to make them our prey. But what of Lot?"

"That's the best news! He and his wife are with the captives." "Unharmed?"

"Yes lord. A soldier told us they were under orders that the wealthy nobility and their women were not to be touched. The kings expect ransom offers or high prices for their unspoiled goods in the slave markets."

"Praise God Most High!" cried Abram. "Then they'll follow the Jordan to its headwaters on Mount Hermon before turning east to Damascus. We should find plenty of places for an ambush. Well done Peleg! Now rest a day and then take your scouts back. I'll tell you what else to do before you leave. Meet us at Mount Hermon about two days before the kidnappers arrive."

Eight days later, Peleg and his team found Abram and his troops on the slopes of Mount Hermon. They gathered in a wadi a couple miles from a small valley with low, gentle slopes. At the end of that valley was a town called Dan, where for the previous hour they had watched the troops and their captives gather to camp for the night. The herds were gathered south of the valley. The invaders slaughtered cattle, sheep, and goats, gathered many large jugs of wine, and stoked great fires. By all indications, a victory celebration was in order. Sered returned from scouting northeast, reporting that the four kings were coming in from Damascus with a small escort. "They've sent the bulk of their forces home. They've kept only a thousand troops or so as escorts 20 miles back at Damascus. Then there's the couple thousand here at Dan with the spoils."

"Excellent!" said Abram. "Then we will catch the true villains as well. Time now to repay them for all the sorrow they've caused. Now men, here's the plan…"

Abram's men along with Mamre, Eschol, and Aner leaned in, huddling for half an hour. "Alright men, night comes. You know what to do. Wait for my signal. The most important thing to remember is once we have them on the run, don't let up until I say! Pursue closely and without pity. Stop for nothing. Victory becomes fact only when the enemy knows he's been whipped. Certain, total defeat is what will keep them from coming back. When the survivors tell their grandchildren about this night, make sure their tale frightens them from even thinking about coming west of the Euphrates under arms!"

Exultant exclamations and war cries rose from the group. "Now to your places. Await my signal. God be with you all!" As they broke up, Abram had Amram distribute the pitchers, lamps, and rams horns to his men.

By midnight, Peleg reported that the party in Dan was in full swing. Abram's men were ready to go. He led them in prayer. "Lord, You are our light and salvation. So we will not fear. You defend our lives. So we have no dread of evildoers or their numbers. Our enemies will stumble and fall because You are our rock and our shield. Fight those who fight us. Rise up as our help. Make our eyes sharp and our arms strong, and we will sing your praises. You have given me Your covenant and protection. Extend Your loving arms about us and all the victims we rescue. Judge our enemies. Do not let them rejoice over us. We have sought your face. Let us dwell in your presence forever. You are our help and our salvation. Amen."

"Amen," echoed his men.

"Men, have no fear; for we are honest men in a righteous cause, pitted against those who will not allow others to live in peace. Their twisted minds conceive twisted gods to put them under slavery to their twisted kings. Think about their foolishness. They chop down a tree, take half the trunk, fashion it into their idea of a god, and cover it with gold leaf. They give it a mouth, nose, eyes, and ears, but it can neither speak, smell, see nor hear (amused looks among the troops). They pray and sacrifice to their log god, not even sparing their children! Yet," Abram winked, "they take the other half of the log, use part to build a cook fire, and build a cowshed with the rest! And they don't get it! (laughter now, elbowing and winks). Now, think of our God! Invisible. All-powerful. His loving-kindness is eternal. He cannot be contained in His creation. His care is personal. We know not His name, but He knows each of us and has numbered the hairs of our heads! Our God is Justice, Mercy, Love, Faithfulness, and Goodness. Our enemies' gods are no greater nor more moral than they are: dressed up firewood worshipped by ignorant, evil men. Remember this as you fight – how great is our God!"

The soldiers cheered and raised their weapons. Abram raised his hand, and the crowd fell silent. "You know the plan. Wait for my signal; then *win*! Move out!"

As the rescuers closed in on Dan, they could hear the drunken revelry around the town. Silently, they occupied the opposite rims of the valley and the low rise astride the road at the South side of the town. Then Abram, Peleg, Sered, and the scout team moved to the outskirts. Surprising ten sentries getting drunk at a campfire, they dispatched them easily. They donned the sentries' thin bronze helmets and leather armor capes as a disguise. The capes clasped just below the neck, with brass studs all over (too far apart to add protection), covering the shoulders and part of the chest, extending down to mid-calf. Completing their disguise with their foes large, wooden shields and heavy thrusting spears, they moved into the confused mass of revelers and toward the town center. Watching from his hiding place, Amram passed the word to his 300 men arranged in teams of 100 on the three sides of the town to light the oil lamps inside their pitchers.

Right behind them were the ranks of Mamre, Eschol, and Aner.

Abram and his squad filtered through the drunken masses, quickly locating the sheep pens just outside the village where the captives were held. Peleg sent two scouts back to lead Mamre to their rescue.

At the center of town, the four kings sat at a long table on a low dais, toasting their subordinates, each other, and their gods. Music played and women whirled amid the drunken merriment. Abram and his squad had edged within a few yards of the dais, when Chedorlaomer rose and signaled for silence. "My brother kings! Generals! Lords! Vassals, allies and troops! I thank you all for a most successful campaign against the barbarians of Canaan! Next year, we'll do the same to the Hurrians and Hittites to the north and east! Then, who knows? After that, why not Egypt?" Cheers and roars of approval rose from the reeling throng. "All hail Marduk, storm god!" Applause and staccato attempts to repeat their leader in unison broke up in self conscious laughter. "All hail Shamash and Ishtar, king of the sun and queen of the moon!" More attempted worship faded to babble in the crowd. At the end of the table, King Tidal leaped up to join in, yodeled one great war whoop, and passed out, falling backwards onto the dais to the mirth of all.

It was at this moment of bedlam that Abram pulled out a ram's horn and blew a clear, distinct call. Few revelers noticed until seconds later, when they heard three hundred horns answer from all around. Startled, they spun their heads to see three hundred lights and the silhouettes of masses of men running in from three sides, shouting war cries amid the continuous blare of the horns. Many assumed this was part of the celebration until the missiles struck. The mob was so tightly packed that sling stones, arrows, and javelins could hardly miss. Men began to scream in agony and fall. Bleary eyes widened, drunken feet tried to coordinate, hands groped for weapons that had been left in tents, and panic set in.

It was every man for himself. Friends, lords, loot, and prisoners were forgotten as heart rates zoomed and bowels and bladders loosed. Frantic men drew daggers and knifed comrades in their frenzy to get out. Trampling, cursing, shoving, clubbing, flailing, and running in every direction with only one focus: escape. The few who could think clearly enough to fight couldn't tell friend from foe and began slaying each other.

Abram shed his cumbersome disguise and sprinted for the dais where

Chedorlaomer stood rooted to the spot, amazement on his beet red face. He hadn't time to drop his goblet and go for his dagger before Abram's sickle sword descended in a great sweeping arc. He died with that surprised look frozen on his face. Peleg rammed his spear through King Amraphel's throat as he sat. King Arioch, rising to run, tangled in his robe and tripped over the supine Tidal. Sered and a scout pinned them both to the dais with spears.

At that moment, Abram's troops crashed into the panicked mob from three sides and began to slaughter. So tightly packed that few could raise their hands to defend themselves, the mob swayed this way and that, finding death at every turn. Pressure from the attackers soon forced them in the one way left open, the road to Damascus. Within five minutes of Abram's signal, all resistance had ceased and the pursuit was on. Mamre and his men secured the prisoners first, finding Lot and his wife. Leaving a few men to help Lot organize the rescued people, Mamre joined the pursuit.

For twenty miles to Damascus, the hunt went on. Abram and his men slew every invader they overran. A few escaped in the kings' four-wheeled mule chariots. Reaching Damascus, they spread fear, telling tales of the huge overwhelming force that had wiped out both kings and army and was on its way to do the same to this city. The Damascenes closed the gates at the sound of the rout, dashing the last hope of the invaders as their remnants flowed around the city and on north.

A few miles beyond, at the village of Hobah, Abram called his exhausted men to a halt. "Enough! Leave a few to tell the tale and spread the glory of the wrath of our God!" Trudging back at midmorning, Amram met them with the pack train. They'd brought provisions. Abram and his men fell on the food and drink; then they slept on their arms for their first rest in two days while Amram and his company stood guard. When they took a head count, God' blessing was clear: though there were several wounded, they hadn't lost a man. They returned to Dan singing and praising God.

That day's reunion with Lot and the others was joyous indeed. The next two days involved stripping the dead of tons of armor, weapons, and treasure. Abram's men added that to the loot from the five cities, which was already on transport. Leaving the dead to the scavengers, Abram led the herds, pack trains, and several thousand former captives southward. After ten days, they came to Jebus, a town on a mountain called Zion in a district called Salem.

Melchizedek was the priest and king of Salem. Unlike the polytheists around him, he worshiped the One God and had been acknowledged as the High Priest of God by the Jebusites. As Abram was on his way to Salem, he sent word to Melchizedek who greeted him at Shaveh, a valley southeast of Zion. Melchizedek brought out bread and wine, greeting Abram with raised hands of peace and proclaiming for all to hear: "Blessed is Abram, beloved of God Most High, the maker and owner of heaven and earth! And blessed be God Most High who gave you victory, delivering your enemies into your hand!"

Then Abram replied, "Truly, the victory of the few over the many, the salvation of the innocent, and the preserving of the rescuers is all because of the Most High God, whom you serve. I have set aside the best tenth of all we captured and recovered: flocks, herds, treasure and arms. As God's representative on earth, I give it to Him through you, as an offering of thanks for His love and care in this matter and throughout my life." They embraced and sat down for a victory meal.

The day before, the new king of Sodom, Enlil-Opher, arrived at Zion with the survivors of his army. He came as a supplicant, not under arms. During the meal, he came to Abram and Melchizedek's table where he went to his knees and bowed, praising Abram for his rescue of the people of the five cities. Enlil-Opher said, "Exalted father, (that is what 'Abram' means) after all you've done, we owe our very lives to you. Please keep all the goods you have captured. You have more than earned it. My people will be happy to return home with only the clothes on their backs."

"Not on my life would I do such a thing," replied Abram. "I undertook this mission for two reasons: so that God's justice, love, and mercy might be evident to my neighbors that they might realize His love and have faith in Him as I do, and to rescue my nephew Lot. So I swore to God that I would take nothing from you or your people, not even a sandal strap. I will not have you boast 'I made him rich' or later resent me because I took what belonged to you. The tenth of all of it I have given to God. Of the rest, I claim only repayment for what my men have eaten and a just division from the recovered goods for the expenses and efforts of my faithful friends, Amer, Eschol, and Mamre."

"I applaud the wisdom and generosity of Abram," said Enlil-Opher, "it shall be done as you say. Our eternal thanks."

Lot and his wife stayed a few days in Hebron with Abram and Sarai. The people of the five cities went on, eager to get home and rebuild. The last night, Abram tried to convince Lot again. "Nephew, stay here. You must see now that life in the cities is too risky."

"We will be family again," added Sarai, smiling, "and I can enjoy getting to know your wife, my new niece."

"But uncle, don't you see that my role in the battle and prestige as your nephew have made me a great man among them? Enlil-Opher says I will be made a judge at the gate of Sodom. My fortune is made!"

"Besides," put in his wife, "it's too quiet in the country. There is so much to see and do, so many goods and delights in the city, and so many opportunities for our children, when they come."

Abram saw the lust for the great city in her eyes, and he sighed. "All right, you're a grown man. I won't tell you what to do. But beware! Don't let where you live define who you are, or what you own begin to own you."

"Dearest uncle," he laughed, "have faith in me. No need to be so concerned."

"Have faith in *God* my son." Abram managed a smile, but his heart was heavy. Lot and his wife left the next morning. Abram never saw them again.

That evening, as Abram prayed at the evening sacrifice, God spoke to him. He told him first that he would have a son, and Abram's name from that moment on would be Abraham (Father of Many). God further told him he would be the first of a People of Faith, whom God would use to bless the whole world. Abraham believed what God told him, and God declared him righteous.

———

Now let's consider a bit of commentary on the lessons we learn from Abram and Lot. First, don't look for any self-doubt in Abram over having to kill murderers (people who'd started an unjust war merely for conquest), robbers (those who take property by force), rapists, and kidnappers. Self-doubt in such a situation is largely a feature of modern times. Not until philosophers like Rousseau, Hume, Kierkegaard, and Hegel made man the measure of all things and truth became

relative has mankind lacked objective standards to gauge right and wrong. Even
the most cursory reading of Psalms (27 and 37 for instance) will show that the
faithful of the Old Testament did not suffer from post-modernist angst about moral
right and wrong – or how to respond to evil effectively.

Abram's belief in right and wrong was grounded in the righteousness of THE
Personal God, as ours should be. In the ancient world of nomads and farmers,
early death by disease, wild animals, accident, or malice was simply accepted as
high probability. Issues of justice and right were stark and concrete. A man must
be responsible and active in preserving his family or lose all. In the absence of
civil government, a man acted with his community and according to its standards.
If the survival of you or yours was threatened by criminal interlopers, then it was
up to you to turn the tables, making survival *their* worry and eliminating the
threat.

Second, Abram's killing in these situations is justified by modern state laws
today. For example, Alabama's self-defense statute allows a victim or the defender
of a third party victim to use "deadly physical force" in response to attempted
murder, robbery, rape, or kidnapping (among other crimes).[1] Other states that
allow the use of deadly force in a kidnapping include Arizona, Missouri, New
York, and Washington.[2] All those crimes were committed in the aggressive war
waged by the four Mesopotamian kings. The ability to use deadly force continues
as long as the crime continues. In the case of kidnapping, the statute says that the
right to kill the kidnapper exists unless and until he ceases the kidnapping by
voluntarily releasing the victim free from injury in a safe place prior to
apprehension.[3] However, under the law, if I catch up with my daughter's
kidnappers while they are still holding her against her will, deadly force is
completely justified under the law.

Finally, let no one doubt the rightness and holiness of Abram's actions in killing
to rescue his kin and neighbors from death and slavery. He loved his neighbor as
himself (Leviticus 19:18b). He did for Lot as he would have wanted done for
himself. Jesus called this one of the two foremost commandments of the Law
(Matthew 22:34-40). Abram was "doing unto others" just as Jesus said we must
(Luke 6:31, Matthew 7:12).

Abram had a realistic view of the world, and he understood the likelihood that evil would need to be confronted. He had 318 trained warriors to protect his people and possessions (Genesis 14:14). Having weapons is useless without proficiency and education in their lawful use. He also lived in a supportive community in Hebron, where he had true friends and a civil infrastructure to help in emergencies (Genesis 13:18, 14:13). There is nothing ungodly about training to use legal force against criminals. David tells us that those who deal with criminals must be armed (2 Samuel 23:6-7). David even stated that God trained his hands for war (Psalms 144:1). Training shows our intent to confront evil successfully, to do so lawfully and with the correct application of force, and to insure good skill level with weapons so as to prevent accidentally harming the innocent.

Do not forget that Abram's actions were declared just and holy by God through Melchizedek, "the priest of the most High God" (Genesis 14:17-20). The writer of Hebrews reiterates this: "For this Melchizedek, king of Salem, priest of the Most High God, who met Abraham as he was returning from the slaughter of the kings and blessed him" (Hebrews 7:1), and "Now observe how great this man was to whom Abraham, the patriarch, gave a tenth of the choicest spoils" (Hebrews 7:4). In Hebrews 7:2, we are told Melchizedek means "king of righteousness" and "king of peace" (Salem). Hebrews 7:3 tells us that Melchizedek was "made like the Son of God, he abides as a priest perpetually." And in Hebrews 7:17, the writer says that Jesus is "a priest forever, according to the order of Melchizedek." So it is clear that Melchizedek's priesthood was ordained and blessed by God and that Jesus' priesthood is modeled after it. Such a man, in obedience to God, would never condone murder.

The point is clear. Abram had just come back from an act of justice wherein he had slaughtered untold numbers of bad guys and chased them over 20 miles to make sure they got the point. Yet even though Abram appeared before Melchizedek with blood on his hands, the priest of God Most High declared him righteous and blessed him with a hearty, "well done!" Melchizedek had the party all set when Abram arrived in order to honor Abram before his own men, allies, the freed captives, and the new king of Sodom. Melchizedek declared to the whole world that God approved of Abram's act of self-defense of Lot and the others. Abram's tithe, conversely, acknowledges gratitude to God for enabling him to kill the bad guys and rescue the victims. There is not the least hint in either man's behavior that Abram has done anything wrong. On the contrary, God praises Abram through Melchizedek for loving his neighbor as himself. God ruled Abram's actions as justifiable homicide and a positive good for all concerned. In fact, it was after this (Genesis 15) that God chose Abram as the "Father of the Faithful" and made specific His eternal promises to him.

The Law

15

Criminals

Who are they? Where do they come from?
What is our proper attitude toward them?

Ask any prosecutor or defense lawyer if in your county there are not certain families that are notorious for being criminals generation after generation. In my county, if we hear that the accused is from one of these several families, all the lawyers say, "he's guilty." As a matter of fact, our local narcotics officers say that if they want to know whether a drug dealer is home so they can serve a warrant, they will call and identify themselves as a member of one of the crime families. A criminal life is so pervasive in these families, some joke that merely by reproducing they are guilty of operating a continuing criminal enterprise under the federal RICO statutes! Part of the message of Exodus 20:5 tells us that ideas, habits, words, and actions of parents have consequences. The bad or good things we teach our kids by example will be practiced by the next generation. Whether we teach them consciously or not, kids catch our values from our actions and habits as part of their environment. We must always keep God's sovereignty in mind. He not only knows the past, present, and future of each individual or group, but also the *effect* that their continued existence will have on their own and future generations.[1]

The next part of the message is this: if children learn to respect and love their parents, they will learn respect for God, true self-respect, and respect for others. Look at the structure of the Ten Commandments. The first four relate to the vertical relationship between God and man: have no other gods before me, do not make or worship idols, do not take the name of God in vain, and remember the Sabbath and keep it holy (Exodus 20:1-11). The fifth commandment is "Honor your father and mother" (Exodus 20:12). Next, are the final five: do not commit murder, do not commit adultery, do not lie, steal, or covet. These last five commandments relate to the horizontal relationship of man-to-man (Exodus 20:13-17). The fifth commandment is not stuck in the middle by accident. God is smarter than we are. Remember, He made us and wrote the Owner's Manual: the Bible (Psalm 100:3). The Fifth commandment is the middle one between our vertical relationship with God (Commandments 1-4) and our horizontal relationship with others (Commandments 6-10). The cross places Jesus at the nexus of this vertical/horizontal relationship and points to Him as the cure for what ails us in our relationship with God and others. Through His completed work, Jesus reconciles us to God and to others. God put the Fifth commandment in the middle to orient our character in the same directions.

When we are infants/toddlers, we really cannot understand the concept of "God." An invisible being might be an imaginary friend, but not an omniscient, omnipresent, omnipotent Creator/Savior of the universe. At that age, the closest we can come to an all-powerful being is our parents. They provide all our needs, set our rules, and seem to know everything. The Fifth commandment requires us to have implicit (and later explicit) respect for parents. We learn obedience, trust, and respect for them and from them. As we grow into adolescence, we learn to respect their wisdom and experience. As I tell my daughter, "Trust me, I've been 14, you haven't been 50." The scriptures support this: "Hear my son, your father's instruction, and do not forsake your mother's teaching; indeed, they are a graceful wreath to your head, and ornaments about your neck" (Proverbs 1:8-9). We respect parents not only for what they know, but for what they do: feeding, clothing, housing, teaching, and loving us; modeling Christ in a hundred ways. "Train up a child in the way he should go, even when he is old he will not depart from it" (Proverbs 22:6). Through this process, we come to learn the eternal truth behind the Fifth commandment: that true self-respect comes only when we learn to respect God first and then others next. From our parents, we learn that through humility and personal achievement, we can have *both* true self-worth and proper regard for and relationships with others. The vertical and horizontal relationships will then be in tune, as God meant them to be: "You shall love the Lord your God with all your heart and with all your soul and with all your might" (Deuteronomy

6:5), and " … you shall love your neighbor as yourself …" (Leviticus 19:18b). Jesus said these two verses sum up the whole Old Testament (Luke 10:25-29). This is what the Fifth commandment did for the Israelites and will do for us, if we follow it.

Instead, we have a society in which respect, manners, and sharing are diminishing. People do not know the difference between fame (being known for an accomplishment that confers benefit on others) and mere notoriety (being known simply for being known). A hero used to be someone who put himself at risk for the good of others. Now, it is a sports star or a swimsuit model, without regard for their character (witness the kids wearing Michael Vick T-shirts who waited to cheer outside his house when he returned from prison). As the media promotes inconsequential, narcissistic people, such as reality show "stars," society becomes further convinced that the point of life is simply to be noticed for any reason. We have lost the wisdom that Solomon provided: "Before destruction the heart of a man is haughty, but humility goes before honor" (Proverbs 18:12).

Contrary to modern thinking, the Bible says kids should learn to respect others first and then themselves. Uncritical, undeserved self-esteem without basis in actual achievement simply produces selfishness. If unchecked, it produces sociopaths. Genuine self-esteem comes from genuine achievement. It is only when we realize that there are boundaries to our whims and actions and we learn to respect the rights of others and the authority of parents that we become responsible, truly self-respecting individuals. God's plan is simple. By learning respect and love for our parents, we learn the same for others in a horizontal relationship and for God in a vertical relationship (Proverbs 22:6).

Crime ultimately is committed by people who grew up believing they are better than others. Criminals, like spoiled kids, believe others are here only to serve their wants and needs. These kinds of people are called sociopaths. For the last 30 years at least, education has put forth a major effort to foster a "me first" mentality among children. This is called "self-esteem" education. The premise is to tell kids they are wonderful little geniuses whose mere existence improves the world and every situation or place in which they appear. Yet this is done without any requirement that these shining tots actually accomplish anything to earn this praise. It goes so far that some schools do not tell kids they are wrong even if they say 2+2=5. They don't get an "F", they get an "L" for "learning" (lest we hurt their self-esteem). Because their self-worth is not tied to achievements, they are trained to assume that they and their every whim and action are God's gift to everyone. They grow up living by their feelings and desires, and if anything goes wrong, it is never their fault. Anyone who frustrates their wishes – parents, cops, or teachers – had better look out. Their philosophy is this: "If I want it, I'm entitled to it!"

Is it any wonder then that teachers often spend more time trying to control their classes than teaching them? As a certified teacher with eight years of public school experience, I can assure you that there are enough narcissistic sociopaths in any given high school classroom to ruin the education experience for everybody. These kids actually revel in being corrected because they are so starved for loving attention at home that they believe any attention is good; disruption is an end in itself. As the Bible says, "A scoffer does not love the one who reproves him. He will not go to the wise" (Proverbs 15:12).[2]

Like these teenagers, many people excuse their bad behavior with a defiant slogan: "Respect must be earned!" The implication is that whatever authority figure they are rebelling against has not "earned" respect. This, of course, allows them to reject anyone or anything that their subjective standards find inconvenient to their selfish desires. Earning their respect means surrendering to their every whim. The 5th commandment tells us unequivocally that respect is first *learned* (not earned). When we learn God's standards from our parents, we gain His objective standards on who deserves respect throughout our lives. Without God's standards, we are merely nurturing more generations of criminals, just as the pre-Flood generations did. To counteract this, we must teach that true self-respect comes only from respecting others.

The Israelites also knew something about sentencing criminals and its relationship to deterrence: "Because the sentence against an evil deed is not executed quickly, therefore the hearts of the sons of men among them are given fully to do evil" (Ecclesiastes 8:11). Our modern day maxim is "justice delayed is justice denied." Lawyers usually say that in the context of encouraging a speedy trial, but Solomon points out that delaying sentencing and its execution denies justice by reducing the law's deterrent effect on criminals. Victims and society as a whole suffer as a result. Never forget that criminals earn their punishment because of their own refusal to evaluate and repent of their stupid and cruel life choices: "A rebellious man seeks only evil, so a cruel messenger will be sent against him" (Proverbs 17:11). The "cruel messenger" is the sentencing statute and the judge who wields it. "The violence of the wicked will drag them away because they refuse to act with justice" (Proverbs 21:7). We can conclude from these verses that the swift effects of justice also result when a cop or private citizen apprehends, wounds, or kills a criminal. Solomon continues to warn us, "He who sows wickedness reaps trouble, and the rod of his fury will be destroyed" (Proverbs 22:8, NIV). "For the upright will live in the land and the blameless will remain in it; but the wicked will be cut off from the land, and the treacherous will be uprooted from it" (Proverbs 2:21-22). The behavior of the unrepentant criminal guarantees a short, unhappy life (Proverbs 11:8). The lesson is clear: when the law is enforced, criminals are deterred from illegal behavior.

I had a client who was army special forces, honorably discharged with sergeant's rank and a computer degree. He went to live in a high-tech city with lots of government contractors who loved to hire veterans. So what did he do? He started a drug habit, got a burglary conviction, and then, ignoring his possible probation revocation, stole from his employer. The evidence against him was overwhelming. I begged him not to go to trial, but he insisted. After his conviction, he called me to complain that I did not care about him. I pointed out how he had separated from the army equipped for a good future and had moved to the right place to live that life, but he had made poor choices. I concluded, "You say I don't care about you, but *you* don't care about yourself! When you begin caring about yourself and making good decisions, your life will get better!" A little later, he called and asked my secretary to pass on his apology to me. His moment of clarity did not stick, however. The District Attorney told me several years later that my former client had committed another felony.

Despite their best efforts, lawyers are often excoriated by the very clients they have worked so diligently to help. The criminal's trouble is that he has dug a hole so deep that *no one* can dig him out. Solomon gives the moral of this story, "If a wise man goes to court with a fool, the fool rages and scoffs, and there is no peace" (Proverbs 29:9). Many times one of my clients has rejected a reasonable plea offer in the face of overwhelming evidence at trial. The rules are such that if the client wants a trial, the lawyer cannot refuse. If I could not logically dissuade the client from a disastrous trial, I would tell them, "Okay, we'll go to trial. But you're on a kamikaze mission."

Solomon tells us repeatedly that the wicked earn their ends. Personifying Wisdom, he has her say: "For he who finds me [wisdom] finds life, and obtains favor from the Lord. But he who sins against me injures himself, all those who hate me love death" (Proverbs 8:35-36). We lawyers express it in other ways. After

> "A rebellious man seeks only evil, so a cruel messenger will be sent against him" (Proverbs 17:11).

seeing people return to criminal folly time and again (despite all that friends, family, lawyers, employers, churches, or probation officers could do) my observation is: "Some people are just too stupid to be free." The Bible says it this way: "a mocker resents correction, he will not consult the wise" (Proverbs 15:32, NIV). One of my best friends (a former assistant D.A., criminal defense attorney, and municipal judge) has the best explanation, "The only thing I can figure is that they're trying to break *into* jail! They like it better there!" The Bible supports this: "A fool finds pleasure in evil conduct, but a man of understanding delights in wisdom" (Proverbs 10:13, NIV). The wisdom books of the Bible contain many other verses about the nature and fate of criminals. Repeatedly, the Bible points out that criminals have worked hard to earn their fate: "He who is steadfast in righteousness will attain to life, and he who pursues evil will bring about his own death" (Proverbs 11:19; 10:16). Their imprisonment, injuries, and untimely deaths are so often tragedies of their own making.

Clearly, the people of the Bible understood the definitions of the word *good, evil, wisdom,* and *folly.* As in all eras, people in the Bible made good and bad choices. They added to their store of wisdom based on the results of these choices. The smart ones learned from it all and taught that reality to their children. In the ancient near east, life's lessons were passed on in the form of "wisdom literature." In the Bible, these books of practical life lessons and philosophy are Proverbs, Ecclesiastes, and some of the Psalms. "The fear of the Lord is the beginning of wisdom; a good understanding have all those who do His commandments" (Psalm 111:10a).

A caveat when dealing with wisdom literature is the need to always consider a passage in context with the rest of Scripture. General statements do not necessarily mean these are universal promises outside their historical and cultural contexts. They offer general guidance for which there may be exceptions. For instance, "A man's gift makes room for him, and brings him before great men" (Proverbs 18:16) does not mean we should bribe judges or give nukes to terrorists. When Jesus says, "Give to him who asks of you, and do not turn away from him who wants to borrow from you" (Matthew 5:42), does not mean I should give the car keys to my 10 year old or a pistol to a guy who says he needs it to rob a bank. Of course not! Remembering that, let's use logical, rational thought about what God has to say about crime, criminals, and self-defense in the wisdom books.

The Psalms are often concerned with deliverance from the wicked. They reflect real anguish of people bearing up under actual, life-crushing problems, who are begging God for assurance of His caring and intervention. David assigns the just fate of criminals at God's hands to himself if he is found guilty of a crime:

"He who sows wickedness reaps trouble, and the rod of his fury will be destroyed" (Proverbs 22:8, NIV).

> O Lord my God, if I have done this [acted criminally]
> And there is guilt on my hands-
> If I have done evil to him who is at peace with me
> Or without cause have robbed my foe-
> Then let my enemy pursue and overtake me;
> Let him trample my life to the ground
> And make me sleep in the dust (Psalm 7:3-5, NIV)

This psalm was obviously written before David's adultery with Bathsheba and the murder of innocent, loyal Uriah. God forgave David for Uriah's murder, but the consequences of David's sin were devastating. David makes clear that God will provide a means to bring the wicked to heel, even though they might get away with it first:

> Arise O Lord; O God, lift up Thy hand.
> Do not forget the afflicted.
> Why has the wicked spurned God?
> He has said to himself, "Thou wilt not require it."
> Thou hast seen it, for Thou hast beheld mischief
> And vexation to take it into Thy hand.

The unfortunate commits himself to Thee;
Thou hast been the helper of the orphan.
Break the arm of the wicked and the evildoer,
Seek out his wickedness until Thou dost find none
Psalms 10:12-15.

David endorses the use of the courts as well: "Appoint someone evil to oppose my enemy; let an accuser stand at his right hand. When he is tried, let him be found guilty, and may his prayers condemn him" (Psalm 109:6-7, NIV).

David believed that God used the direct armed resistance of honest citizens to bring down criminals. "Blessed be the Lord, my rock, who trains *my hands* for war, and *my fingers* for battle ..." (Psalm 144:1, emphasis mine). In the next verse, David expressed his belief that his self-defensive actions were part of God's preservation: "My loving-kindness and my fortress, my stronghold and my deliverer; my shield and Him in whom I take refuge; who subdues peoples under me" (Psalm 144:2). He advises that those who deal with criminals must be armed: "But the worthless, every one of them will be thrust away like thorns because they cannot be taken in hand. But the man who touches them *must be armed with iron and the shaft of a spear,* and they [criminals] will be completely burned with fire in their place" (2 Samuel 23:6-7, emphasis mine). By sanctioning David's weapons and training, God encouraged him to defend himself physically from enemies (he's called "an expert at war" in 2 Samuel 17:8). God blessed David's actions and provided him a "shield" and a "refuge" that allowed him to "subdue" criminals. Even though David did violence, it was in God's cause (except his murder of Uriah), and he is called "a man after God's own heart" (1 Samuel 13:14). Armed citizens today also understand the definition of the word *emergency,* and like David, they prepare for it.

"He who is steadfast in righteousness will attain to life, and he who pursues evil will bring about his own death" (Proverbs 11:19; 10:16).

Rest assured, God knows the difference between murder and legally killing in battle, law enforcement, or self-defense. "Be pleased, O Lord, to deliver me; make haste O Lord, to help me. Let those be ashamed and humiliated together who seek my life to destroy it; let those be turned back and dishonored who delight in my hurt. Let those be desolated because of their shame" (Psalm 40:13-15a). Such is the prayer of the honest citizen faced by a criminal. David would approve the modern way I would shame and humiliate a knife-wielding mugger by showing him that he had brought a knife to a gunfight! The gun is the modern version of "the iron and the shaft of the spear" from 2 Samuel 23:6-7. In Psalm 119:153-159, the Psalmist begs God to preserve him according to His promise, His laws, and His love. (His laws allow self-defense.) The logical conclusion is that God blesses good people who use countervailing force to stop criminals bent on harming the innocent. Moreover, God says through David that the use of weapons is necessary when facing criminals. That is how "he who pursues evil brings on his own death" (Proverbs 11:19).

Does the Old Testament give us clues as to the attitude that Christians should take once the criminal is defeated? Yes. First, you must never forget that it is the criminal who sought this confrontation and forced you into a position where you had to act to stop him. His injuries are not your fault, they are his! He planted the wind and he reaped a tornado upon himself (Hosea 8:7). However, if the criminal survives your counterattack, you must start first-aid (but only if it is safe to do so) and call 911. Leaving your attacker to bleed out would be vengeful and taking the law (punishment) into your own hands. Since you have acted legally, you stay and wait for the police. Do not be surprised though if the criminal does not appreciate your mercy: "Though the wicked is shown favor, he does not learn righteousness; he deals unjustly in the land of uprightness, and does not perceive the majesty of the Lord" (Isaiah 26:10).

16

"Judge not, that ye be not judged"

What is the most well-known and oft-quoted verse in the Bible? Most Christians (and sports fans) would say John 3:16. But I believe the most frequently quoted and well known verse is Matthew 7:1, "Do not judge, lest you be judged." Some might quote it in the King James, "Judge not, that ye be not judged" or in today's vernacular, "That's your personal opinion!" No matter how they say it, people use it to prevent anyone from negatively evaluating their actions. Many in our post-modern society believe there are no standards for right and wrong, but, at a loss to justify their actions, they default to this verse. Their ploy is often effective in stopping the conversation because their challengers have no more insight into the context and meaning of Matthew 7:1 than the person quoting it. But if we cannot decide whether a person's acts are good are bad, how can we decide whether or not to defend ourselves?

"Who are you to judge me?" is the challenge flung by quoting this verse. They are implying that whatever action being judged is merely a matter of personal preference without relevance to anyone but them. In the 70s, many a criticism was answered with "That's just your value judgment!" People used this phrase to deflect negative comment without having to explain what values they deemed worthwhile or worthless. Criticism deflected, those of the "Me Generation" could get back to disco, CB radios, having sex with as many partners as possible, and pushing the outer limits of wearing lethal doses of polyester.

The problem is that when these people quote Jesus, they quote Him out of context, and, therefore, they misquote Him. We have all done this at one time or another to support our own selfish agendas. By taking verses out of context, we can prove any viewpoint we care to justify. Our relativistic moral outlook comes from the fact that the Judeo/Christian ethic has failed to hold the moral center since the second half of the 20th century. Since the mid-18th century, the Bible has receded as the moral standard, and now we refer to ourselves as living in a "post-Christian society." Even many professing Jews and Christians choose their own way when certain behaviors conflict with God's commands. This has diminished the regard for Biblical authority among believers and non-believers.

Rules for Interpreting Scripture

If we sincerely seek God's will for our lives, we must handle accurately "the word of truth" (2 Timothy 2:15c). We should never attempt to put our own spin on a subject; rather, we should examine everything the Bible has to say on a matter before coming to a conclusion on it. "First of all, no prophecy of Scripture is a matter of one's own interpretation, for no prophecy was ever by an act of human will, but men moved by the Holy Spirit spoke from God" (2 Peter 1:20-21). Moreover, accuracy is vital because God Himself will refute us. "Every word of God is tested. He is a shield to those who take refuge in Him. Do not add to His words, or He will reprove you and you be proved a liar" (Proverbs 30:5-6).[1]

God is our creator. He is a loving God, and He has communicated with us in a knowable way, giving us sufficient information to have a personal relationship with Him. The Bible is the owner's manual for successful human life. Absolute standards for ethics, morals, and theology come from the Bible. As Paul tells Timothy:

> From childhood you have known the sacred writings which are able to give you the wisdom that leads to salvation through faith which is in Christ Jesus. All Scripture is inspired by God and profitable for teaching, for reproof, for correction, for training in righteousness, so that the man of God may be adequate, equipped for every good work (I Tim. 3:15-17).

Therefore, if we attempt to determine God's will on an issue like self-defense where He has not expressed a specific command or position, we must honestly examine every relevant verse. God has not said, "Thou shalt/shalt not exercise self-defense," but I believe that careful study can lead us to a Biblical conclusion on the matter.

So when we use a verse like "Judge not," we must be sure to use it as the Bible intends. To properly interpret Scripture, we need to be aware of some basic rules. First, never take a verse out of context. That means we read the verses before and after the verse in question to determine its meaning in light of those other verses. That way we do not stray from the author's meaning. For instance, when a Bible writer begins a verse with "Therefore ...," we should read (at least) the whole chapter before that verse so we can see what it's "there for."

Rule two is "let Scripture explain Scripture." When interpreting laws, attorneys read all legislation that has to do with a legal issue. This is called *reading in pari materia*. A lawyer will not come to a conclusion until he has read all the laws pertaining to a subject and the leading court cases construing them. When analyzing Matthew 7:1, we must also look at Luke 17:1-4 where Jesus tells his disciples, "Be on your guard! If your brother sins, rebuke him and if he repents, forgive him" (verse 3). If we are to tell whether our brother is sinning, then there must be objective criteria by which we can do so (in other words, by judging his actions). In Matthew 18:15-17, Jesus elaborates, saying that if our brother refuses to listen, we should take one or two other Christians with us. If he still refuses to listen, his sin should be told to the congregation, and we are to treat him as an outcast until he repents. Again, how could we do this if we are not to judge by some specific standard?

That standard is, of course, God's. It is not only objective (without human mistakes of fact or perception), but it assures lack of bias on the part of those acting upon it. Any serious Bible reading will show that Jesus meant for us to evaluate our own and other's actions in the light of His Word. Consider what He told His disciples before He sent them on their first mission trip: "I came to convince people to choose me. This will create conflict. If you don't love me more than anything else, I will not recognize you on Judgment Day" (Matthew 10:34-39, my paraphrase).

Does Jesus sound like He's saying, "Well, this is what I say, but you can take it or leave it. You don't have to live by it, especially if it offends others." No, He demands we decide for Him and then live it no matter what others say (including family). Implicit in this speech is the idea that we must judge (distinguish) between the righteous and unrighteous acts of ourselves and others.

Jesus told his audience during a sermon that they could predict the weather but refused to evaluate what He was doing by God's Word: "You hypocrites! You know how to analyze the appearance of the earth and sky, but why do you not analyze the present time? And why do you not even on your own initiative judge what is right?" (Luke 12: 54-57). When some challenged Him because He had healed on the Sabbath, he said, "Do not judge according to appearance, but judge with a righteous judgment" (John 7: 21-24). Jesus teaches that there are both proper and improper choices to be made and conclusions to be reached, but we must use the right standard. In John 3:19-21, He declares that those who do evil hate the light, and those who do good love it, and the deeds of both groups will be exposed at the Judgment. He continues in John 5:28-30 by saying that those who have done evil will be resurrected for condemnation, while those who do good will rise to eternal reward. He concludes by saying His judgment is just because it is based on the revealed will of His Father.

Finally in John 12:44-50, Jesus says anyone who has seen Him has seen the Father and that those who believe in Him will be rescued from darkness.[2] However, He warns us that those who reject Him will be judged by His Father. The standard will be the words Jesus spoke.

These are just a few of the New Testament verses that command us to make decisions on right and wrong. Therefore, the only way to interpret that Matthew 7:1 says we cannot evaluate, criticize, or correct another person's words and actions is to take that verse out of context. I must conclude that God wants and even commands me to judge good and evil and to make life and death decisions based on His Word. "I call heaven and earth to witness against you today that I have set before you life and death, the blessing and the curse. So *choose life* in order that you may live, you and your descendants" (Deuteronony 30:19, emphasis mine). Choosing life for me and my descendants logically includes making decisions that lead to self-defense.

The Right to Judge

God never forces us to accept or obey Him. He tells us the consequences of obedience and disobedience, and then He lets us make our own choices and reap the consequences. God's explicit will leads to righteousness and our maximum happiness, yet His permissive will allows us to act disobediently and suffer the consequences (hoping we, as individuals and as a society, will learn from our mistakes). In either case, His sovereign wisdom and power achieves His ultimate will for both individuals and mankind (Romans 8:28).

Our next rule for explaining a verse is "if the normal sense makes good sense, look for no other sense."Most verses are fairly clear when read in context. For example, *shall* is a legal term. Any lawyer will tell you that *shall* in a statute means *must*, leaving no room for discretion

> *I call heaven and earth to witness against you today that I have set before you life and death, the blessing and the curse. So choose life in order that you may live, you and your descendants (Deuteronony 30:19).*

(as there would be when a statute says *may*). So when God says, "you shall not murder" (Exodus 20:13), we know that statute prohibits the intentional, unlawful killing of a person. But what if modern English is sometimes inadequate or imprecise to interpret a word or phrase accurately? In those cases, we must refer to the original languages: Hebrew and Koinonaea (marketplace as opposed to classical) Greek. God has helped us here by having the Bible written in dead languages. The meanings of words are fixed in ancient Hebrew and Greek. In living languages, the meanings and connotations of words change over time (for example *gay, cool, text, I love ice cream/I love my wife*). We don't have this problem with Greek and Hebrew. When these civilizations (ancient Rome, Greece, and Israel) ended, their languages were frozen in time, leaving us plenty of examples of each to build complete vocabularies, grammars, and context. Therefore, we need not guess as to the meanings of all except a few of the words at the time they were written. Admittedly, some few words and phrases are disputed. Though scholars may not agree as to the meaning of every word (otherwise we would not have different translations), those disputes are so few that none of the doctrines of the Bible are in doubt. In addition, historical and archeological facts can be used to explain the cultural, religious, social, and other contexts of the subject of a passage. Within these guidelines, our interpretation of a verse can be trusted as reliable.

In light of all that, let's return to Matthew 7:1-6 and see whether Jesus meant to say we cannot judge other people under any circumstances. The context is the whole Sermon on the Mount (Matthew 5-7). At several points, Jesus condemns the actions and motives of hypocrites (Matthew 6:2, 5 and 16), so obviously He could judge them. He was God on earth, though, and He could read minds (Matthew 9:4).[3] He knew people's innermost motivations and intentions. We are left to guess. His specific lesson about us judging is the following passage:

> Do not judge lest you be judged. For in the way that you judge, you will be judged; and by your standard, it will be measured to you. And why do you look at the speck that is in your brother's eye, but do not notice the log that is in your own eye? You hypocrite, first take the log out of your own eye, and then you will see clearly to take the speck out of your brother's eye. Do not give what is holy to dogs, and do not throw your pearls before swine, lest they trample them under their feet, and turn and tear you to pieces (Matthew 7:1-6).

First, we must recognize that Jesus is *not* telling us to disregard objective right and wrong. Otherwise, He would not have earlier confirmed the Sixth and Seventh commandments (Exodus 20:13-14), "You shall not commit murder" (Matthew 5:21) and "You shall not commit adultery" (Matthew 5:27). In both commandments, God tells us what we must not do and implies that we can tell the difference between good and evil acts. Thus, we must conclude that Jesus wants us to uphold absolute standards of right and wrong AND that *we* can judge *words and acts* that God says constitute moral and legal right and wrong. In verse two of Matthew 7:1-6 ("For in the way you judge ..."), Jesus contrasts our own dishonest standards for others by setting *objective* standards, which means the rules are the same for everyone. Whose rules? God's rules. They are true. They are universal and everlasting (true in every society in every age). They are more real than this book in your hand. "Heaven and earth will pass away, but My words shall not pass away" (Matthew 24:35). They are published in the Bible, so they are available to everyone. Jesus said His teaching was not His own, rather He conveyed it straight from His Father (John 7:16). His word is a plumb line, given to us so we need not guess at, argue about, or stumble around searching for standards of right and wrong.

Instead, Jesus is telling us not to judge others' thoughts, intentions, and motives by our own subjective standards. If we do, our own standards will be applied against us on Judgment Day, so we had better use the most merciful and just standard available: God's. He tells us in Matthew 7: verses 3-5 that we must *first* make sure that we are not doing the same thing (especially to a much worse degree) as the person we are criticizing. Even if our own life is clear of their kind of sin, we cannot criticize their motives, intent, or thoughts – only their actions. Verse 5(c) says that once we have made sure we do not have the same kind of sin, we can lovingly correct their actions. If we share the same sin, we should suggest we both work on it together, as followers of Christ, instead of condemning them.

However, we must *never* say, "I know what she really meant by that," or "I bet he did that because …." We are *not* God! We *cannot* get inside the heads of others and make conclusions as to their inmost thoughts. If we do so, Jesus promises to judge us by the same selfish, unfair, rigid, unmerciful standards we have dealt to others in life. Jesus forbids us to judge thoughts, intentions, and motives of others because we do not know the whole story behind the way they think. Neither do we judge impartially, because we are neither all-knowing, all-wise, nor omnipresent for every event in everyone's lives. God, however, is all these things, and we lack those very attributes that allow Him to judge people's hearts. We are only to judge what is apparent: words and actions.

But how do we know Jesus is referring to judging behavior and not thoughts? We know because of what He says next in verse six. He states that some people are untrustworthy dogs and vicious swine. Jesus simply says some people are not worth our time and effort. How would we know that? He is telling us that we can judge them as such by their *words* and *actions*. If Jesus never meant for us to have an opinion, He would not have added this verse (calling people "dogs" and "swine") into the conversation. By doing so, He clarifies and delineates what is permissible (actions and words) and impermissible (motives, intentions and thoughts) by which to judge in a godly manner.

Jesus is also talking here about judging things that are merely matters of personal opinion. Just because I disagree with it or have a strong contrary opinion does not mean that those with whom I disagree are sinning. Where God has not spoken about a subject, I need to be quiet. It is none of my business. "For through the grace given to me I say to every man among you not to think more highly of himself than he ought to think, but think so as to have sound judgment, as God has allotted to each a measure of faith" (Romans 12:3). The Bible often reminds us not to think we are always right or that our opinions should apply to others.

"For you were called to freedom, brethren, only do not turn your freedom into an opportunity for the flesh [thinking I'm better or smarter than others], but through love, serve one another" (Galatians 5:13).[4] When I give my opinion on Scripture, I always try to make sure everyone understands that it is just my opinion. They can take it or leave it. I warn them by saying, "This is just my humble opinion, which is rarely humble and always opinionated!" Whatever Jesus or His Word says on a given subject, however, is what is important.

Jesus requires everyone to make a decision about who He is and to respond to His claims.

> Everyone therefore who shall confess Me before men, I will confess him before My Father who is in heaven. But whoever shall deny Me before men, I will also deny him before My Father who is heaven. Do not think that I came to bring peace on the earth. I did not come to bring peace, but a sword. For I came to set a man against his father and a daughter against her mother, and a daughter-in-law against her mother-in-law; and a man's enemies will be the members of his own household. And he who loves father or mother more than Me is not worthy of Me; and he who loves son or daughter more than Me is not worthy of Me. He who has found his life shall lose it, and he who has lost his life for My sake shall find it (Matt.10: 32-39).

Jesus sets the standard here. If we do not love Him more than anyone or anything else in the world, then our lives will never be in balance in this world or the next. He forces us to judge between life in Him and living under this world's standards, and He warns us that even our close relatives could become hostile. When Jesus talks about believing in Him, He doesn't mean a mere mental assent, such as: "I believe it will rain today." Instead, He means a belief that is life-changing; a belief that causes us to change the way we think, speak, and act; a belief that places Him and His Word as the standard for all our attitudes and actions; and a belief that may cause some to hate us, and some to love us. In any event, we must speak the truth in love (Ephesians 4:14-16; 25-32), and let others make their own decisions.

Therefore, based on the objective standards of the Bible, we are commanded to analyze both our own behavior and that of others and to act on what is right and wrong in life. God wants us to decide between right and wrong. Remember Deuteronomy 30:15, where God said He shows us the difference between good and evil, life and death? God would not order us to make such choices if He hadn't given us the mental and moral ability and objective standards by which to choose. This means that we can, and should, decide whether to stop criminal attack. In so doing, we choose life for ourselves and our descendants. It is the criminal who chooses the curse of sin. His acts of assault, burglary, rape, kidnapping, robbery, and murder *force* us to reply with the threat of deadly force. He brought on the confrontation. He chose sin. He chose to commit crimes so dangerous that the law allows his potential victim to kill him. Thereby, he has also chosen death. When we stop him with force (including deadly force), we have judged his sinful actions, and we obey God's command in Psalm 82:4, "Rescue the weak and the needy, deliver them out of the hand of the wicked."

Moses and the Law of Self-Defense

The following story from Exodus 2 is a fictional account of Moses explaining to his son Gershom the events that brought him to Midian. During the interview, Moses describes his deadly encounter with the Egyptian taskmaster. The story is followed by a brief legal analysis of the killing with regard to self defense.

Days passed slowly in Midian. To pass the time among their peaceful flocks, shepherds taught their children the history of their people and their own life stories. Moses had many tales from his own illustrious life in Egypt, but he preferred to tell the histories of his forefathers: Abraham, Isaac, Jacob and his sons, and of their nameless God who made man and the universe. He had often prayed for God to show him and help him understand his place in the story and for justification of his faith. As of yet, no clarity had come.

"What would you like to hear, Gershom?"

The boy hesitated, then looked up imploringly and said, "Could you please tell me how you came to Midian?"

"Perhaps another time, son, it's a hard tale to tell."

"Please father? I'm a man now. Twelve!" His pleading eyes and hopeful looks persuaded Moses.

"I suppose it *is* time," he thought. "All right son," he sighed. Then he gazed a moment at his flocks grazing at the foot of God's mountain. The boy smiled, waiting eagerly for his father to begin.

"You know, son, about the story of my birth and how in the fullness of God's time I learned I was a Hebrew. As you know, in Egypt the word *Egyptian* means *human being*. However, we Egyptians referred to Hebrews as the Hapiru dogs. I did too until I gained new perspective."

"What's that?" asked Gershom.

"A different way of seeing people and things," replied Moses. "As I secretly learned about my heritage, I realized that Father Abraham taught us to love God first and to love our neighbor as we would ourselves."

"Mother and you have shown me that since I can remember. Doesn't everyone realize that?"

"Sadly no, son. They don't. It means we can't stand by and let evil happen."

"But father, I've heard some of our Midianite relatives say that as long as you don't cause any bad to happen to others, then you're righteous. They say: 'Don't do to others what you wouldn't want done to you, and God is pleased.'"

"What do you think of that idea, son?"

Gershom pursed his lips and knit his brows for a minute, then slowly replied. "I think … that … it's kind of backwards, father."

"How so?" grinned Moses, guessing the track the boy was on, and proud of the youngster's reasoning.

"Well, doesn't it give the impression that … as long as I don't cause any harm to others, then I'm holy – even if I never do anything to make it better? Like when cousin Makor's prize ram fell between the rocks in the ravine last week, and he couldn't get it out by himself. If we hadn't helped him, he'd have lost his best breeder, and his flocks would've been much the poorer because of it."

"So?"

"Sooooo," drawled Gershom, thinking hard, "if we'd followed the 'do *not* do' idea, Makor would have lost money on his flocks, and his family would have had a harder life and had to beg help from everyone else, and …"

"And what?"

"And I wouldn't have this great feeling I have for helping him!" beamed the boy.

"Right!" affirmed Moses. "You're reasoning is sound. You really *are* becoming a man."

Gershom's face shone.

"Yes, my son, any faith based on merely *not* being responsible for someone else's misfortune is selfish and ultimately detrimental to a good society. Our motto must be 'Do to others, as you would have them do to you'; then loving families and healthy communities are formed and sustained. You see, there's a very practical side to loving your neighbor as yourself."

"But dad, that seems so clear when you think about it. Why doesn't everyone see it that way?"

"Remember Father Abraham was taught by God Himself. It took him awhile, I'm sure, to realize this – a long time working out God's wisdom in his own life until it made sense, I guess. Many think it's a lot easier to pass by our neighbor in need and blame him for his own problems. And truly, life can get complicated when you step in to help others."

"How dad?" coaxed Gershom, sensing that Moses was coming to the story he'd asked for.

Moses raised his eyes to God's mountain and once more prayed silently. "Our help is from you, Lord, but when will your promises be fulfilled? What is *my* place in them?"

Returning his attention to Gershom, he began. "When I discovered my true identity, I was beset by a hunger to learn of my people and the God they worshipped. As a prince of Egypt and a commander of her armies, it was easy to find official excuses to go to Goshen. There, at the most eastern part of the Nile delta, our people built the great treasure cities, Per-Atum and Avaris, under the lash of their taskmasters.[1] In Goshen I found my brother Aaron and my sister Miriam. It was from them and the tribal elders that I learned the history of our people and our God."

"From Noah, I learned that the Creator loves mankind, but His justice will not tolerate sin. From Abraham, I learned that God wants a personal relationship with each of us. Abraham also taught me that since God's ways and purpose are immeasurably superior to ours, we must patiently trust that He will bring His words to pass in His own ways and times. From Joseph, I learned that even when all seems lost – family, justice, gratitude, and future – God is actually near to us and working all the while for those who love Him. I hoped that God had placed me in my station at just this time for His own purpose."

"Gradually, the trappings of my rank had become a burden. The religion of Egypt seemed childish and hollow. Wealth, power, fame, and privilege, I realized, were brief and had no significance once the mummification process began." Moses' eyes suddenly sparkled and he grinned. "After all, how dignified *are* you when they're pulling bits of your brain out through your nose?" Gershom chuckled at the irony.

"God's people made me realize that the quest to know our God and to live in His will counted for more than all the kingdoms of the earth could give. According to the elders, their captivity should end in a few years. They dreamed of their day of deliverance when they would bear Joseph's bones and all their people back to Canaan, the land promised by God to Abraham and his descendants."

"Did they know how it would happen, father?"

"No. God hadn't said *how*, only that He *would*. He said after 400 years, after the sins of Canaanites were complete. Some urged revolt. After all, the Egyptians were killing us slowly by work, drowning our sons, and by despair. But many of them thought it was not God's will to free us by any mortal means, but rather by His own mighty arm; a demonstration that would tell the world His power, glory, and love for us."

"Is that what you thought, father?"

"I wasn't sure *what* to think. Revolt against Egypt's professional armies would be disastrous. I've told you how chariot archers can herd infantry and slaughter them like sheep. Yet it was hard to understand that if God *really* loved us, why would He leave His people so long in misery. Nights I tossed, worn out with prayer and wondering. I was sure I had some part to play, but I couldn't see what it was. Though I had studied in the universities of Egypt, no plan came to me – except a small, still voice inside that said, 'Wait.' So I studied and searched the tales of God and our ancestors from Adam forward. As I did, my faith grew that God was true. With that faith, calm came. Though the long evil was real, I knew somehow God was working to make His promises come true. I began to pray that He would use me to accomplish this. I did know one thing. I was sick of who I was, so I asked God to make me His man, no matter what else.

Then one evening at the worksite in Avaris, after most of the workers had left, I heard shouting on the other side of a large stone lion, one of a line of seven in front of the Temple of Thoth. As I rounded the corner, I saw one of the Egyptian foremen beating a Hebrew. He raged, cursing and striking with a short shovel. The Hebrew's face, forearms, and shoulders were badly cut. As I ran up, the foreman's long sweeping, two-handed blow split the Hebrew's ear. He was killing a man of my people! I had to act! A quick look over the worksite assured me there were no Egyptians around to see or interfere. I ordered him to stop. He never even looked up, so intent was he on hurting that man. The Hebrew fell against the stone lion's base. Too close to swing now, the foreman began kicking his torso. Against the stone, the man's unconscious body couldn't recoil from the blows and took the full force. I heard ribs crack as I lunged. When I pushed the foreman away, he backed just a step. He didn't recognize me or my rank, and he cursed me for interfering even as he swung the shovel one-handed at me. I was too quick, reflexively stepping inside his swing. My punch landed with all my weight on his throat. His eyes bulged as he dropped the shovel, his tongue out, his hands clawing for his neck as he dropped to his knees; his face purpling as he struggled for air. I'll never forget it. I had killed in battle many times before this, but it was always impersonal and the immediate need to engage the next foe left no time to watch the former foe die. His pleading, wide eyes begged for help, but there was none to give. His voice box had caved in on his air pipe forever.

I pulled my gaze away from his gurgling form to check the Hebrew, who was still unconscious. I carried him to the worker's huts across the sand dune and left him with them. Eyebrows were raised, but none dared to question why a Prince should care about one of them enough to bring him to aid. I simply told them the man was injured when he stayed late at work, then left quickly. I ran back to the dead Egyptian. Taking his shovel, I buried him at the rear of the lion. It was fully dark when I finished, so I slipped back to my house, thinking no one was the wiser.

I couldn't sleep. I was too nervous. Even the labor of burying the man failed to calm me down. I knew I had done right in saving a helpless man from brutal, certain death, yet Pharaoh's court would never see it that way. 'What, in the grand scheme of things, is the life of one Hapiru slave?' they'd say. 'Certainly it was not worth the life of one human being.' Other thoughts disturbed and excited me. 'Was this the opening act of God's deliverance of Israel? Was I the Deliverer?' My mind raced all night.

Yet I could be sure of one thing: no one knew. If anyone at court ever found
out, my life would be worthless. Like any royal court, there were factions, and
the one against me was strong. I had risen too far too fast for there not to be many
jealous eyes cast my way. While the merit of my deeds kept Pharaoh thinking I
was useful, I was not secure. Politics saw to that. If I was ever found out, I would
be lucky to receive only banishment. My foes would want a sure, permanent
solution; while friends (looking to their own interests and families) would shy
away from me. But those worries were mere phantoms. No one had seen
anything. The victim never saw me. His fellow workers only knew I brought him
for treatment. Finally, the foreman was well hidden.

After a sleepless night, I returned to the city building site. After forty years of
work, the treasure city was nearly half complete. Most of the temples and houses
were done, but public buildings, the large treasure houses, and the great circuit of
the wall was yet to be built. The city wall was necessary since Avaris was directly
in the path of any invading eastern army that managed to breach Egypt's first line
of defense. That first wall is miles to the east, blocking the habitable strip between
the sea and the Sinai desert. Do you recall its name, Gershom?"

Standing with a wide grin, Gershom threw out his chest and with his deepest
dramatic 12 year old voice, declared: "The-Wall-of-the-Keeping-Out-of-the-
Miserable-Asiatics!"

After sharing a chuckle, Gershom sat and Moses resumed. "Pharaoh's mansion
and grounds were to be located outside the city walls. He could relax there
anytime he visited. It would be at least another 50 years work. I resolved to forget
the trauma of yesterday and lose myself in the work. It was just after the mid-day
meal that I strolled over to the Temple of Thoth to check the finishing touches
there. Part of my purpose was to check the scene where I had saved the Hebrew
the day before to make sure I'd not left any evidence. Turning into the lane at the
rear of the statue, I saw only a slave on a scaffold about six feet high, painting
hieroglyphs on the upper left foreleg of the stone beast. Suddenly, another slave
rounded the corner carrying a hod of bricks. Since he was walking right next to
the statue when he turned the corner, he couldn't see the scaffold until it was too
late. He collided with it, falling backward with the hod, which had dropped some
bricks on the painter's feet, causing him to fall to the sand. Neither was seriously

hurt, but the painter, upon checking his scratches, jumped up and went for the hod man. Both began trading furious blows.

I ran up and shoved them apart ordering them in my command voice to stop. They did, looking at me and my half-heartedly brandished taskmaster's whip with fire in their eyes. No one spoke. I thought to give them a moment to calm down before ordering them back to work. So I asked, 'Why such anger and blows over an accident? Do you two have a history?'

With fire in his eyes, the painter shoved me, spitting out 'Who made you a prince and judge over us? Are you going to kill me, like you did the foreman yesterday?'

I was horrified! Someone had seen! 'Yes Master,' he mocked. 'I was high up on one of Thoth's columns, painting in the last rays of Ra, and saw your deed. I've been wondering if it would be worth my freedom to tell the authorities.'

Now the hod man's eyes grew wide as he put two and two together. The foreman's absence had been noticed. The victim, who could not yet speak, was hurt near sunset. I could see he knew it was I who'd brought him to the other Hebrews for help. Word of my deed would spread fast. I tried to keep my composure and ordered them back to work. They complied, but I saw the smirk on the painter's face as he remounted his scaffold. As I walked away, I realized that other things besides building and painting take place on scaffolds.

My blood ran cold in the afternoon sun. When I reached the master builder's command tent, he remarked that I looked pale and inquired after my health. I agreed I wasn't feeling well, and excused myself for the day. At my house, I called for my chariot while I gathered food, water, and other necessities for a trip into the desert. My only chance was to hide among the 'barbarian' tribes of Sinai. Telling my servants that I had urgent orders from Pharaoh to return to On immediately, I left that evening.[2] For an hour, I headed south on the road to On, then cut back northeast across the desert for Sinai. I would miss my friends and my adopted mother. My enemies at court would fan Pharaoh's wrath. My flight would assure judgment of guilt upon me. My life in Egypt was now forever in my past. 'But what of my people?' I thought. Obviously, I was not the one that God would designate to help them. I had lost my wealth, rank, fame – all the power by which I might have helped the Hebrews. They must stay in captivity. That fact alone filled me with greater sorrow than any other," sighed Moses.

Gershom looked at his father, thinking, not speaking.

Moses resumed, "It took a month or so before I could sleep well again. Although I'm convinced that there was no other way and I did the right thing – still, it is a heavy thing to have to kill a man. Besides, there has always been the knowledge that I can't ever help my people, the Israelites. The rest you know, my son: how I arrived here in Midian, rescued your mother and aunts, married your mother, and was taken in as a son by your grandfather Jethro, the priest of God here. I found healing and a new life. And now, it's been 40 years since all this happened."

By then the western sun had begun to cast long shadows in the narrow defiles and valleys of Midian. They sat quietly for a while, listening to the soft bleating of the grazing sheep. Finally, Gershom spoke. "I suppose in Egypt they'd call you a murderer. That's not true though."

"Why son?"

"Because you didn't kill that man because you hated him or wanted to take something of his. You were just trying to keep him from killing someone else. And when you did try to stop him, he tried to kill you, too. You were just defending the other man and yourself. What could be wrong about that? I'm sad though."

"Why?" questioned Moses.

"Well, who will God use to save our people? When will He end their bondage?"

"Gershom, I'm proud of you. You really are becoming a man."

"I'm proud of you too, dad" said the boy, beaming again. They hugged.

As they embraced, he looked over Gershom's head up the side of the mountain of God. Then he did a double take, focusing. In one of the now dark crevices near the top of Sinai was a bright light. A bush was burning.

"Odd," he thought, "no one lives up there. There's no grass for herds. Why would someone …" then he paused and stared hard. "The bush!" he thought. "It was on fire, *but it wasn't being burned up!*"

"Gershom! Do you see?" he pointed.

"Yes! Father, why doesn't it burn up?"

"I don't know, son. Take the flock back to our tents. I must go and see this marvelous sight for myself."

The boy gazed a moment at the bush, then obeyed. Moses began trudging up Sinai toward his destiny.

———

Moses' killing of the Egyptian has been written about many times. I have read several Christian authors who refer to it as murder. Some are great Bible teachers, men whose writings have inspired, uplifted, and instructed me in my walk with Jesus for many years. But on this point, I must disagree with them. (After all, they are theologians, I am a lawyer; so in this instance, I am right.) What Moses did was definitely *not* murder. Remember, murder is the intentional, unlawful killing of a human being. If Moses had committed murder, he would have fallen under the sentence of Genesis 9:6 for murderers. Yet, nowhere in the Bible is Moses ever condemned for this act! When David murdered Uriah after his adultery with Bathsheba, God confronted him through Nathan the prophet.

In contrast to David, there is not one word of condemnation for Moses' act of killing the taskmaster. Rather, the Lord spoke to him "face to face, as a man speaks to his friend" (Exodus 33:11).[3] Had Moses been guilty of murder before God, would not God have mentioned it? Would not God have explicitly forgiven him somehow *before* designating him as the Deliverer of his people? Surely He would have, if there had been anything to forgive. Those who call Moses a murderer might be fine theologians, but they are not lawyers. I am, and I tell you Moses did not commit murder.

What Moses did would not be called murder in modern times, either. The Greeks, Romans, and all cultures in history up through the Anglo-American justice systems have recognized the right of self-defense and the defense of third parties. For example, Section 13A-3-23 of the Alabama Code is the self-defense statute cited in other chapters. Subsection (a) says:

> A person is justified in using physical force upon another person in order to defend himself *or a third person* from what he reasonably believes to be the use or imminent use of *unlawful physical force* by that other person, and he may use a degree of force which he reasonably believes to be necessary for the purpose. A person may use *deadly physical force* if the actor reasonably believes that such other person is: (1) using or about to use deadly physical

force; or (3) committing or about to commit ... assault in the first or second degree ... (emphasis mine).

Section 13A-6-20 defines Assault 1st Degree as a person who:

1. With intent to cause serious physical injury ('which creates a substantial risk of death, or causes serious or protracted disfigurement, protracted impairment of health, or protracted loss or impairment of the function of any bodily organ' (13A-1-2(14)) *by means of a deadly weapon or dangerous instrument;* or

2. With intent to disfigure another person seriously and permanently, or to destroy, amputate or disable permanently a member or organ of his body, he causes such an injury to any person; or

3. Under circumstances manifesting extreme indifference to the value of human life, he recklessly engages in conduct which creates a grave risk of death to another person, and thereby causes serious physical injury to any person. (emphasis mine)

Section 13A-6-21, 2nd Degree Assault is similar. Of course, my story with the Egyptian imagines an Assault 1st subsection (1) scenario, but it could have been a subsection (2) or (3) situation. The point is that the Egyptian was clearly doing something that unjustifiably would have resulted in the death or permanent maiming injury of the Hebrew had not Moses stepped in. Whatever the Egyptian *was* doing, we can be sure that Moses' act of killing him to stop the carnage he was wreaking on an innocent person was justified by the laws of God and Man, then and now. Arizona, Colorado, and Idaho also allow use of deadly force for felony assault.[4]

Notice again, that just as God finalized His blessing and covenant with Abraham after his justifiable homicides, He did the same with Moses, although this time with a 40-year gap. Clearly, when loving one's neighbor as oneself results in the justifiable killing of criminals, it does not disqualify a person from a dynamic, useful, and personal relationship with God.

However, doing the right thing can sometimes get us into a great deal of trouble. Though Moses righteously intervened, his actions caused a great deal of trouble, including his 40-year exile to Midian. To make sure any defensive action we might take will be legal, we must get competent legal advice and defensive training. Even if we do everything right in a self-defense situation, our lives can quickly go from short-term scary to a long-term nightmare. That is why the first book I recommend is Massad Ayoob's *In the Gravest Extreme* for those who are interested in self-defense. Our goal must be legal and physical competence. Otherwise, our good intentions can put us on a path that leads to lawsuits and possible jail time.

Jesus, Self-Defense,
and Pacifism

The Pacifist Christian

My working definition of a pacifist Christian is a person who believes that Jesus was a pacifist, that defensive use of force is not allowed by Jesus or the Bible, and that the advocacy of pacifism in Christian circles is biblically based. I also assume that the vast majority of pacifist Christians honestly believe that pacifism is the best solution to handle conflict. Always remember, though, simply believing that an idea is true does not make it so.

Having seen that legal remedies are applicable to criminals in the Scriptures, we know Christians can certainly defend themselves and others with appropriate force. Paul says, "If possible, *as far as it depends on you*, be at peace with all men" (Romans 12:18, emphasis mine). We should always be ready with alternatives to using any force, but failing that, we should be ready with non-lethal force, if possible. However, if I am in a fast food establishment and some maniac strides in, heavily armed and shooting, then peace no longer depends on me. He has made it impossible for me to be at peace with him. German theologian and member of the underground resistance in WWII, Dietrich Bonhoeffer asserted that Christians must speak for those who cannot speak for themselves: "Open your mouth for the dumb, for the rights of the unfortunate. Open your mouth, and judge righteously and defend the rights of the afflicted and needy."[1] My presence in that restaurant means I can "speak" for the helpless, saying "Stop!" to the criminal in the only effective way he would understand.

A pacifist Christian can choose to die there and go to heaven (rather than shoot the attacker) while praying that the criminal might someday find salvation. The pacifist Christian who shrugs and says, "Well, if it's my time to go ..." totally misses the fact that his attitude is tantamount to committing suicide. (Note that the Bible does not say suicide is an unforgivable sin. If you are in Christ, that one isolated act of rebellion would condemn you no more than if you told a lie and then died of a heart attack before you could repent.) Like a suicide, he refuses to consider what plans "for good and not evil" (Jeremiah 29:11) and "the more abundant life" (John 10:10) God has in store for him. Furthermore, to take that attitude with the lives of others is at best, arrogance: "I'm going to die and go to heaven; everyone else can take their chances." At worst, it is clear disobedience to Leviticus 19:16, Psalms 82:4, Proverbs 3:27-28 and Proverbs 24:11-12, which teach us to save those in deadly peril. His alternative ignores the high probability that everyone in that restaurant is not a Christian. Do you grasp the irony of a pacifist Christian who, on the one hand, would agree that he is under a duty to win the world for Jesus under the Great Commission (Matthew 28:18-20) but who becomes passive when it comes to saving lives instead of souls? Suddenly, without consulting Jesus, he has declared that the job Jesus gave him is over. If the criminal has his way, many people will meet their Creator without their Savior. In effect, the pacifist Christian is saying, "Oh well, it's their time to go. Mine too. Nothing I can do." Not true! You can at least stick around to aid the wounded and comfort the dying! There is no love or virtue in the pacifist Christian's embrace of death; instead, the attitude is lazy, selfish, and a dereliction of duty owed to Jesus!

As for me, I am going to obey God and "Respect what is right in the sight of all men" (Romans 12:17b) and refuse to succumb to the criminal's evil. God is not willing that "any should perish, but for all to come to repentance" (2 Peter 3:9b). If God wants people to have a chance to come to Him in faith, and if my handgun can give them an opportunity to do so, then I am doing God's will. The criminal made both his choice and mine. I can no longer be peaceful under Romans 12:18; Hebrews 12:14-15. He is forcing me to choose either his survival and possible salvation or the survival and eventual salvation of his intended victims. Forced to that choice, the biblical, moral, and humane decision is to shoot him to save innocent lives. "A worthless person, a wicked man ... his calamity will come suddenly. Instantly he will be broken, and there will be no healing" (Proverbs 6:12a and 15). The only way I can live in peace with him is by doing all in my power to make him "peaceful" as quickly as I can.

When criminals put others in immediate danger, it is our duty to bring them under control. Since we are not God, we cannot miraculously blind them and speak to their innermost spirit, as Jesus did to Saul on the Damascus road. Instead, we must use the means at our command to stop them. Remember, God Himself gives us the technology to make weapons to stop the ungodly (Isaiah 54:16; Hosea 7:15). The good news is that most criminal activity can be met with non-lethal responses, such as pepper spray.

However, the attacker has to be convinced that you will actually use the gun if he does not immediately stop or leave. If he is not convinced, beware! Seasoned criminals can sense fear and indecision. If you do not convey your earnestness, they will disarm you and kill you (and maybe any other possible witnesses on the scene). For example, I know of an 80-year-old woman who bought a 20 gauge pump shot gun in response to a rash of burglaries in her neighborhood. But she refused to buy shells for it. "Oh, I'll just scare them real good," she assured the clerk. A week later, two crooks broke in. When they realized her weapon was not loaded, they beat her to death with her shotgun. The moral of the story: guns are great intimidators, *but only if* you can convince a criminal that you will use it if he does not stop instantly. Otherwise, buy a rabbit's foot, not a gun. Guns are tools for defense, not movie props or good luck charms.

As I have stated before, when violence occurs, you will have two to five seconds to recognize it and react. Long before that emergency, you must decide whether and when you will use opposing force. You must also be convinced and certain of the moral and legal parameters under which you can act. Paul agrees by saying we should not be wishy-washy when making a decision:

Do you think I talk out of both sides of my mouth – a glib *yes* one moment, a glib *no* the next? Well, you're wrong. I try to be as true to my word as God is to his. Our word to you wasn't a careless yes canceled by an indifferent no. How could it be? When Silas and Timothy and I proclaimed the Son of God among you, did you pick up on any yes-and-no, on-again, off-again waffling? (2 Corinthians 1:17-19, *The Message*, emphasis mine).

Moreover, Paul says, "Therefore take up the full armor of God that you may be able to resist in the evil day, and having done everything to stand firm. Stand firm (Ephesians 6:13-14a).

This book is intended to guide you into a moral commitment, but it is only the start of your necessary preparation. Do not consider using defensive force unless, by study and prayer, you first reach a rock-solid conviction that self-defense is legal, ethical, moral, and approved by God. Then learn the self-defense laws of

your state to the level that you know the legal maximum force-level for felonies
and misdemeanors or personal versus property crimes. Next, equip yourself and
train, so if a mugger confronts you, he will see your gun's muzzle and the calm
determination in your eyes. Suddenly he is forced to contemplate his future on
earth and in eternity. He must ask himself that popular movie question, "Do I feel
lucky?" and he will likely back down. But first you must believe that what you
are doing is right. That starts with having convictions, not suppositions. As Jesus
said, "Make no oath at all... but let your statement be yes, yes or no, no, anything
beyond these is toward evil" (Matthew 6:34a and 37; James 5:12). Be convinced
that self-defense is holy, and then act accordingly.

Slaughtered Like Sheep?

Does Paul advocate pacifism anywhere in the New Testament? Some may think
that Romans 8 supports pacifism in verses 35-37, which goes like this:

> Who shall separate us from the love of Christ? Shall tribulation, or distress, or
> persecution, or famine, or nakedness, or peril, or sword? Just as it is written,
> 'For Thy sake we are being put to death all day long; we were considered as
> sheep to be slaughtered.' But in these things we overwhelmingly conquer
> through Him who loved us.

If read out of context, this passage could give the casual reader the impression that
martyrdom is to be a normal part of the Christian life. Especially since the passage
seems to say we conquer by doing so. "Conquer how?" you might ask. The pacifist
Christian's answer would be, "We have faith that God will use our martyrdom to
witness to Jesus' love, and our non-violence will somehow increase His kingdom."

My response is this: "If God has such a plan, where is it located in Scripture?" I
have presented the Bible's many commands and examples that teach us to defend
ourselves and others, and that armed citizens are part of God's plan to control
crime. Where are the similar verses that command and provide a rationale for the
practice of martyrdom? There aren't any.

So what do these verses from Romans 8 mean in context? Romans 8 is one
of the most triumphant and uplifting chapters in the Bible. We are promised
that God will eventually work out all the events of history and our lives for our
ultimate good and for His ultimate triumph. This chapter does not say everything

that happens to us is good, but that God will weave even tragedies and disasters into history so that they are part of His final victory.

In this victorious assurance ("if God is for us, who can be against us?"), verses 35-37 appear only after assuring us that no matter how Satan tempts and accuses us of sin, Jesus intercedes for us continually before God, obtaining forgiveness and victory to God's glory. "The sheep to slaughter" passage is quoted from Psalms 44:22, which is also ultimately a message of hope. In verse 22, the psalmist writes, "But for Thy sake we are killed all day long" because they would not conform to and assimilate with false gods and foreign culture. Consequently, the Israelites are "considered as sheep to be slaughtered." They are in danger of being exterminated at any time, but not actually being killed at that time. After asking why God has forsaken Israel, the psalmist ends with the hopeful plea: "Rise up, be our help, and redeem us for the sake of Thy loving kindness" (verses 24-26).

Likewise in Romans 8:35-37, we are "considered as sheep to be slaughtered" not by Jesus but by our enemy, Satan, and his earthly representatives, such as criminals. By quoting Psalms 44:22, Paul is echoing the psalmist's optimism that even though our enemies are numerous and powerful, God is greater and will get us through. How do we know that? By referring to the thesis of this part of the chapter, "If God is for us, who can [possibly, ultimately] stand [or prevail] against us?" (Romans 8:31b).

When we know all that the Bible says about self-defense, it is silly to assume that Romans 8:36 orders us to seek out martyrdom and allow, consent to, and endorse the murder of innocents instead of doing our best to prevent such things. Neither here nor anywhere else in the Bible are we encouraged to seek martyrdom. In all of the persecutions that Paul experienced, he did not stick around to be killed. He went on to the next town to preach. He submitted to being taken to Rome to spread the Gospel to Nero's court, not with the purpose of being martyred. The fact that he and Peter were martyred in Rome was just coincident with Nero's tantrums, Rome's fire, and Nero's need to find a scapegoat (Christians) for the fire. Romans 8:36 is not a proof text for pacifism. Instead, it is part of a glorious assurance that we can face life, death, and the hereafter with complete confidence in God's love.

The last three verses of Chapter 8 illustrate that the threat of death under any circumstances should hold no fear for the Christian:

But in all these things we overwhelmingly conquer through Him who loved us. For I am convinced that neither death, nor life, nor angels, nor principalities, nor things present, nor things to come, nor powers, nor height, nor depth, nor any other created thing, shall be able to separate us from the love of God, which is in Christ Jesus our Lord (Romans 8:37-39).

Like good soldiers in all ages, armed citizens and cops must deal with the fear of death. With Jesus' promise of eternal life and reward (John 14:1-4) and the surety of resurrection (1 Corinthians 15:42-58), Christians have no need to fear death. Only when fear of death or injury is no longer a major concern can we do our best to defend ourselves and others. Then we are free to respond legally to a felon's threat.

The Duty to Act

Now we return to our scene in the restaurant and the criminal attack. Is there a New Testament verse that clarifies a Christian's duty in this situation? Yes. Romans 15:1-3 says this:

Now we who are strong ought to bear the weaknesses of those without strength and not just please ourselves. Each of us is to please his neighbor for his good, to his edification [growth, building up]. For even Christ did not please Himself, but it is written, 'The reproaches of those who reproached you fell on me.'

Consider this: if I am armed that day and you are not, which one of us is able to "bear the weaknesses" of others (the victims), and who is the person "pleasing himself" by his helplessness? On my first shot, the criminal will turn his sole attention on me. The innocents can now escape.

The Message was written with the intent that the verses should have the same impact on a person in 21st century as it did on the first century readers. Author of *The Message*, Eugene Peterson renders Romans 15:1-3 this way:

Those of us who are strong and able in the faith need to step in and lend a hand to those who falter, and not just do what is most convenient for us. Strength is for service, not status. Each one of us needs to look after the good of the people around us, asking ourselves, "How can I help?"

That's exactly what Jesus did. He didn't make it easy for Himself by avoiding people's troubles but waded right in and helped out. "I took on the troubles of the troubled" is the way Scripture puts it.[2]

The Bible tells us to study diligently to be approved by God in all our actions, accurately handling scripture when teaching it and living it in a practical manner (2 Timothy 2:15). My study of the Bible tells me that self-defense and defense of others is part of God's mission for me. Convinced of that, I do not have to be timid about legally using force. Assured by His Word and trained by legal knowledge and physical discipline, I stand ready to demonstrate God's love and mine for others in any situation. Whether the need is a comforting word or an accurate shot, I am ready. How about you? If you are a pacifist, have you actually researched and tested your philosophy of pacifism based on the Bible? Is your pacifism approved by God? "Beloved, believe not every spirit, but test the spirits to see whether they are from God; because many false prophets have gone out into the world" (1 John 4:1). Have you prayerfully considered your beliefs in light of the new information presented in this book?

Before we apply an idea or concept to our lives, we need to test it biblically. Pacifism and self-defense are such concepts. To adopt either idea without critical study is to presume we know the will of God.

> Also keep back Thy servant from presumptuous sins, let them not rule over me; then I shall be blameless, and I shall be acquitted of great transgression. Let the words of my mouth and the meditation of my heart be acceptable in Thy sight, O Lord, my rock and my Redeemer (Psalms 19:13-14).

When Peter saw Jesus walking on the water, he did not presume that he also had that same power. Instead, he asked Jesus' permission to walk on the water (Matthew 14:22-29). If you are a pacifist, you must ask yourself whether your ideology is an unscriptural presumption of God's will and whether because of this presumption, innocent people might needlessly die.

Men and women of God have a clear biblical duty to show their love for others by actual, physical aid whenever possible. Any philosophy that negates or limits this doctrine to passive measures when lives are in danger is wrong. "See to it that no one takes you captive through philosophy and empty deception, according to the tradition of men, according to the elementary principles of the world, rather than according to Christ (Colossians 2:8). In the following chapters about Jesus, I will show you that Jesus did not preach pacifism (just the kind of manmade idea Paul warned us about). It is an extra-biblical idea that did not appear until over a hundred years after Jesus' ascension.

I urge my pacifist readers to consider prayerfully the information presented here. Our purpose as Christians is to leave this world a spiritually and physically better place than we found it. "For we are His workmanship, created in Christ Jesus for good works, which God prepared beforehand, that we should walk in them" (Ephesians 2:10). Is saving innocent life good work only when you can do it passively? If so, where is that qualification in the Bible? Pacifism's refusal to render aid by force is the same kind of self-righteous, manmade ethic as the Pharisees used in trying to forbid Jesus from healing on the Sabbath. "So He asked them, 'Is it lawful on the Sabbath to do good or to do harm, to save life or to kill'? But they kept silent" (Mark 3:4). They could not answer because they knew their passivity was indefensible under Proverbs 3:27-28: "Do not withhold good from those to whom it is due, when it is in your power to do it, Do not say to your neighbor, 'Go, and come back, and tomorrow I will give it,' when you have it with you."

So if the criminal strides into that restaurant, and I have never considered or prepared for such a situation, or if I hold the philosophy that responding with force is wrong, then I believe Jesus would be as angry with me as He was with those Pharisees (Mark 3:5). He created me to do good works (Ephesians 2:10), and to save lives is a good work.

These are serious subjects to be handled with adult logic applied by scriptural reference. Life and death decisions should not be based on tradition, historical inertia, careless interpretation, biblical hearsay, or unwillingness to obey God when His will is clear.

As a result [of our maturity in Christ] we are no longer to be children, tossed here and there by waves, and carried about by every wind of doctrine, by the trickery of men, but speaking the truth in love, we are to grow up in all aspects to Him, who is the head, even Christ (Ephesians 4:14-15).

Does Jesus Support Self-Defense?

Before we consider whether Jesus took a stand on self-defense, we must first consider His mission. He described His purpose several times: "For even the Son of Man did not come to be served, but to serve, and to give His life as a ransom for many" (Mark 10:45) and "For the Son of Man has come to seek and save that which is lost" (Matthew 18:11). Jesus primarily came to show us who God really is. We are finite, God is infinite. By the definitions of these two words, we know that the finite cannot fully comprehend the infinite (at least not in this world).

Jesus was here for a specific, unique mission. As both God and man, He had abilities, knowledge, and powers that we do not. That is why "What would Jesus do?" is not applicable to self-defense or many other situations we might confront. For instance, if someone is drowning 100 yards from shore, what would Jesus do to save them? He would walk across the water, part the water, or maybe fly them out. We cannot do that. We have to rely on lifeguard training and select from the options of "reach, throw, row, or go." Jesus was divinely protected from assault or harm until He declared it was time for his martyrdom. We are not protected in that way. So we should not dismiss the necessity of self-defense for ourselves by glibly saying, "Jesus would not do that." Self-defense was not in His job description. When we find ourselves in situations that Jesus did not experience while on earth, we should ask, "What would Jesus have *us* do?" We can only do that by studying His Word.

Some information God has reserved for Himself, but what He has revealed through His word is a completely sufficient guide for a successful life. "The secret things belong to the Lord our God, but the things revealed belong to us and to our sons forever, that we may observe all the words of this law" (Deuteronomy 29:29). Jesus came to give us the opportunity to live the most successful life possible in this fallen world: "I came that you might have life, and might have it abundantly"

(John 10:10b). However, how can you have an abundant life, or any life, if Jesus forbids you to defend yourself?

Jesus did not condemn the use of defensive force under any and all circumstances. The Gospels do not portray Jesus as a pacifist. While many believe that Jesus lived and taught pacifism, this opinion does not have a scriptural basis. Pacifist misconceptions about Jesus and Christianity started in the second century A.D. after the apostles and other New Testament writers had died. Like many misapplications of Scripture, its origins lie in bad scholarship, personal agendas, politics, ignorance, and inertia.

Many misconceptions about Christian life and doctrines resulted when Christianity morphed from a personal relationship with a living, breathing Savior into a *religion*: a mode of relating to God, which is controlled by people. "Religious" people make up rules that others must follow, regardless of what God says. This is how the rule-makers acquire power. Judaism under the Pharisees had changed into a religion long before the time of Jesus. However, God always intended a personal relationship with each of us.

When we find ourselves in situations that Jesus did not experience while on earth, we should ask, "What would Jesus have us do?" We can only do that by studying His Word.

Jeremiah prophesied about the personal relationship with Jesus that would begin with the indwelling of the Holy Spirit.

> 'But this is the covenant which I will make with the house
> of Israel after those days,' declares the Lord, 'I will put my
> law within them, and on their heart I will write it, and I will
> be their God, and they shall be my people. And they shall
> not teach again, each man his neighbor and each man his
> brother, saying, "Know the Lord," for they shall all know
> Me, from the least of them to the greatest of them,' declares the Lord,
> 'for I will forgive their iniquity, and their sin I will remember no more'
> (Jeremiah 31:33-34).

Jeremiah was foretelling the indwelling of the Holy Spirit. Once we become Christians, Jesus Himself lives in us and teaches us through the Holy Spirit: "For all you who were baptized into Christ have clothed yourself with Christ" (Galatians 3:27). Jesus said in John 16:13-14, "But when He, the Spirit of truth comes, He will guide you into all truth; for He will not speak on His own initiative, but whatever He knows, He will speak and ... He shall glorify Me; for He shall take of Mine, and shall disclose it to you." Peter expressed it this way: "But you are a chosen race, a royal priesthood, a holy nation, a people for God's own possession, that you may proclaim the excellencies of Him who has called you out of darkness into His marvelous light" (1 Peter 2:9). Based on this verse, Martin Luther expressed it as "the priesthood of all believers" in describing the right of each person (within Scriptural limits) to conduct his own spiritual walk. Of course, there are those designated for church leadership: elders (also called bishops, overseers, presbyters, and pastors in various New Testament translations), deacons, preachers, and teachers. But all are to act within the confines of scriptural authority. James 1:27 gives the Biblical definition of true religion as a way of life (holiness and helping the needy) lived according to God.

The Roots of Christian Pacifism

Over time, though, as the historian Eusebius and the writings of second and third century "church fathers" reveal, certain extra-biblical ideas began to take root, including pacifism. In *Decline and Fall of the Roman Empire,* Edward Gibbon contends that pacifism was a direct cause of the Empire's fall. He states that so many men were drawn into "church work" that the Roman army could not raise enough recruits to defend its borders. By the fourth century, he says that many in the church accepted the view and preached that Jesus was a pacifist.[1] Whether this was to justify and secure their professional status in the Church without having to join the army he does not say. Gibbon mentions refusal to serve in the army based on pacifism as a characteristic of the "primitive" church, citing as authorities the "church fathers," Origin and Tertullian.[2] However, Origin did not write until the early third century and Tertullian until the middle/end of that century. Tertullian even suggests that Christians should desert the army.[3] These men are at least 130 years removed from the date of the last book of the New Testament, and are merely fallible commentators on the Word. Unlike the authors of the Bible, they were not divinely inspired. Origin and Tertullian are merely two of the various "fathers" who led multiple sects or held opinions that vary more or less from Scripture. Despite Gibbon's assertion that pacifism is an early doctrine, the earliest Christian/soldier/martyr that he (or anyone) can cite is the centurion Marcellus in 298 A.D.[4]

In *The Story of Civilization, Volume III: Caesar and Christ,* Will Durant disagrees that pacifism contributed to the fall of the Empire. Durant claims that Christianity grew because Rome was already in decline as to its morals, intellect, and values: "Rome was not destroyed by Christianity, any more than by barbarian invasion; it was simply an empty shell when Christianity rose to influence and invasion came." Christianity filled the moral vacuum in the lives of the citizens of Rome. Durant does appear, however, to agree with Gibbon on one point: that so many men had become exempt from military service by taking church positions that Constantine had to ban able-bodied men from joining the ministry.[5]

Obviously, there was no church doctrine of pacifism taught or observed throughout the church. Shortly thereafter (302 A.D.), the anti-Christian emperor Diocletian ordered the discharge of Christian soldiers who refused to sacrifice to Roman gods, but other than the instance of Marcellus, there is no record of a general refusal to fight among them.[6] The editors of *Roman Civilization, The Empire* comment that Marcellus' defection was merely an occasional occurrence among "numerous Christians in the Roman armies" rather than the rule.[7]

In *How Rome Fell,* Adrian Goldsworthy explains that even before the reign of the first Christian emperor "[t]here were Christians in many walks of life, including the army and imperial administration, and only occasionally did some of them find that their beliefs became incompatible with their official duties."[8] He further states that when Diocletian required sacrifices to his genius in 297, some Christians resigned their posts, while others refused outright and were executed, but there is no mention of resignations on pacifist grounds.[9] Thus, pacifism was not a rule of faith, but a matter of opinion by the late third century. I can find no historical evidence of it in the first 150 years after Christ. Pacifism was a later, extra-Biblical opinion.

When Constantine became emperor in 312 A.D., Christians fought in his army. As the proportion of Christians grew, they served in the ranks in increasing numbers until the end of the Roman Empire. In the conclusion of *How Rome Fell,* Goldsworthy, one of today's most respected classical scholars, does not even mention Christianity as a possible cause. In any event, after Constantine made

Christianity the official religion of the empire, there was no longer any serious controversy about Christians serving as soldiers.[10]

As the western church slowly became the Roman Catholic Church and moved into the Middle Ages, it never took a doctrinal stance on pacifism. Had the Roman Catholic Church endorsed pacifism, it would not have survived barbarian and later Muslim invasions. Though the church inherited some of the law-giving functions of the now defunct Western Roman Empire and took definite stands on many doctrines, it never developed a consistent policy toward war. In the Middle Ages, warfare became so prevalent that by the 1100's at least one third of days were saints' feast days in which "The Peace of God" was declared to keep Christians from slaughtering each other so often.[11] Yet the church still recognized the need for self-defense in a dangerous world. Knights were to spend the evening before their elevation in prayer at the church altar, dedicating themselves as God's defenders of justice and the weak.[12] Conversely, the church sponsored the naked aggression of the Crusades, not only against Muslims, but against Jews and heretic sects in Europe as well. Even churchmen often took up the sword. William the Conqueror's brother, Bishop Odo, wielded a mace at Hastings in 1066. There were the military orders of "warrior monks," the Knights Templar, and the Hospitallers of St. John. What about the wars of the Reformation, which had both religious and political causes? Christians slaughtered each other over both. The final bits of official schizophrenia were the "warrior pope" Julius II of the Renaissance and the inexcusable Inquisition.

Since their beginnings, the Quakers, Mennonites, and Amish have always held pacifism as doctrine. In the 20th century, pacifism gained ground with some mainline Christian denominations that even considered removing "warlike" songs (*Onward Christian Soldiers, The Battle Hymn of the Republic*) from their hymnals in the 1980s.[13]

Was Jesus a Pacifist?

Does the Bible tell us Jesus was a pacifist? I saw a bumper sticker once that stated so. When I read it, I thought, "The Temple moneychangers would be surprised to hear that!" Did Jesus preach pacifism? No, He did not. Pacifists unknowingly model themselves more on Ghandi and his mistaken perception of Jesus than on Jesus. Never forget, Gandhi would not have prevailed or survived had he dealt with Nazi Germany rather than democratic, Judeo-Christian Great Britain. The Nazi's would have dealt with Gandhi as they did with Bonheoffer and Niemuller, who were Christian ministers fighting against the Nazis. My dad always says, "Opinions are like belly buttons: everybody has one and knowing anything about the subject is not a prerequisite." For an opinion to be worth anything, it must be based on facts. "Jesus the pacifist" is not based on fact. So what is the deal with Jesus and pacifism?

Jesus Teaches Self-Defense

Jesus never directly addresses the subject of self-defense. Yet in various conversations, he expresses spiritual themes using analogies to self-defense. While straightening out the Pharisees about His healing a demon-possessed man who was blind and dumb, He makes this comparison to binding Satan: "Or how can anyone enter the strong man's house and carry off his property, unless he first binds the strong man? And then he will plunder his house" (Matthew 12:29).[14]

Jesus assumes several things in this homespun analogy. The homeowner is described as strong. This means that he has the health, vigor, and training with weapons and hand-to-hand combat (Luke 11:21-22) to defend his home, family, and property. From Exodus 22:2-3, Nehemiah, and other Old Testament references, we know that the Hebrews were allowed to defend their homes with deadly force. In Luke 11:21-22, Jesus follows this reasoning by describing the homeowner as fully armed, including defensive armor, and actively guarding his own house. This agrees with Paul's command to Timothy about a man having a duty to care for his family or he is worse than an unbeliever (1 Timothy 5:8). Furthermore, we know from the Sermon on the Mount that Jesus would often restate Mosaic law and place it on a higher plane, but when He found man-made traditions replacing God's word, He specifically refuted those ideas. It is interesting that Jesus never refutes any of the self-defense passages from the Old Testament. He never said, "You should help others *unless* it requires the use of force."

Second, according to Jesus' example, the strong man obviously has the will to resist and the conviction that he has the right before God and man to defend his own. Therefore, he has no moral qualm about doing so. By implication, Jesus has no moral qualm about home defense either. Finally, the burglar knows he must capture and tie up the homeowner or face resistance from him. This statement implies that if the burglar cannot figure out a way to bind the strong man, he will not attempt the burglary. Jesus' matter-of-fact use of this analogy means that both He and His audience logically accepted that self-defense was practical, proper, moral, and beneficial to society. Jesus treated home defense as good common sense (going back to Exodus 22:2-4).

Had Jesus meant to propose a doctrine of pacifism, He would never have used this analogy. He would have used home defense in a distinctly disapproving way to make that point or to simply declare it as sin. Jesus never turned down an opportunity to declare a moral standard if there was a point to be made. Here, though, He cites armed self-defense as a proper, moral, and logical act without qualification or disapproval. In Matthew 12:30, Jesus follows His analogy by saying, "He who is not with me is against me, and he who does not gather with me scatters." Jesus states here that in the battle against evil, we cannot stand by or ignore it. His terms "gather" and "scatter" mean that He does not expect cheerleaders in the battle against evil. He wants players! As explained in several Old Testament passages, we need to act to rescue those in need to prevent the success of evil men.[15]

In Mark 12:1, Jesus tells The Parable of the Vineyard. He mentions the owner building a wall and manning a watchtower to protect it. Again, Jesus could have commented on the "selfish moral depravity" of passive defensive measures (a wall) to keep those "in need" from freely taking his grapes. Of course, that would mean Jesus is against burglar alarms and barking dogs. Biting dogs would be really sinful. He could have further condemned using guards in a tower to actively protect the field (since guards imply the willingness to use force to protect the property), but He does not. He mentions both defenses as simply logical measures to protect private property in a fallen world filled with sinful people. His casual, matter-of-fact manner in mentioning passive and active defense of self and property in both the strong man and vineyard analogies leads me to conclude that

Jesus never intended to prevent us from protecting our own.

Jesus also tells us to be on the alert for His second coming in Mark 13:33-37. He uses the example of a householder going on a journey who appoints his servants to guard the place (again, active defense of property). In Luke 12: 35-40, Jesus gives the same example, but He adds in verse 39: "And be sure of this, if the head of the house had known at what hour the thief was coming, he would not have allowed his house to be broken into." Are we to assume that these guards were only allowed to tell a burglar not to enter? Or if the burglar ignored their warning, were the guards given full authority to use physical means to keep him out? Jesus dispels any qualms about the morality of self-defense in this verse (Matthew 24:43). He states approvingly that the homeowner *will* actively resist the burglar (as in Exodus 22:2-3). His attitude in all of these verses is of one of the logical and practical affirmation of defense of self and property. Jesus gives no hint in any of these examples that the owners have committed any sin by defending their lives and property.

It is interesting that Jesus never refutes any of the self-defense passages from the Old Testament. He never said, "You should help others unless it requires the use of force."

Jesus misses another chance to preach pacifism in Luke 14:31-32 when he uses this example:

> Or what king, when he sets out to meet another king in battle, will not first sit down and take counsel whether he is strong enough with ten thousand men to encounter the one coming against him with twenty thousand? Or else, while the other is still far away, he sends a delegation and asks terms of peace.

In this passage, Jesus is speaking of us making a cost/benefit analysis whether to follow Him (Luke 14:25-35). He does not say the king should simply meet his enemy with unarmed flower-bearing crowds singing, "Give Peace a Chance" or with a force incapable of winning. Rather, He portrays the king as deciding whether he can successfully make war or whether his country's best interest lies in a peace treaty. Jesus did not take this opportunity to preach against war. Instead, He says war should not be undertaken when there is no chance for success any more than a person should thoughtlessly swear loyalty to Jesus. In this example, Jesus implicitly agrees with Solomon that there is "a time for war and a time for peace" (Ecclesiastes 3: 8). Thus, going to war is not against Jesus' morals; there are justifiable reasons for war, and if we go to war, we should be in it to win. However, Jesus would surely require that the reasons for war and its conduct be moral.

Jesus actually confirms that arms should be used against criminals. When He was arrested on the Mount of Olives, He said, "Have you come out with swords and clubs to arrest Me, as against a robber?" (Mark 14:48). Do not think that Jesus is just asking a question. His comparison, "as against a robber," contrasts what authorities might lawfully and morally do against a person who is actually committing a violent crime versus what they were illegally and needlessly doing that night. He implies that weapons can be properly used against felons, but He had not broken any law. The arrest was illegal. He also points out that they could have arrested Him any time He preached in the Temple, but they did not because the people would have known the arrest was illegal. He juxtaposes the proper use of weapons against violent offenders versus the need to use minimal force against those who do not resist. This mirrors our modern sliding-scale *force continuum*, taught to police and civilians so they can apply the appropriate amount of force in a given situation. Luke gives us Jesus' prophecy from a few hours before as He quotes Isaiah: "For I tell you, that this which is written must be fulfilled in Me, 'And he was numbered with the transgressors' for that which refers to Me has its fulfillment" (Luke 22:37 quoting Isaiah 53:12b).

That night in the Garden, Jesus again had a perfect opportunity to preach pacifism and condemn the use of weapons by the police, but he did not. Instead, He says that police using swords and clubs against robbers is appropriate. By predicting that He would be considered a common criminal by the authorities, Jesus further establishes that the posse's weaponry was appropriate for a "transgressor." Jesus tells us here that lethal weapons are sometimes appropriate to keep civil order.

Jesus sent the twelve out on their first mission trip with these words: "Behold, I send you out as sheep among wolves; therefore be shrewd as serpents, but innocent as doves. But beware of men" (Matthew 10:16-17a). Jesus tells us here that the world is a tough neighborhood. Some people are not to be trusted. So do not sin against anyone, but do not be a patsy and trust everybody either. As a Christian armed citizen, I am one of Jesus' sheep, but I am also a shepherd with a duty to protect other sheep (my family at least). Jesus wants the very best for us: the best possible life that can be lived in the midst of a fallen world. He said, "The thief comes only to steal, kill and destroy; I come that they might have life, and might have it abundantly" (John 10:10). If Jesus intends that we have the more abundant life, then He surely does not intend that we allow our lives and others to be cut short by random criminal violence. But do not miss how Jesus distinguishes Himself (the totally devoted shepherd) from the hired hand who runs away (John 10:12-13). We know from David that the true shepherd will defend his sheep with his life against any foe (1 Samuel 17:34-35). Jesus says He will lay down His life to save His sheep (John 10:11) to prevent Satan from getting them. He fulfilled that promise on the cross. Again, this is a spiritual analogy to a physical truth: the good shepherd actively, physically defends the sheep; the bad one simply stands by or runs away. The conclusion is that Jesus says defending the innocent is the will of God; running away or standing by (pacifism) is not.

Do not miss another point here. Jesus calls the devil a murderer in verse 10. In John 8:44 He says "[T]he devil … He is a murderer from the beginning, and does not stand in the truth, because there is no truth in him. Whenever he speaks a lie, he speaks from his own nature; for he is a liar, and the father of lies." If Jesus had ever wanted to say that any killing is wrong, He could have done it in these two verses (John 8:44; 10:10). He takes time to condemn murder, lying, malicious destruction, theft and robbery (John 10:8-10). Yet He only uses "murder" and "kill" in this context in the common-law legal term for murder: "the intentional, unlawful killing of a human being."

Section 13A-6-1 of the Code of Alabama defines "criminal homicide" as "(a) (1) Murder, manslaughter, or criminally negligent homicide … and (2) a person commits criminal homicide if he intentionally, knowingly, recklessly or with criminal negligence causes the death of another person." Murder is defined in Section 13A-6-2 (a) (1) as "with intent to cause the death of another person, he or she causes the death of that person or another person." Definitions of murder are similar in other states, such as Iowa. Both Texas and Utah statutes have exactly the same definition as Alabama's statute.[16] Jesus always uses the term *murder* in the legal sense and always condemns it, but He *never* equates it with justifiable self-defense.[17]

Finally, Jesus says that the hired hand flees and leaves the sheep in danger because he does not care about them (John 10:13). If pacifists flee or refuse to act when others are endangered, Jesus seems to imply that they do not care about others, like the hired hand in His example. The only way Jesus could defend us "sheep" spiritually was to give His life sacrificially according to God's plan. Jesus' ancestor, David, risked his life to defend his father's sheep and the people of Israel (1 Samuel 17:34-37). Regarding ourselves, Jesus declares that the shepherd who stays to defend the sheep is concerned about them and is acting as Jesus would. So what would Jesus have us do? He wants us to fight spiritual and physical evil with the proper means in the proper context.

The good shepherd actively, physically defends the sheep; the bad one simply stands by or runs away.

Jesus and the Battle of Armageddon

I have never heard pacifist Christians address this question: "If Jesus is a pacifist, why will He fight the Battle of Armageddon?" Do they say, "He was a pacifist on earth, but when He comes back ... that's different?" No. "Jesus Christ is the same yesterday, today and, yes, forever" (Hebrews 13:8). Jesus may change His methods over time, but His nature, His personality never changes. So if He were a pacifist then, why will He not be a pacifist when? The answer is: He never was a pacifist, and He never will be. (Consumer Alert Disclaimer: I used to be an expert on the book of Revelation, until I met someone who had read it.) Check out the description of Jesus in the Second Coming from Revelation 19:11-21: "And I saw heaven opened, and behold, a white horse, and He who sat on it is called Faithful and True, and in righteousness He judges and *wages war*" (verse 11b, emphasis mine). So there is such a thing as a "just war." "And from His mouth comes a sharp sword, so that with it He may smite the nations ... He treads the wine press of the fierce wrath of God, the Almighty" (verse 15a and c). "And the rest were killed with the sword which came from the mouth of Him [Jesus] ..." (verse 21). Does this sound like the emasculated, indecisive, Jesus who pacifists so easily envision? "The Lord is a warrior, the Lord is His name" (Exodus 15:3). Under the doctrine of the Trinity, Jesus was the warrior Lord who drowned the Egyptian army

in the Red Sea, and He is the same warrior Lord who will wreak vengeance at
Armageddon.[18] "The Lord will go forth like a warrior; He will arouse His zeal like
a man of war. He will utter a shout, yes; He will raise a war cry. He will prevail
against His enemies" (Isaiah 42:13).

Examining the foregoing verses shows us that Jesus had plenty of opportunities to
endorse and expand on pacifism, yet he passed up every one. Instead, He implicitly
endorses self-defense and will return one day to lead armies against the wicked.

Clearing and Re-clearing the Temple

If Jesus is a pacifist, why did he use force to clear the Temple – probably
twice? John places the first cleansing early in His ministry in John 2:13-22. The
cleansing recorded in the synoptic Gospels is placed after the triumphant entry
into Jerusalem.[19] In his excellent edition of The Daily Bible, F. LaGard Smith joins
many other scholars in saying that there were two cleansings: one near the outset
and one at the end of Jesus' ministry.[20] Jesus could certainly have had excellent
reasons for doing it twice, but the significance for this study is that He did it at all.

In the second cleansing, the synoptic Gospels agree that Jesus drove out the
moneychangers and those selling sacrificial animals by overturning their tables
and benches and stopping anyone from carrying merchandise through the Temple.
How did Jesus accomplish this if He was a pacifist? Would a pacifist overturn
tables and benches in a flea market, strike people, and intimidate them to stop
doing business? Did the moneychangers not resist because they thought His
followers would hurt them if they did not comply? That would still make Him as
guilty as a mob boss who orders a crime committed but who does not personally
participate. However, Jesus did personally participate. He knocked over their
tables as He preached His sermon and condemned the merchants as "robbers"
(Matthew 21:13). The disciples apparently watched Jesus in stunned silence.

John gives us the details of how Jesus proceeded the first time (John 2:13-
22). Jesus entered the Temple, investigated, and comprehended the situation.
Historians have described what was going on. By an agreement with the
Pharisees, the Sadducees controlled the Temple and the priesthood. Scripturally,
Sadducees were conservatives who rejected the oral traditions of the Pharisees,

who valued their oral law on a par with the Law of Moses.[21] Sadducees, for instance, did not believe in the resurrection. While paying lip-service to Scripture, though, they collaborated with the Romans and embraced pagan cultural practices, especially those of the Greeks.

Jesus became angry when he saw the rampant, open dishonesty and misuse of God's house. However, Jesus was not enraged. John tells us that He took the time to make a whip of several striking ropes with knots at each end called a "scourge of cords" (sort of like a cat-o'-nine-tails). Then, Jesus began to drive them out while preaching to them. He knocked over their tables and seats (Mark 11:15), poured their cash boxes on the ground, drove out the animals (John 2:15), and forbade anyone to carry merchandise through the Temple court (Mark 11:16).

Jesus twice used violence and the threat of it to clear the Temple. He also took the time to make a non-lethal weapon to enforce His will. He either struck the offenders with the whip, or He convinced them that He would strike them. The Scriptures say that He "drove" them out. This implies actual force. His anger was righteous and real. John says the disciples remembered Psalms 69:9, "Zeal for Thy house has consumed me." Yet, Jesus never lost control. His zeal according to knowledge was always subject to God's righteousness. (Contrast Paul's description of his fellow Jews in Romans 10:1-4 about their misplaced zeal for God). Jesus' audience, actions, words, deeds, and His weapon were all appropriate for the time, place, situation, wrongdoers, and their crimes. So must our defensive actions be when we confront criminals. Were Jesus' actions those of a pacifist, or were they actions of a person who knows more about good and evil than anyone else and thus knows that sometimes evil must be physically fought and defeated? Like Caesar, Jesus came, saw, and conquered. Unlike Caesar, He twice accomplished a righteous deed and taught a righteous lesson with righteous actions.

Jesus on Unexpected Friends

Let's consider the story of the Good Samaritan. It can help us understand how Jesus would have us think about self-defense. Found in Luke 10:25-37, our text begins with a lawyer's question. Lawyers of Jesus' day were experts on Old Testament law and the added traditional laws and commentaries on them (later called Talmud and Mishnah) that had been built around it over time. Like the Scribes, they had memorized the Old Testament.

A lawyer approached Jesus and asked Him what he had to do to inherit eternal life (Luke 10:25). Luke says he was testing Jesus, maybe to see if Jesus knew the law as well as he did. Perhaps he was trying to lure Jesus into an argument about an obscure point of interpretation. We lawyers sometimes do that. Semantics is our life.

The lawyer's question was a good one, but his motive was questionable. Was he trying to get Jesus to delineate who he had to be kind to and who he could ignore? Based on Jesus' answer, that may have been it. God says "be holy, for I am holy" (Leviticus 11:44). Yet so often our request is, "Preacher, please draw me a line I can walk that is just as close to the pit of Hell as I can get without falling in." Maybe this lawyer was asking Jesus to give him a rule that would let him look good without having to do good.

Employing some verbal judo, Jesus posed the question back to him, "What is written in the Law? How does it read to you?" (Luke 10:26). Jesus forced him back to the standard of God's Word. The lawyer's answer combined Deuteronomy 6:5 and Leviticus 19:18: "You shall love the Lord your God with all your heart, and with all your soul, and with all your strength, and with all your mind; and your neighbor as yourself." Interestingly, the lawyer added "all your mind" and left out the part of Leviticus 19:18 that says not to take vengeance or to bear a grudge against your countrymen. Maybe he wanted to emphasize his personal effort but minimize his application of love. What these verses mean to me is that if I love God with every intention, word, and deed, I will also love my neighbor in such a way that I intend and act to secure the same best outcomes for him that I want for myself.

Jesus told the lawyer he had answered correctly. We can see the self-satisfied smile on the lawyer's face fade into a frown as Jesus finished with a quote from Leviticus 18:15: "do this, and you will live." Jesus left him with a central Bible message: hearing and understanding the Word is no good unless you put it into practice.[1] Apparently stung by Jesus, the lawyer then resorted to a common legal tactic: hairsplitting. "But wishing to justify himself, [before the onlookers and Jesus] he said to Jesus, 'And *who* is my neighbor?'" (emphasis mine). This legalist really asked Jesus to set the boundary of people he had to deal with. Like most of us, he was probably thinking, "Draw the circle very close to me, though."

Jesus answered his legalistic question with a true story of two men. This was not a parable, which is an earthly analogy to a heavenly truth, such as the Parable of the Sower (Luke 8:4-15). Jesus usually labels a parable as such and often provides the explanation to it. In this case, however, Jesus does neither, apparently relating an actual event in verses 30-36.

A man was traveling "down" from Jerusalem to Jericho. While we tend to say we travel "down" when headed south, the Jews referred to going to Jerusalem, situated on Mt. Zion, as "going up." So leaving Jerusalem, which was spiritually the highest point in Israel, was "going down" to wherever, regardless of the actual compass heading. On the way to Jericho, the man was attacked, robbed, stripped, wounded, and left for dead. As he lay there, a priest came down the road. The priests and Levites served by turns in the Temple, so the priest was apparently going home after his duties.[2] Seeing his fellow Jew injured and helpless, he merely moved to the opposite side of the road and passed on. Priests became ceremonially unclean *forever* if they touched the dead, except for immediate family. Even then, they could not perform their duties until purified, which took one week (Leviticus 21:1-2; Ezekiel 44:25-26). If the priest had touched the victim and found him dead, his career would have been over. On the surface then, he had an excuse for avoiding the victim. However, he did not even bother to see if the victim was alive. Jesus repeatedly condemned those who valued ceremony, position, and procedure over mercy.³ Jesus would clearly have risked His career to help someone, and we should, too.

Then a Levite passed by on the way home from Jerusalem, saw the victim, and also passed by on the other side. If a Levite touched the dead, he had to be purified for seven days, but he could thereafter resume his duties. If he failed to purify himself and tried to work in the Temple, though, he was to be executed (Numbers 19:11-13). In this case, his shift was over for several months, so touching the dead would not have affected his career. There were thousands of other Levites to do the work. Regardless of their religious offices, both of these leaders violated the verses I have quoted many times in this book where God commands us to help others.⁴ These church leaders did not know whether the victim was still alive, but they did not want to know, either. Even though their duties were over, getting home on time was more important than helping someone. They neither tried to summon help ("Call IXII! Call IXII!") nor planned to send help after they reached a populated area. They preferred to let the victim die rather than risk interrupting their "holy," busy lives.

We have examined Leviticus 19:16b before: "You shall not stand by and watch your brother's blood be shed" (paraphrase). The Talmud says this verse puts a duty on a person to help another if he can. These guys both had a choice and refused to do their duty. Jesus says our best choice is to serve others (Mark 9:35). Under Leviticus 19:16-18, the victim had the right to expect help from his fellow Jews, but help came instead from an unlikely hero.

This hero was a Samaritan. The Samaritans were a group of Israelites left by the Assyrians (circa 516 B.C.) after they deported most of the "valuable" people. This remnant was mixed with pagan settlers transplanted there from other parts of the Assyrian empire. Because of the mix of cultures and religions across some 700 years, the Jews considered them as mongrels and their religion defiled (2 Kings 17:1-18; 24-41). The Samaritans built a temple to Jehovah on Mt. Gerazim about 388 B.C. and established a rival, hereditary priesthood to that of Jerusalem. Samaritans considered just the Pentateuch (the five books of Moses) as the only true Word of God, while the Jews recognized the rest of what we call the Old Testament as well. Each side deemed the other as heretics. The Jews destroyed the Samaritan temple in 128 B.C., creating permanent hatred between the two peoples.[5] Since that time, both sides had avoided each other's territory and personal interaction if they could help it.

After the priest and Levite had passed by the injured man, a Samaritan appears on the road to Jericho. When he sees the victim, he does not ignore him. He has compassion and empathy: "That could have been me." He even disregards the chance the robbers might return. Whatever his business was, he put it on hold, and went over to the victim. Finding him alive, he administers first aid, using olive oil and wine. The Samaritan's wine was probably mixed with barley to make vinegar (an antiseptic), with myrrh added to make an anesthetic.[6] That was the type of wine offered to Jesus on the cross, which he did not drink (Mark 15:23). The Samaritan bandaged the victim's wounds, exercising effort, skill, and his own resources. He put him on his own donkey and took him to an inn, where he "took care of him" (verse 34). Then he dropped his own plans for the rest of the day and night to care for a stranger who should have been his enemy.

Before the Samaritan left the next morning, he gave the innkeeper the equivalent of two days wages and instructed him to take care of the victim. Then he promised that he would return and pay for any additional expenses (verse 35). I have always wondered about the innkeeper, who was certainly a Jew. Did he allow a Samaritan under his roof simply because he was a paying customer or because he was astonished by his care for a Jew? Maybe he did it out of sheer respect in the face of such a holy, selfless act. I am reminded of the courageous and faithful black preacher who guarded the critically wounded white trucker during the Rodney King riot. Neither man thought for his own safety. Neither the preacher nor the Samaritan thought of repayment or reward. Neither man quibbled about racial, social, or cultural differences. Each only saw his neighbor in trouble and saw him through the crisis, just as Jesus would have him do. Each demonstrated to the whole world what "Love thy neighbor" is all about.

Jesus then confronted the lawyer (who had head-knowledge of everything and thought that was enough to be righteous), asking him, "So which of the three proved he was his neighbor?" The lawyer admitted it was "the one" who had shown mercy. (Notice the lawyer did not and perhaps could not even say "Samaritan.") Jesus then commanded him, "Go do the same!" (verses 36-37). Note that Jesus is not giving us good advice or a suggestion. "Go and show love to any

human being by helping him
in need" is a direct command!
Jesus tells the lawyer, "Go and
demonstrate that you can love at
least as well as that Samaritan."

We are not saved by good works (Jesus has taken care of that). However, the Good Samaritan shows us that our good work can save others, both physically and spiritually.

We are expected to treat love as a verb, not a noun. Jesus' story of the Good
Samaritan encompasses all of the "get in there and help them" verses of the Old
Testament.

I wish Jesus had told the story so that the Samaritan had shown up while the
robbery was going on and had driven off the robbers using a Colt .45 automatic.
Of course, He did not. The hero of the story enters after the action, and Jesus
does not mention active defense of others. However, the moral of the story is that
we show our love for God and man by meeting others' needs when they are in
trouble. If the emergency requires jumper cables, a first aid kit, a fire extinguisher,
or a gun, we should be ready and willing to capably respond. It does not matter
how much Bible we know or how often we are in church, Jesus is not truly our
Master until we do what He says: "If you know these things, you are blessed if you
do them" (John 13:17, emphasis mine).

Turning Good Intentions into Action

In 1976 while pursuing my teaching certificate, I had a class with a professor who called himself "an evangelistic agnostic." His class was entertaining but challenging to students of faith. As part of his many efforts to detach budding teachers from their moral moorings, he gave us handouts that took shots at Christianity. One was titled "All Religions Are the Same" and quoted Matthew 7:12: "Therefore, however you want people to treat you, so treat them, for this is the Law and the Prophets." Listed below this quote were pronouncements from Islam, Confucianism, Taoism, Buddhism, Hinduism, and a couple of others that were similar to the Golden Rule. I raised my hand and commented that something was not quite right about the comparison, but I was not sure what. He kindly invited me to think about it and tell the class my conclusion at the next meeting.

At the next class, I told the professor I had figured it out.

"So?" he said.

"Well," I began, "notice that Jesus said, '*Do* unto others ....' but every one of the others are versions of '*Do not* do unto others what you *would not* have done to you'."

"So?" he repeated.

"Take Hinduism," I said. "Let's say a baby is born to an Untouchable in Benares, the holy city on the Ganges. His mother will break his legs so he can legitimately beg as a cripple for life. Meanwhile, a Brahmin can sit by the river, 10 feet from that crippled child, counting his prayer beads and ignoring the cripple. Yet he is considered holy because he has not personally caused the misery. Neither Hinduism nor any of these other religions or philosophies imposes responsibility on the Brahmin to help cripples, beggars, or anyone. In fact, he is not even allowed to teach the Untouchable how to improve his lot in his next life cycle. This 'don't do unto others' philosophy is a recipe for an uncaring, irresponsible world. 'Do unto others …' is on a much higher moral plane with vastly different results."

Like the verses we have examined from the Old Testament, "Do unto others" is a direct command from God to help those in need. The standard is to help as we would like to be helped if we were a victim. The Samaritan who helped the robber's victim understood this, yet today's pacifist Christians do not. If you are a pacifist Christian, you likely do not believe in personally using violence to protect yourself and your family, but if you are awakened some night by the sounds of a break in, you will call 911 and ask armed, capable police to come and use whatever force necessary to stop that threat. Or you will call your gun-savvy neighbor to hurry with his shotgun. Perhaps then, if help comes in time, you will realize that Jesus, the police, and your neighbors all stand ready to "Do unto others" according to the real emergencies that occur daily. You will understand that helping others as you would like to be helped means preparing mentally, spiritually, and physically to thwart unlawful attacks on you, your loved ones, and your neighbors. I urge you to prayerfully consider whether defense of yourself and third parties could possibly be encompassed by Matthew 7:12 and Luke 6:31.

"Do unto others" comes from the Sermon on the Mount, which has been called the greatest expression of moral ethics in history. Found in Matthew 5-7, this beautiful passage of Scripture gives us Jesus' Word to practice, not to praise, as He tells us how to change the world by living and loving on a personal level in a life-changing way. Jesus wants us to believe that. To live like God, others must come first. This is especially relevant to those who carry concealed weapons because the attributes Jesus sets forth are the marks of an authentic Christian, and these attributes must control our thoughts and actions in all social contexts, including self-defense.

The Heart of a Servant

Jesus begins the Sermon on the Mount with the Beatitudes: basic attributes that, if cultivated, lead to a happy, successful life in Christ because they are modeled on Him. The practice of those attributes lead to the blessings that flow from being in Jesus. "Blessed are the poor in spirit, for theirs is the kingdom of heaven" (Matthew 5:3). "Poor in spirit" does not mean we convince ourselves that we assume a false humility that results in passivity.[1] It is not walking with downcast eyes, believing we have nothing to contribute. "Poor in spirit" means we recognize that we are not smart enough to run our lives without God's help. We need His love, wisdom, rules, people, and forgiveness. When Jesus said, "I came that they might have life, and have it abundantly" (John 10:10b), He meant that if we turn our lives over completely to Him, we will live life in the best and most satisfying way that humans can live in this fallen world. The catch is that we must be humble enough to admit we cannot do it on our own; we must put Him in charge. For the armed citizen, "poor in spirit" means we see ourselves as servants prepared to help others, not as superheroes or avenging angels. We do not fantasize about confrontations; we try to avoid them. We simply realize that we all live in a tough world, so we are prepared to step in with the level of action that fits the situation.

Turning Sorrow into Joy

"Blessed are those who mourn, for they shall be comforted" (Matthew 5:4). The word *mourn* here is a Greek word connoting deepest sorrow.[2] It refers to those who have suffered the deepest tragedies of life: the loss of a close family member, a divorce, or being the victim of senseless, brutal crime. C.S. Lewis said that when we stay close to Jesus in tragedy, He stays closest to us, and that is also when we exercise our faith to the fullest. In other words, God is proudest of us when we cannot see Him but we carry on in faith.[3] Those who have been through trouble can empathize with and effectively help those who are now suffering through horrible circumstances.

An example of a comforter who turned her mourning into good is Susanna Gratia Hupp, who lost her parents in the Luby's massacre. After their deaths, she ran for and won a seat in the Texas state legislature where she pushed through Texas's concealed carry law. She turned her loss into statewide safety, significantly reducing the chance that other Texans would suffer a similar tragedy. I am certain that she found some comfort in taking the opportunity to turn madness into compassion. God never disregards our pain. Instead, over time, He gives us chances to reach out to others in ways we would never have anticipated, with wisdom we would never otherwise have earned.

Meek is Not Weak

"Blessed are the gentle (meek), for they shall inherit the earth" (Matthew 5:5). Do not make the mistake of equating "meek" with "weak." Meek does not exactly mean outward behavior toward others. The Greek word denotes submission (meekness) toward God as King of our lives.[4]

Like "poor in spirit," meek is based on the conviction that since all His dealings with us are for our good, we submit to His will without argument or resistance. In other words, meekness is an attribute of faith.

However, does meek mean that if we are accosted by a robber, it is God's will that we submit to his evil? Good question, but no. Vine's *Expository Dictionary of Old and New Testament Words* points out that Jesus described Himself as meek (Matthew 11:29 and 30).[5] While we often equate meekness with weakness, the opposite is true.[6] Jesus was meek while simultaneously having all the power of God at His command. He used His power sparingly but forcefully when necessary, whether casting out demons or the money changers. The Greek conveys the idea of "power under control." In classical Greek texts, the word meek is used to describe a highly trained war horse or a fine hunting dog, both ready to spring into action at their master's command. The word applies to a condition of mind and of heart: gentleness in action, thought, word, and deed, yet constant readiness to act vigorously for the right. Jesus was meek but not weak. Ask the Temple moneychangers. This is the very concept that all competent self-defense instructors try to convey in their classes: a measured, intelligent, lawful, reasonable, necessary, and moral response to criminal threat by a properly trained person.

Crave Righteousness

"Blessed are those who hunger and thirst after righteousness, for they shall be satisfied" (Matthew 5:6). This means we cannot live fully unless our minds, hearts, and actions are guided by the quest to know and live by God's Word. This means we are open to any instruction that helps us walk closer to Jesus. That is when we are happiest. If you are truly concerned about righteously helping others, then this craving is the attitude that compelled you to read this book. Like me, you could not live with the practice of self-defense if Jesus required pacifism. So you began to study to see whether you have been misinformed by those who thought they knew something about the subject. Hungering and thirsting for righteousness means you care enough about what God says to change your ways.

Give the Other Guy a Break

"Blessed are the merciful, for they shall obtain mercy" (Matthew 5:7). We are most like God when we are giving and forgiving. Those are the main components of mercy.

God's mercy however, is not necessarily getting what we want. It is getting what He knows we need. For instance, if the criminal you have captured wants you to drop the charges or to let him go before the cops show up, nothing doing. What he needs is to take personal responsibility for his crime. Sociopaths are not used to doing that. They avoid responsibility like a kid avoids Brussels sprouts. They have always got an excuse for why their criminal actions are someone else's fault. Like the prodigal son who "came to his right mind" (the Greek translation) when he hit bottom in the pigpen, some people have to be knocked flat on their backs to make them look up (Luke 15:11-32). Even though we speak the truth in love (Ephesians 4:15), it is going to hurt sometimes before the person starts to heal.

What is not merciful is failing to reach out to the criminal in the hospital, jail, or prison. We may be met with indifference or rejection when we try to show mercy, but we must try anyway. Jesus never promised that if we obey Him and love others, the others will change. He does promise that if we cast ourselves in Love's direction, we will be changed! "But love your enemies, and do good, and lend, expecting nothing in return; and your reward will be great, and you will be sons of the Most High; for He Himself is kind to ungrateful and evil men" (Luke 6:35). Jesus also promises that the mercy we give will come back to us from others when *we* need mercy (Luke 6:38). It is not merciful to refuse to forgive others. We lack mercy when we gossip, judge others by appearances, or fail to listen. There are a thousand unmerciful sins, all falling under the word that also explains their cause, which is selfishness. I once taught Micah 6:8 (Do justly, love mercy, walk humbly) to a group of junior high kids and asked them what it meant. One boy volunteered, "Give the other guy a break." Exactly.

Mercy is the quality that motivates us to protect the innocent, preserving their lives so they can realize their potential. Mercy means that we preserve, protect and defend, but we do not seek vengeance. This is the motivation behind the laws' mandate that when defending, we use only the force reasonably necessary to stop the criminal act.

In real life, mercy means that whether we are a cop or a civilian, as the bad guy stops resisting so must our force. Mercy works through the force continuum: up and down, depending on the level of control versus the threat faced right up to deadly force level (as long as it is reasonably necessary). Once control is gained, our force must de-escalate proportionately. We do not throw one more good kick or punch to teach our attacker a lesson. The legal system will give the lesson. Not only that, mercy requires us to render first aid, if possible, not because it makes us look good in court but because first aid is a merciful response. Mercy embodies "do unto others" in the force continuum. This means we only fight when forced to fight, we never use more force than appropriate, we decrease force as the bad guy does, and we aid him when it is over. It also means we never use *less* force than appropriate to stop a criminal act and save lives. Otherwise, we and innocents might get hurt needlessly. We defend with skill, determination, even with anger, but without malice. Here is the difference: Anger says, "How dare you?" Malice says, "I'll get you for that!"

We can fight without vengeance and malice because we have no ulterior motive beyond defending the innocent. Momentary anger during the fight is not sinful. It is a God-given physio-psychological reaction to an unjustifiable criminal assault that focuses our skills and strength, but we let our anger pass when combat is over, never disengaging our brains. Hence, our anger is not malice because after our necessary defensive response, we will treat the criminal's wounds to give him a chance to fulfill his potential.

The Wisdom that Leads to Peace

"Blessed are the peacemakers, for they shall be called the sons of God" (Matthew 5:9). Many today equate "peacemaker" with the aim of eliminating all war and interpersonal conflict in the world as if the absence of war equals peace. Just because war is over does not mean there is peace. Ask anyone from a country occupied by Germany or Japan or from the Iron Curtain countries after WWII. We know that Jesus was not a pacifist, so what did He mean by "peacemaker?" During His temptation in the desert, Jesus did not try to appease Satan by negotiating with him. Jesus was no Chamberlin at Munich to Satan's Hitler. Jesus does not want us to be starry-eyed optimists about peacemaking. It was only when Reagan walked away from the table at Reykjavik that Gorbachev got serious about arms control. Jesus does not mean that a peacemaker is a go-along-to-get-along-regardless-of-the-stakes kind of guy.

Jesus' Gospel causes conflict. He intended that it do so. The establishment hated Him. Followers abandoned Him. One disciple betrayed Him. A king and a Roman governor feared Him all because He demanded they make life choices based on His objective Word. He had no time for appeasers or anyone who refused to face up to the questions: "Whom do you love?" "Whom will you serve?" "But who do *you* say that I am?" (Luke 9:20, emphasis mine). Rather, He demanded that we use His definition of peace, not a man-made concept that merely describes absence of conflict at any price. He says we are blessed when we share the Gospel even when it is hard, when we are trying to soothe hurt feelings and reconcile people even as they ridicule us.

Mercy is the quality that motivates us to protect the innocent, preserving their lives so they can realize their potential. Mercy means that we preserve, protect and defend, but we do not seek vengeance. This is the motivation behind the laws' mandate that when defending, we use only the force reasonably necessary to stop the criminal act.

Since 1991 when I started teaching self-defense classes to police and civilians, I have always emphasized that unarmed force and weapons are a last resort. I teach the maxim that your mind and communication skills are the best weapons you have. On the street, the peacemaker is one who can out-talk and out-think his opponent.

Those without inner peace end up hurting others. And we will not get inner peace by being friends with this world rather than with Jesus (James 4:4). Peacemakers can help and influence other folks because they themselves are at peace.

From Rejection to Glory

"Blessed are those who have been persecuted for the sake of righteousness, for theirs is the kingdom of heaven. Blessed are you when men cast insults at you, and persecute you, and say all kinds of evil against you falsely on account of Me. Rejoice and be glad for your reward in heaven is great, for so they persecuted the prophets who were before you" (Matthew 5:10-12).

As Christians, someone is always watching us. Some watch only to snipe, criticize, and justify their cynicism. Others are genuinely impressed by our lives and witness and are watching to learn more. When we stumble, the critics will condemn us for not being perfect. Those who put us on pedestals may hate us if they think we have disappointed them. (They have forgotten that it is Jesus who belongs on the pedestal.) The best we can do is to admit our faults and remind them only Jesus is perfect. However, there are those who actively oppose God and therefore oppose us ("so they persecuted the prophets before you," verse 12b).

If you are being snubbed, accused, lied about, slandered, libeled, and generally hung out to dry because you stand for Jesus, rejoice! But be self-aware if you are being criticized. You are either doing something right and God is proud of you, or you are doing wrong and making Him look bad. Hang in there if it is the former and knock it off if it is the latter.

Turning the Other Cheek

Now we come to one of the proof-texts of pacifists: "But I say to you, do not resist him who is evil; but whoever slaps you on your right cheek, turn to him the other also" (Matthew 5:39). Pacifist Christians believe this verse says we are forbidden to use force to defend ourselves or others no matter the cause, situation, or provocation. Instead, they believe they might influence the mugger, robber, or rapist to turn to Christ because of their refusal to fight back.

As discussed in the "Bringing the Criminal under Control" chapter, we cannot influence someone until they are willing to listen. If that someone is in the process of committing a violent crime, he is certainly not ready to listen until he realizes he has run out of options. Consider our hypothetical situation where an attacker enters the restaurant and starts shooting. Does Jesus expect us to turn not only our cheek to the shooter's second bullet, but to do so also on behalf of every innocent person there? Wouldn't Jesus want a trained person to intervene and try to save others by stopping the criminal with force?

Consider a martyr's actual potential to witness in the event of a mass shooting. The press will feature a few victim stories for public interest but only if there is a hook to their story. Is "Victim Dies Because He was a Pacifist" going to be one of those stories, or will it be "Korean War Vet Dies Stopping Mass Killer"? Turning the other cheek in the face of pure, violent evil creates a crime statistic, not a martyr. Jesus wants us to assess the world realistically. That is why He said, "Behold I send you out as sheep in the midst of wolves; therefore, be shrewd as serpents, and innocent as doves" (Matthew 10:16).

Jesus would have me be serious about serious subjects. If a man charges me, loudly threatening death with a knife, bat, or gun in hand, his intent is clearly to murder me. He will not stop until either he succeeds or until I stop him. In this scenario, if the pacifist stance is correct, a Christian's only hope of surviving is to run. Otherwise, there are only two possible outcomes. First the Pacifist Christian dies in the hope that somehow his death was a witness to the killer. Alternatively, his survival must be delegated to non-Christian cops and the military. But that means the Pacifist Christian is forcing police officers and soldiers to endanger their own souls by going against Jesus' commands. You see the problem. We need to use some common sense. "Therefore be careful how you walk, not as unwise men, but as wise, making the most of your time because the days are evil" (Ephesians 5:16-17).

What did Jesus Mean?

So what did Jesus mean by "turn the other cheek"? As always, we must consider this verse in its scriptural, historical, cultural, and practical real-world contexts. As I have shown, Jesus refers to examples of self-defense on several occasions, so I must consider all His relevant statements along with the "turn the other cheek" statement. Next I must consider the context. Jesus' statement is part of the Sermon on the Mount. Beginning with the Beatitudes, the first part of Jesus' sermon (Matthew 5) is about forming relationships and re-establishing broken ones. Jesus is not addressing nations or institutions. He is teaching us God's principles for successful interpersonal relationships (Matthew 5:13-48). As we saw with the lawyer in the Good Samaritan story, the Jews of Jesus' day had taken institutional principles of the Law and misapplied them so they did not have to deal with others on a personal level. So Jesus sets a new standard and teaches them to change their outlook to God's way of thinking. Each time Jesus says, "You have heard …. But I say to you …," He redefines a commandment or rejects a prominent teaching of the Pharisees. From verse 21 to the end of Chapter 5, Jesus addresses forging and repairing relationships with those we see most often: family, neighbors, co-workers, clients, and church members.

In Matthew 5:21-22, Jesus makes it clear that murder begins in the heart, with hatred (malice aforethought):

> You have heard that the ancients were told, 'You shall not commit murder, and whoever commits murder shall be liable to the court.' But I say to you that everyone who is angry with his brother shall be guilty before the court; and whoever shall say to his brother 'Raca' [good for nothing] shall be guilty

before the supreme court; and whoever shall say, 'You fool' shall be guilty enough to go into the fiery hell.

In Mark 7:20-23, Jesus says, "That which proceeds out of the man, that is what defiles the man. For from within, out of the heart of men, proceeds the evil thoughts ,… murders …. All these evil things proceed from within and defile the man." John said, "Everyone who hates his brother is a murderer, and you know that no murderer has eternal life abiding in him" (1 John 3:15). Murder starts with frustration, grows with resentment, and finally executes with hatred. When we act in self-defense, we have neither hatred nor pre-planning to kill a particular person for personal gain. We kill only as a last resort to save innocent life. Therefore, killing in self-defense cannot be murder by Jesus' definition.

In Matthew 5:23-26, Jesus says that the way to diffuse anger and hatred in our hearts is to refuse to let it fester. He says before I try to worship God, I must first make sure that I repair broken relationships. Jesus teaches us to ask God to forgive us in the same way that we forgive others (Matthew 6:12). He warns us that if we refuse to forgive others, then God will not forgive us (Matthew 6:14-15).

After addressing how God's absolutes for marriage and truthfulness relate to relationships, Jesus addresses vengeance in Matthew 5:38-48. When he quotes the Mosaic Law on "eye for an eye," He refers to the criminal and civil legal systems God established for Israel. Damages were awarded only after a trial and legal adjudication, not personal retribution exercised on whim or for vengeance.[1] He says, "You have heard that it was said, 'an eye for an eye and a tooth for a tooth.' But I say to you, do not resist *him* who is evil." It is clear from the context of this chapter that Jesus is not referring to general evil, such as Nazi Germany or criminal activity, but to a person with whom you have a relationship who is hurting you. Remember that Jesus is dealing with those closest to us, not with random strangers. He is not making a blanket prescription under all circumstances toward all people, because He speaks of an individual personally hurting us. These people are those we know best and with whom we have regular contact: the insufferable boss, the back-stabbing co-worker, the vicious gossip at church – *not* a criminal stranger.

Realizing this, let's consider the pacifist Christian's proof text: "but whoever slaps you on your right cheek, turn to him the other also." It is from this example that we know Jesus does not refer to criminal assault. Note what Jesus says: He posits being slapped on the right cheek. Now if you slap someone on the right cheek while facing them, you must use your open left hand. Ask anyone who has been to the Middle East, and they will tell you the significance of the left-handed slap: it is a pointed public insult, not an attempt to do physical harm. Why is it such an insult? Because for thousands of years before Jesus and ever since in the Mideast, the left hand is the one you use to wipe after defecating! To slap someone or even shake their hand with your left is the highest order of insult.[2] Biblically, the right hand is the hand of power if force is intended. God's right hand is associated with His active, creative, sustaining, and destructive power in over 34 verses of the Old Testament.[3] This connotes the left as the weaker, non-destructive hand. Therefore, the left-handed slap is not a reference to dangerous physical attack but to a public or private insult with the intent to humiliate.[4]

Jesus is also paraphrasing Lamentations in a passage that states if we are persecuted, the Lord will vindicate us in time: "Let him give his cheek to the smiter, Let him be filled with reproach. For the Lord will not reject forever. For if He causes grief, then He will have compassion according to His abundant loving kindness" (Lamentations 3:30-32). Jesus' message on turning the other cheek concerns our interaction with people who know us and who realize we can retaliate if we wish. Thus, Jesus is continuing the theme of his sermon: how to handle personal relationships. He has not suddenly changed the subject to discuss how we should respond to a criminal trying to attack or provoke us. There is no risk of life, limb, or liberty here. He is talking about ignoring a public insult from someone you thought you could trust, whose snide, hurtful comment left you with red, burning ears. He is talking about a stinging unjustified rebuke from a boss or co-worker; a vicious rumor about you from a fellow church-member; the false accusation from a frustrated neighbor; or even an angry blow during a political disagreement. Bystanders might expect us to hit back, reply in kind, or justify ourselves. Our tormenter may even think we are completely justified in hitting back, blow-for-blow, insult for insult, but we will refuse in Jesus name. Instead we practice "Bless those who persecute you, bless and curse not" (Romans 12:14) and turn the other cheek (perhaps by giving him a compliment). Trust God that He will use your self-control to change your opponent. If you do not affect him, you have still witnessed to the bystanders by your forbearance.

These are the scenarios envisioned by Jesus and Jeremiah when they exhort us to reject anger and retaliation by "turning the other cheek" because God will vindicate us in the end. If we are in private with the insulting person, inviting them to strike again will surely impress him that his concept of us is all wrong. He must ask himself, "Why is he treating me this way? Why will he not retaliate? What is wrong with him?" You have just created a chance to witness. If we are in public, the person will probably be too ashamed to strike a second time while our forbearance is on display for all to see. Bystanders will get a favorable impression of Jesus from our restraint. Remember, someone is always watching you if you are a Christian to see if your claim is genuine. This is the purpose of ignoring personal insult and injury.

In verse 40, Jesus describes another way to turn the other cheek by forbidding vengeful actions at law. He is reiterating that nothing Christians do should stem from vengeful motives (see also Romans 12:9-21). He does not forbid legitimate civil actions, just those with vengeance as a motive. He is still discussing the theme of interpersonal conflicts between folks who know each other, not strangers committing criminal violence or a chemical company polluting a town's water. He is not telling us to refuse to prosecute criminals. Paul clarifies verse 40 in 1 Corinthians 6:1-11 when he says that Christians should never air dirty laundry in court before non-believers. Rather than dishonor Christ that way, he says it is better to be wronged and accept it (verse 7b). In verse 40, Jesus says, "For the sake of good church family relationships and the preservation of your witness, agree, compromise, even be defrauded, but do not shame Me in court!" To accept Christ is to accept the fact that your entire life is now a teaching witness, for good or bad, on behalf of Christ. "Let your light shine before men in such a way that they may see your good works, and glorify your Father who is in heaven" (Matthew 5:16).

Going the Extra Mile

In Matthew 5:41, Jesus teaches us about making peace and forging interpersonal relationships even after an association is forced upon us, as with strangers or criminals. He says, "And whoever shall force you to go one mile, go with him two."

Since the time of the Persian Empire from the sixth to the fourth century B.C., the law enjoined a citizen to help a royal messenger in any way he could. The official could requisition help as needed. This custom was adopted by the empires of Alexander the Great and his successors. When the Romans conquered the East, they also used the rule. By the first century, the rule was that any Roman soldier could force a Jew to carry his pack (which could weigh 70-80 pounds on campaign) but for one Roman mile only (a bit shorter than our modern mile). Once the Jew completed the required distance, he could drop the pack without further obligation. The Roman could then order another Jew to replace him for the next mile.[5]

Why would Jesus order the Jew (and us) to go a second mile? Because the service of the first mile is forced on us. No matter how cheerful and friendly the Jew acted while carrying the pack, the soldier would be skeptical.

"Hi! My name is Gideon. What's yours? Pleased to meet you, Marcus! You from outta town? Capua! Cool! Hey, you like jokes? You'll love this one. Pontius Pilate and the High Priest go into a bar ...."

The soldier's natural assumption would be, "Yeah, he's making the best of it because he fears my sword and the law. I know these Jews. They'd rather do anything than be near one of us 'unclean Gentiles.' At the next milestone, he'll drop my pack and his happy act and run like I've got the plague."

By going the extra mile, Jesus is telling us to shock the oppressor and take control by volunteering when our service is no longer required. When the cheerful Jew volunteered to go the next mile, the cynical Roman could not help but be impressed and interested enough to ask why. He would realize that the Jew's friendliness during the first mile was not just a show. A relationship would begin in which the Jew could now witness because control of the situation had now passed to him. Jesus is saying that there is no witness unless the oppressor or criminal knows our kindness is voluntary!

Today, cheerful compliance with a robber's demands creates no impression on him either. We are merely a compliant victim, forced to carry his "pack" the required distance. However, if we hospitalize or hold him for arrest and visit him in the hospital or jail, then like the Roman he will see there is something different about us. Now we have control, having chosen to care for and to care about the bad guy. He knows we have no obligation to meet anywhere but in court; thus, he might be intrigued by our action and witness. What is Jesus saying? That there can be no witness without control over the situation. We can minister grace to our former attacker only when we gain undisputed control and then go the second mile.

We must make sure that we do not draw the wrong conclusions, as some Christians have for centuries, regarding "turn the other cheek" and "go the second mile": that Christian strategy is a suicide pact. When confronted by organized persecution (Romans, pagans, Mongols, radical Muslims, Nazis, Communists, and so forth), some have assumed that attempts to eradicate Christians by force are "God's will." There are those who believe that if these murderers want to lock us inside our church and burn us alive that Jesus would require us to submit. That is not the case! In Matthew 5:41, Jesus teaches us that there is NO witness unless our tormentor realizes that we have a choice whether or not to submit.

When teaching armed church security teams, I spend two or three hours on the principles of this book, and then another seven hours on the self-defense and trespass laws of Alabama. Author of *On Killing*, Lt. Col. Dave Grossman believes that the next terrorist attacks will occur at churches, schools, or sporting events.[6] Such attacks would be modeled on the 2005 attack by Muslim terrorists on the Beslan, Russia, Junior High School. Just as at Beslan, the terrorists would enter with firearms to torture and kill as many as possible, and they would not plan to come out alive. If this type of incident happened at your church or school, would the popular definition of "turn the other cheek" and "go the second mile" be rational responses? Based on all the evidence, scriptural and otherwise, I conclude that Jesus did not mean for Christians to stand by and let that happen. Neither does our submission to such evil promote the Gospel.

Then there are the mentally deranged or common criminals who attack churches, synagogues, and mosques every year. A preacher with a Ph.D. in

Psychology once spoke to my college church group. One student asked why there seemed to be so many weird people in and on the fringes of the 1,000+ member congregation. He replied, "You see, many desperate people consider the church their last stop before the mental hospital. If they perceive that the church is not helping, they might to decide to retaliate."

Study how to survive such emergencies. The book *Surviving Workplace Violence* by Loren Christensen is excellent. On YouTube, view the video *Run, Hide, Fight* from the City of Austin, Texas. The best book I know on church security and general risk management is Ron Aguiar's *Keeping your Church Safe*. As security chief for the 25,000 members of Southeast Christian Church, he knows the subject well and has many helpful suggestions.

Understand that you cannot turn the other cheek on behalf of another person. As I have shown, the biblical command is to jump in and help those in trouble, not order your family or congregation to keep singing and be slaughtered like sheep. Responding to corporate or private evil, its nature, and the possible witness to the tormentor is a private decision, but a desperate criminal striding into your worship service with a shotgun and a twisted sense of grievance needs to be met by armed resistance. If he survives, you can use psychological counseling and Jesus' love to try to help and convert him. Simply calling 911 while he decimates the choir *is against God's law!* Remember that when the Jews fought their oppressors in the book of Esther, they won peace for themselves ever after (Esther 8 and 9). *That* is the biblical model!

We can minister grace to our former attacker only when we gain undisputed control and then go the second mile.

God allowed the Hebrews to fight their oppressors throughout their history. He did not stand by and order them to be exterminated just to be a "witness" to their enemies. Yes, God did allow the nation of Israel to be destroyed because of its sin, but He announced His judgment beforehand and gave Israel a chance to repent and turn His wrath away. Those who repented fled to Judah; however, Judah was later conquered by Babylon because of their sins. Yet, God brought the Jews back after 70 years when they had learned their lesson.

Some might say, "But what about early Christians? They did not fight back." Early Christians attempted to hide and avoid combat instead of fighting back.

Their persecutions were connected to their refusal to worship the Spirit of Rome (as embodied by the Emperor), and thus they were considered traitors or rebels and risked the wrath of the Roman Army. For centuries there were no successful citizen revolts against Rome. Their generals, tactics, and morale simply could not be matched, and they never admitted defeat, no matter how long it took. Those rebels who were not exterminated were enslaved and dispersed. As Tacitus said of his own people, "They make a desert and call it peace." The ruthlessness with which the Romans put down organized revolt was not limited to rebels but often included innocent neighbors. Christians did not want their neighbors counted as collateral damage – not a good witness. Revolt meant extermination. So they did not use armed resistance. Second, Roman persecutions were not universal. Even under the Emperor Domitian and other dedicated haters of Christianity, individual Roman officials were spotty on their enforcement of Imperial edicts. Moreover, Christians usually worshipped at night in private homes, so they were generally "under the radar" of government. There were always many areas where persecution was not enforced, and Christians could move from hotspots to places of greater tolerance. The rapid spread of the Gospel converted so many that they could hide among the sympathetic population. Even unbelievers acknowledged their charitable acts to all, which won them many friends who later became converts. Finally, these early Christians believed that Jesus would return at any moment and set things to right, so armed resistance was considered unnecessary.

In the face of the actual threats to churches from terrorists, criminals, and the insane, armed church security teams make perfect sense. Such measures allow us to take control of the situation from the criminal. Sometimes deadly force will be the only option he gives us. Remember, there is a 98 percent chance that when we pull a gun we will not have to fire.[7] Unfortunately, sometimes a criminal's actions demand a response that results in his death. Jesus said that the head of the house must be alert so the burglar cannot take him by surprise (Matthew 24:43; Luke 12:39). We do not wish the attacker's death, nor do we gain satisfaction or vindication from it. Our goal is simply to preserve innocent life. That is why police and responsible firearms instructors teach to shoot to stop by aiming for the trunk of the body. A person shot there with a handgun has a 25 percent chance of dying, but the only reason we shoot at all is to prevent him from inflicting death, permanent maiming injury, or a heinous assault like rape or kidnapping. The criminal who forces our decision by breaching our home or church defenses and continues his unlawful advance after we order him to stop compels us to protect the innocent in the most decisive way we can. Our intent and deed are righteous, while his intent comes from a perverted (and likely drug induced) sense of entitlement.

God takes no pleasure in the death of the wicked (Ezekiel 18:23) and neither do we. Yet God says, "The person who sins will die" (Ezekiel 18:20a). Remember, it is the felon who deliberately put us in the position of having to harm him: "They lie in wait for their own blood. They ambush their own lives. So are the ways of everyone who gains by violence, it takes away the lives of its possessors" (Proverbs 1:18-19). "He who is steadfast in righteousness will attain to life; and he who pursues evil will bring about his own death" (Proverbs 11:19). We do not presume to be God when we use deadly force. We are only trying to save innocents legally and morally by the only means the bad guy has left to us in that moment. In Matthew 5:38-40, Jesus says our witness is only effective when we have control of the situation. To do that, we must first convince the bad guy that we are in control by assuring him that we will shoot if he does not stop.

Final Thoughts on the Sermon on the Mount

In Matthew 5:42-48, Jesus continues His theme of repairing and forging relationships by going the second mile. In verse 42, He says, "Give to him who asks of you and do not turn away from him who wants to borrow from you." This echoes Solomon: "Do not withhold good from those to whom it is due when it is in your power to do it. Do not say to your neighbor, "Go, and come back, and tomorrow I will give it'" (Proverbs 3:27-28). In Luke 10:25-37, Jesus defined "neighbor" as anyone in need whom we can actively help. In doing good, we are to first target our family in Christ. "And let us not lose heart in doing good, for in due time we shall reap if we do not grow weary. So then, while we have opportunity, let us do good to all men, and especially to those who are of the household of the faith" (Galatians 6:9-10). One of the basic tenets of the Bible is generosity to those in need. Jesus says, "By this all men will know that you are My disciples, if you have love for one another" (John 13:34).

I am sure we have all been able to show such kindness to friends and strangers. Many Christians refuse to give money to beggars because they are afraid the person will spend it on booze or in another harmful way. For me, Jesus settled that argument in Matthew 5:45(a): "[F]or He causes the sun to rise on the evil and the good and sends rain on the righteous and the unrighteous." I do not think it is my responsibility how the person uses my money. How often has God given me good gifts that I have squandered? Yet He still blesses me. Jesus tells me to give, and God will hold that person responsible for how he uses my gift. However, we must use common sense. Matthew 5:42 does not mean that I am so generous that I endanger my family's survival. I will control the situation as far as I can. In college, we would often have people come by the campus ministry who said they were looking for a meal. They would ask for money. Instead, we would let them pick a place to eat and take them there. Once there, we would say, "You can have anything you want to eat, but no booze."

Sometimes they would ask, "Why no booze?"

"Because it's *my* money," we would reply. We never had an argument.

However, "Give to him who asks of you" does not mean that I give a loaded gun to a four-year-old, hand a beer to a recovering alcoholic, or give up my gun when a criminal orders me to do so. Jesus continues his theme from verses 42-48 that I forge or repair relationships. That is the point behind His command for generosity and why it follows the "go the second mile" command.

After this, Jesus quotes a statement that had become proverbial for the Jews of His day. "You have heard that it was said, 'You shall love your neighbor, and hate your enemy'" (Matthew 5:43). The first part of the saying is from Leviticus 19:18: "You shall not take vengeance, nor bear any grudge against the sons of your people, but you shall love your neighbor as yourself. I am the Lord." In fact, Leviticus 19:13-18 mirrors much of Matthew 5:21-48: it is all about godly relationships with others. But the Jews at some point had deleted the part about refusing vengeance and grudges or even loving your neighbor as yourself. Instead, they added, "and hate your enemy." This is based on a specific command from Deuteronomy 23:3-6 about the Ammonites and Moabites, descendants of Lot (Genesis 20:30-38). These people were forbidden to enter the tabernacle/temple until the eleventh generation after Moses because they opposed the Israelites on their journey to enter Canaan. It says not to seek their peace or prosperity all your days (do not trade or make treaties with them). It never says to hate them or to hate enemies in general. "Hate your enemy" was made up. In fact, Ruth, an ancestor of Jesus, was a Moabite (Ruth 1:1-4, 4:13, 18-22; Matthew 1:5). In other words, the people of Jesus' day had cooked up a convenient saying: "Love your neighbor" (and we know from the lawyer in Luke 10:17 how narrowly they liked to construe that) and "hate your enemy." So according to the common wisdom of their day, it was okay if you do not like someone. This was an easy way of ignoring everything God said in the Old Testament about loving others.

In fact, the Bible never tells us to hate anyone. We are told to hate evil (Psalms 97:10), the works of evil people (Psalms 101:3), false ways (Psalms 119:104, 128), vain thoughts (Psalms 119:113), and lying (Psalms 119:163). In other words, we are to hate the sin but not the sinner (Amos 5:15). In Psalms 139:21-22, David says he hates those who hate God and that they are his enemies. That is David's opinion, not a command from God. He is expressing poetically his fervent opposition to those who actively deny God and work against Him, and, therefore, he hates the misery they cause. For instance, think of the long-term effects of child molestation. David might have been referring to foreign enemies who served gods other than Jehovah. If those enemies defeated Israel, they would eliminate His worship and impose their god's worship on the Israelites. This may have been the source of the vehemence in David's verses, but they clearly are not a command from God to hate anyone.

So Jesus negates the Jews' apostate saying with the following: "But I say to you, love your enemies, and pray for those who persecute you in order that you may be sons of your Father who is in heaven; for He causes the sun to rise on the evil and the good, and sends rain on the righteous and the unrighteous" (Matthew 5:44-45). Praying for others is the start of getting our attitudes right so we can begin to start or repair relationships. I know of several lawyers who refuse to sue deadbeat clients because they know how poor they are and the harm that payment would cause to the client's family. So they forgive and forget, trusting that God will make up the difference.

Verses 44 and 45 are the conclusion of the theme that Jesus started in verse 21.

We are told to love our enemies because Jesus does. He loved Judas as much as the other disciples. When Jesus washed the disciples' feet, I am sure He washed Judas' feet as thoroughly and as gently as He did the others (maybe more). "For God so loved the world…" (John 3:16) emphasizes Jesus' love for everybody, but John 3:17 brings it home when Jesus says He was not sent to condemn anyone but so that everyone could be saved through Him. Jesus tells us in Matthew 5:21-48 that we are most like God when we are giving and forgiving. When we are forging new relationships and repairing broken ones, without regard to our own image, status, or advantage, we act like Jesus.

Near the end of the Sermon on the Mount, Jesus makes one of His best known statements: "Therefore, however you want people to treat you, so treat them, for this is the Law and the Prophets" (Matthew 7:12; also Luke 6:31). Now if I am hungry, lack shelter, need clothing, my car breaks down in the middle of nowhere, or if I am drowning, I want some help. By the same token, if someone is trying to rob, rape, kidnap, burglarize, cripple, or murder me, I want some help. All of these are bad things. In every situation, I hope that someone will respond to my distress with appropriate help. In the case of the crimes listed, I need a neighbor to intervene with countervailing force, not to wish me well, bake me cookies, ignore my plight, or even call 911. I need help now! When Jesus said, "Do unto others …" He *does not* qualify it by saying, "unless it means you have to use force." His qualification is "as you would have them do unto you."

In his masterful work *The Jesus I Never Knew*, Phillip Yancey advances the idea that Jesus left us here to do His work. While that idea is traditional doctrine (2 Corinthians 5:14-6:3), he proposes a novel, yet soundly biblical viewpoint of Matthew 25:31-46.[8] This is one of Jesus's last private talks with His disciples. He tells them that when He returns to judge the earth, He will divide humanity into sheep and goats. The sheep will be those who fed Jesus when He was hungry, took Him in though he was a stranger, clothed Him when He was naked, visited Him when He was sick, and visited Him in prison. The goats will be the ones who saw but ignored Him. The goats will be sentenced to eternal punishment, but the sheep will be rewarded with eternal life (verse 46). Both groups will say in amazement that they did not recognize Jesus in any of those circumstances. They just saw other people in those dire straits. But to the sheep, Jesus will reply,

"Truly I say to you, to the extent that you did it to one of these brothers of Mine, even the least of them, you did it to me" (verse 40). To the goats, He says the same but omits the phrase "these brothers of Mine." He shows them that they dismissed the needy as "the least of these," not regarding them as brothers, but simply as not worthy of their attention. The Hebrew writer commands hospitality to strangers and to help those in prison because some have hosted angels without knowing it (Hebrews 13:1-3). Yancy emphasizes that Jesus left fallible Christians here to be His literal body and to share His love.

I agree. We are to be His arms to hug and protect, His hands to serve the needy and restrain evil, His eyes to perceive good and identify danger, and his voice to teach, warn, comfort, soothe, and encourage. Matthew 25:31-46 teaches us that if we ignore Hell on earth, Hell will be our destination. German theologian Dietrich Bonhoeffer said, "To believe is to do." Once again, if a criminal comes into that restaurant and Jesus has ordered us to preserve life by feeding, clothing, and healing people, would He frown on me if I use force to defend them from murder? Jesus defended His disciples (John 17:12a). If angels rejoice over any sinner who repents (Luke 15:10), would they not rejoice if I save the lives of many sinners who will now have a chance to repent? I would hate to look Jesus in the eye on Judgment Day and try to explain why I "turned the other cheek" when I had the means and ability to help while others had no choice or chance.

If a gang is beating me to death, I want intervention, not sympathy or nostrums about bearing all things with patience. If I would want intervention, then Jesus commands that I do the same for others in a similar situation. Jesus goes on to say that we will be known by what we do (our fruits), not what we say (Matthew 7:17-21). This is why Christians in occupied Europe had no problem lying to the Nazis when asked, "Are there any Jews in this house?" Jesus commands "Do unto others," and there is nothing evil if that help comes in the form of a .45 caliber slug.

Living and Dying by the Sword

Our witness becomes effective when we and our adversary both know that we are in control. Jesus exercised that control in Gethsemane, and told His captors so (Matthew 26:53). He could have called 72,000 angels to rescue Him, but He chose obedience to His Father's plan (Matthew 26:54). Jesus told Pilate the only reason that he had control over Him was because Jesus submitted to God's will (John 19:11).

"But," some will ask, "didn't Jesus deny us the use of weapons by saying, 'Those who live by the sword shall die by the sword'?" Good question. Yes, He said that, but in saying so He did not deny us the use of weapons or self-defense. We have already seen that Jesus made and used a weapon to clear out the Temple. Yet He did not chide Himself by saying, "He who lives by the scourge will die by the scourge." Was He a "Do as I say, not as I do" kind of guy? Of course not. His statement in the Garden pointed out that there is a proper time and place for everything, and that particular time was not the right time for using force on His behalf.

To see what Jesus meant, we must look at all four Gospel accounts of what happened that night in context. Just as reading the four accounts of the Last Supper give us a look at a complete Passover service, reading all four versions leading up to and through the events at Gethsemane give us the whole "die by the sword" story. First, let's examine Luke 22:35-38 to see how this episode began. Just before they all went to the Mount of Olives, Jesus addressed them in the upper room.

> And He said to them, "When I sent you out without purse and bag and sandals, you did not lack anything, did you?" And they said, "No, nothing." And He said to them, "But now, let him who has a purse take it along, likewise, also a bag, and let him who has no sword sell his robe and buy one. For I tell you, that which is written must be fulfilled in Me, 'And He was numbered with transgressors'; for that which refers to Me has its fulfillment."

And they said, "Look, Lord, here are two swords." And He said to them, "It is enough" (Luke 22:35-38).

Jesus refers to the time when He sent the Twelve out in pairs on their first mission trip.[1] He instructed them to take nothing extra with them so they could see how God would provide during that particular mission. They confirmed that all their needs were met on that mission. He later sent them out with 58 other disciples and when they returned, He confirmed His divine protection was on them: "Behold, I have given you authority to tread on serpents and scorpions and over all the power of the enemy and nothing will injure you" (Luke 10:19).

At the Last Supper, however, He told them that very soon He would no longer be physically with them to deflect the assaults by Satan's servants and the misfortunes of life (John 13:33,36; 14:1-4). Throughout His ministry, Jesus and His followers were physically protected from hostile people. His fellow Nazarenes were enraged at Him when He preached there. They tried to throw Him off a cliff, but He simply walked through them (Luke 4:16-30). Neither He nor the disciples were harmed by the crowd. The violent Gerasene demoniac fell at Jesus feet instead of attacking Him or the disciples (Luke 8:26-29). While preaching in the Temple, no one could lay hands on Him or the disciples (Luke 19:47-48, 20:19-20; John 8:20). God prevented it because Jesus' mission was not completed yet (John 7:31). Temple officers who were sent to arrest Him simply left, dumbfounded at the grace of His message (John 7:32, 43-46; 11:57). Jewish leaders even threatened to kill Lazarus after he was raised from the dead, but nothing came of it (John 12:9-11, 19). Finally, in His prayer in John 17, Jesus states that the safety of the disciples had been in His hands. "While I was with them, I was keeping them in Thy name which Thou has given me; *and I guarded them,* and not one of them perished but the son of perdition [Judas], that the Scriptures might be fulfilled" (John 17:12, emphasis mine). Logically, each time Jesus was threatened, the disciples were, too. Part of His job was to keep them safe to the end of His earthly ministry.

As He was leaving, He said they must be prudent in all things (Luke 22:36). In Matthew's account of Jesus sending them out on their first mission, Jesus warned them to "be shrewd as serpents, and innocent as doves" and to beware of treacherous men (Matthew 10:16-17). In other words, they were not to be naïve about the world. Paul says he was "in danger of death" many times during his missionary journeys and in danger from robbers, countrymen, the wilderness, Gentiles, the city, the sea, and from false brothers (2 Corinthians 11:23c and 26). Surely his experience of physical danger was not unique to Paul but was shared by all the apostles throughout their careers.

How high a priority did Jesus set on the disciples' need for swords for personal protection? He said swords were such necessary equipment that if they did not have one, they should sell their cloaks and buy one (Luke 22:36). The cloak, or robe, was a Jew's outer garment and one of his chief possessions. If a cloak was taken as collateral on a loan, the lender could not keep it from the borrower overnight, "for it is his only covering; it is his cloak for his body. What else shall he sleep in?" (Exodus 22:26-27). Since He was about to leave them, Jesus tells the disciples that swords would be more important than even their most valued possession. In a tough world, our lives and those of loved ones are, of course, more precious than possessions.

If you say, "Well, I just believe God will protect me, I do not need a gun," that is fine. That is your choice. But I bet you do not live that way in other aspects of your life. I will bet you buy the safest car you can afford, and you would use seatbelts even if it was not mandatory. You might have smoke alarms in your home and regularly see your dentist and doctor, too. If God will keep you from being a crime victim, why would He not prevent a car accident and a house fire? Do you truly believe the only victims of crime are non-Christians? Jesus said we would have a need for personal weapons. Paul had the need under various situations. You should prayerfully think it through. Remember, Jesus said that we are not to be naïve about the world. And 1 Timothy 5:8 says that a Christian man who does not take care of his family is worse than an unbeliever.

When Jesus told them to get swords, they replied, "Lord we have two swords." "That is enough," He answered (Luke 22:38). (If I had to guess, it was Peter and Simon the Zealot who had the swords!) Jesus told the disciples that they would need weapons when he left them. So then, what did Jesus mean about living and dying by the sword? [2] Was Jesus "the pacifist" playing a trick on them? Did He tell them they would need swords just to set Peter up to make the point that Christians are not to use weapons under any circumstances? Of course not! Not in this instance or at any other time in the Gospels do we find Jesus engaging in such theological bait-and-switch. God is not the author of confusion (1 Corinthians 14:33a). He did not tell them to bring those swords with them to the Garden that night because He was still there and had them under His protection. They had come to *pray*. Jesus had indicated at the Last Supper that the swords were a prudent precaution and would be needed *after* He had left them (Luke 22:35-38).

Jesus knew everything that would happen in the Garden that night: "You will all fall away because of Me this night, for it is written, 'I will strike down the shepherd, and the sheep of the flock shall be scattered'" (Matthew 26:31, quoting Zechariah 13:7). His first concern was that the Scriptures should be fulfilled, the same Old Testament prophecies by which His disciples would convince the Jews that He was the Messiah.[3] He would not let anyone hinder that goal. "How then shall the Scriptures be fulfilled, that it must happen this way? ... But all this has taken place that the Scriptures of the prophets may be fulfilled" (Matthew 26:54-56).[4] John 18:4 says, "Jesus therefore, *knowing all the things that were coming upon Him*, went forth, and said to them, 'Whom do you seek?'" (emphasis mine). Jesus did not fight in the garden because Judas, the priests, and their posse were not the enemy. Satan was. Jesus knew He would defeat Satan on the cross and with the empty tomb.

Peter's use of the sword was in total opposition to Jesus' goal that night. He needed no help since He was in complete control of the situation. Those in the arresting crowd were already terrified of Him. When He asked, "Whom do you seek?" they answered, "Jesus the Nazarene." Jesus responded, "I am He." When He said this, "*they drew back, and fell to the ground*" (John 18:1b-6, emphasis added). Jesus knew that even token resistance would have upset God's plan for the perfect Lamb to go to the cross as an unprotesting sacrifice. "He was oppressed and He was afflicted, yet He did not open His mouth. Like a lamb that is led to slaughter, and like a sheep that is silent before its shearers, so He did not open His mouth" (Isaiah 53:7). "Not by might nor by power, but by My Spirit, says the Lord of hosts" (Zechariah 4:6b).

After the trembling posse hit the dirt, Jesus asked again, "Who do you want?" and they said, "Jesus of Nazareth." "I told you that I am He; if therefore you seek Me, let these go their way." He said this so the prophecy would be fulfilled that

He would lose none of His faithful followers (John 18:7-9). The posse then surged forward to seize Jesus. Realizing what was about to occur, at least one of the disciples asked, "Lord, shall we strike with the sword?" (Luke 22:49). Without waiting for a reply, Peter impetuously struck off the ear of Malchus, a servant of the high priest. "Stop!" ordered Jesus, "Sheathe your sword! For all who live by the sword shall die by the sword. Do you realize I can snap my fingers and have 12 legions of angels here instantly? But then I wouldn't be the compliant sacrifice that God requires." Then He healed Malchus' ear and submitted to the arrest, while the disciples broke and ran.[5]

Look at Jesus' reaction to Peter's untimely defense. "Put the sword into its sheath; the cup which the Father has given me, shall I not drink it?" (John 18:11). Peter probably reacted out of anger or sheer bravado to disprove Jesus' recent prophecy that Peter would deny Him. Peter's misguided act was a perfect example that "[T]he anger of man does not achieve the righteousness of God" (James 1:20).

When Jesus stopped Peter and healed Malchus' ear, He prevented a possible riot. A melee between the disciples and the posse would have forced His divine intervention and thwarted the fulfillment of Scriptures that the disciples would escape (Zechariah 13:7). He said He could have summoned His angel army. (A Roman legion of the first century numbered 6,000 men.) Had He called 72,000 angels (12 legions) to defend Him and His men, He would not have been the prophesied submissive Lamb of God. He could have allowed the riot or stopped the arrest, but He wanted to prove once and for all that He was willingly submitting to the cross so the Scriptures would be fulfilled (Matthew 26:53-54).

Remember the power of angels from the story of Sennacharib, King of Assyria, and his siege of Jerusalem? Remember how one angel came down and slew 185,000 Assyrians? The point is that if *one* angel can do that, 12 legions of them can ruin your whole day!

So we return to the question: "Did Jesus tell them to buy swords just to set Peter up?" Definitely not! Can anyone find a place in the Gospels where Jesus asked His disciples to do something ungodly just to set them up for a fall and a lesson? Never. It is *not* in Jesus' nature to do so. What then did He mean by "Live by the sword and you'll die by it"? (Matthew 26:52). Remember, Jesus could read minds.[6] He knew they had brought the sword, but knowing already what would happen,

He could also accomplish several things since Peter had it.

First, He tells us not to resist legitimate authority with force. Those who do so can be lawfully harmed by law officers. The vast majority of the posse had no reason to suspect that arresting Jesus was not a lawful act. They were simply doing their jobs. Some felons have actually argued in court and on appeal they had a right to shoot at cops because the cops pulled their guns first! No court in the nation will allow a felon a self-defense claim against police. Despite the fact that many states allow you to resist an unlawful arrest, no lawyer worth his license will advise a client to do so. Instead, we always advise people to submit to unlawful arrest peacefully and to prove it is unlawful in court later. Once a police officer decides to bring you in over your resistance, he will not give up until you are in his control. He will either increase legitimate force levels or call in reinforcements until you are under control. Peter's resistance that night put the innocent lives of both the posse and the disciples at risk. Notice that Peter did not cut off the ear of Judas but that of Malchus, an innocent servant. Peter's downward slice was a cowardly strike at a non-threatening man who could not know the strike was coming. Jesus is telling Peter that those who use deadly force against the police or the innocent deserve death.

Secondly, He tells us that the Gospel is not defended by force but by love, which He showed by healing Malchus' ear (Luke 22:51). Jesus would *not* have endorsed the Crusades (an aggressive war "to recover the Holy Land"), the wars of the Reformation where Christians killed each other over theological differences, or the forced conversion of unbelievers as done by Charlemagne. Nor would He have supported the Inquisition or various aggressive "holy" wars against Turks, Jews, Incas, Aztecs, or "heretics." Neither would He endorse such "holy wars" today because none of these can be justified by Scripture. He certainly does not endorse shooting abortion doctors or bombing their clinics. As He told Pilate, Jesus' kingdom was not of this world; otherwise, He would have allowed His men to fight to advance it (John 18:36). Jesus told Peter He would neither tolerate forcing anyone to accept Him nor fighting to thwart God's will.

Third, when He said two swords were enough, Jesus predicted that when Peter brandished his sword, the skittish posse would assume that all the disciples were armed and let them escape rather than try to arrest them (John 7:12; 18:8-9).

Peter's sword convinced the posse that since they had Jesus, the small fry were not worth the trouble. Jesus' comment on living and dying by the sword told Peter that it was not the right time, place, attitude, or *purpose* for the use of a weapon. Remember, Jesus used a weapon (a whip) when He cleared the Temple. So Jesus is telling Peter that there is a proper time, place, and purpose for appropriate weapons, but the situation in the Garden was *not* appropriate for *any* resistance, let alone deadly force.

Next, when Jesus said, "Those who live by the sword shall die by the sword," He meant that those who resort to force in any argument to get their way, make their living by illegal violence, or rely on weapons *without* relying on God and His Word will end up dying outside of Christ. Those who rely on force alone are those who do not rely on the Fruit of the Spirit (Galatians 5:22-23). That night, Jesus was trying to teach Peter to trust Him alone and to save the sword for a proper time. Teaching the same reliance, Moses said:

> And you shall remember all the way which the Lord your God has led you in the wilderness these forty years, that He might humble you, testing you, to know what was in your heart, whether you would keep His commandments or not. And He humbled you and let you be hungry, and fed you with manna which you did not know, nor did your fathers know, that He might make you understand that man does not live by bread alone, but man lives by everything that proceeds from the mouth of the Lord (Deuteronomy 8:2-3).

In other words, if I think I am protected, successful, or a "real man" because I have a gun, talent, wealth, looks, or smarts, then my perception of the world is very narrow and spiritually bankrupt. If "Happiness is a Warm Gun" is the basis of my personal security, it is a dangerous life philosophy.[7] Believing that, I will never depend on God or develop godly relationships with anyone.

Jeremiah puts it this way:

> Thus says the Lord: Cursed is the man who trusts in mankind and makes flesh his strength and whose heart turns from the Lord. For he will be like a bush in the desert and will not see when prosperity comes, but will live in stoney wastes in the wilderness; a land of salt without inhabitants (Jeremiah 17:5-6).

Peter's' worldly outlook caused him to make "flesh his strength" that night and miss entirely what Jesus was doing. He missed the "prosperity" that Jesus' sacrifice and resurrection would bring. He refused to see that Jesus was fulfilling God's will, and he did not remember that Jesus had foretold all this many times.

The moral is that the self-made man worships his creator (himself) and nothing else. Jesus had been teaching the disciples for three and a half years, yet they still did not get it. In the Garden that night, Peter ignored Jesus' prophecies about His sacrificial death and attempted to substitute his own outcome over the one God had planned from the beginning.[8] By using his sword that night, Peter exemplified the saying that, "If your only tool is a hammer, pretty soon every problem starts to look like a nail." Instead, Jesus' statement to him was an admonition to "Trust in the Lord with all your heart, and do not lean on your own understanding. In all your ways acknowledge Him, and He will make your paths straight" (Proverbs 3:5-6). Just as a man cannot live a successful life by focusing on materialism (bread) alone, he cannot do it by forcing his way "by the sword" either. Only by total reliance on God's Word, Jesus, and His Spirit can we have "the more abundant life" (John 10:10).

Finally, notice that Jesus did not tell Peter to throw away the sword. He told him to "Put your sword back into its place" (Matthew 26:52b), "Stop! No more of this" (Luke 22:15), and "Put the sword into the sheath" (John 18:11b). He told him to re-holster it, not to throw it away. As Jesus had previously told the disciples, they would need swords later, but not now. Peter's mistake was not that he owned a sword, but that he used it at the wrong place, at the wrong time, and for the wrong purpose. Like Barney Fife, Peter was going off half-cocked. Like Sheriff Andy, Jesus was limiting his Barney to one bullet, only allowing him to load his gun (pull his sword) when He authorized it (which is the theme of this book!). Peter would learn from all this, so Jesus told him to keep it where he could still carry it until he really needed it and could use it in a godly manner.

Peter's mistake was not that he owned a sword, but that he used it at the wrong place, at the wrong time, and for the wrong purpose.

Jesus told Peter that no matter what tool we use to succeed or survive in life, that tool must be guided by God's Owner's Manual, the Bible: "But seek *first* His kingdom and His righteousness, and all these things shall be added to you" (Matthew 6:33, emphasis added).

Conclusion: Jesus was NOT a Pacifist!

So what can we conclude from studying Jesus on self-defense? First, we cannot say that He was a pacifist in the style of Ghandi or the modern day "surrender-first-and-ask-questions-later" crowd. He defied both religious and secular authority, refusing to be intimidated. When the Pharisees passed on death threats from Herod Antipas, Jesus replied that no one would hinder Him from His goal in Jerusalem (Luke 13:31-35). He was never namby-pamby-wishy-washy on things that mattered. He only got angry when religious people refused to recognize or allow the works of God as when He healed on the Sabbath or when they showed disrespect for His Father's house.[9] He told those in power directly when and how they were sinning and called on them to repent (Matthew 23). He neither fought anyone nor took any lives because that was not part of His earthly mission (Luke 9:56a). When rejected by some Samaritans, James and John wanted permission to zap them with lightning, but Jesus replied that He was not here to kill people but to save them. He then told them they were "of the wrong spirit," not only because that was not their mission but that giving the death penalty for an insult is the deed of a homicidal egomaniac, not a law-abiding person or a follower of Jesus (Luke 9:51-56).

Note that when humility was called for (in the boat during a storm, when unable to heal, accepting those not of their group) the disciples had little faith, but when they were irritated and vengeful, they thought they had God at their beck and call. In Luke 9:55, Jesus tells them "You don't even know yourselves." During His time on earth, fighting simply was not part of His mission: "He will not cry out or raise His voice, nor make His voice heard in the street. A bruised reed He will not break, and a dimly burning wick He will not extinguish" (Isaiah 42:2-3). He was here to give direction and hope and to rescue those whose faith was floundering and those trapped in sin.

Second, we can say that at least once, and probably twice, He used a weapon and physical force against defilers of the Temple. Therefore, He was not opposed to the use of force in every circumstance.

Third, Jesus states that weapons are proper for police and civilians against criminals. He asked those arresting Him, "Have you come out with swords and

clubs as against a robber?" (Luke 22:52b). Jesus contrasted the fact that though
He was innocent, they were nevertheless appropriately armed for dealing with
a known, violent criminal. To Him it was simple common sense and practice.
Likewise, He used armed householders and property owners as positive examples
on several occasions.

Fourth, He never explicitly condemned the use of force except in three
situations: in retaliation for an insult from a person with whom we have a
relationship, to force others to accept God's will, or to change God's prophetically
declared plan. He never condemned legitimate self-defense or just wars. In fact,
He commanded the ownership of weapons for His followers' protection after He
ascended.

Fifth, Jesus passed up every opportunity to preach pacifism each time He
referred to defense of self, property, or the practice of warfare. Instead, He used
the story of the Good Samaritan to reiterate the Old Testament's admonitions
to aid others in need in a timely fashion by appropriate means, which logically
includes use of weapons to help others.

Sixth, neither He, nor John the Baptist, nor any of the disciples condemned the
career of soldiering. In fact, Jesus called the Roman centurion the most faithful
person he had met (Matthew 8:5-13).

Finally, Jesus will be the general of an avenging army when He returns. This act
is totally opposed to the assertion that He is a pacifist. During His time on earth,
His primary mission was to persuade by example and words: to seek and save the
lost. On His return, He will be general, judge, jury, and executioner (Revelation
19:11-21). Read every word in red in the Gospels. Look at the historical, cultural,
and biblical context of what He said and did. In so doing, you will not find any
basis for the argument that Jesus rejected the appropriate use of force for Himself
or for us. "Jesus the Pacifist" is not in the Bible. Jesus did not fight because He had
God's protection, and the nature of His mission called for force only twice. We,
however, have no such explicit promise of physical protection at all times because
we are neither that unique person nor do we have His unique mission. Just
because He rarely used force *does not* mean that He forbids its use to us under the
legally proper circumstances. Rather, through His words and example, Jesus says
that use-of-force is proper to defend life and home, that warfare for proper reasons

is permitted, and that we should have weapons on hand for personal defense.

> Read every word in red in the Gospels. Look at the historical,
> cultural, and biblical context of what He said and did. In so doing,
> you will not find any basis for the argument that Jesus rejected the
> appropriate use of force for Himself or for us. "Jesus the Pacifist" is
> not in the Bible.

Opponents of the
Death Penalty

Considering the Death Penalty

When discussing self-defense, I must consider whether God allows us to take life for any reason, such as in the case of capital punishment. If God allows capital punishment, then He allows society to defend itself from murderers. And if society can defend itself, then so can an individual. I contend that the right of the government to execute criminals extends to police and deputized citizens, including those with carry permits.

The second most misquoted verse is the King James Version (KJV) of Exodus 20:13, "Thou shall not kill." It is constantly misquoted, especially by death penalty opponents. However, the actual Hebrew meaning is not *kill*, but, rather, *murder*. The command in Hebrew is *lo tirtzah*, "Thou shall not murder." *Lo taharog* is "Thou shall not kill." The commentary from ETZ HAYIM says, "Unlike other words for the taking of life, it [lo tirtzah] is never used in the administration of justice or killing in war."[1] All modern translations of the Bible, such as NKJV, RSV, NIV, and NASV properly translate it to read "Thou shall not murder." Murder is the unlawful, intentional killing of a human being. Other words are used in Hebrew for capital punishment, for killing in war, and for self-defense. Just as in modern penal codes, the Bible differentiates between intentional killing (which is divided into justifiable homicide and various degrees of murder) and accidental, unintentional homicide (manslaughter or criminally negligent homicide). Yet death penalty opponents take this one mistranslated verse out of context without ever considering that Jesus properly uses the term *murder* when quoting Exodus 20:13 in Matthew 5:21 of the KJV. He spoke Hebrew; He ought to know.

God is Sovereign

The controlling principle here is that God is sovereign. God has control over life and death, and life may not be taken without His permission. "Behold all souls are Mine. The soul of the father as well as the soul of the son is Mine" (Ezekiel 18:44). The soul who sins will die.[2] God is the giver of life. He united flesh with spirit, "and man became a living soul" (Genesis 2:7). Therefore, "do not murder" forbids the unlawful separation of the flesh and the spirit. Life belongs to God, and it is only under His objective absolutes that life becomes precious and immune from man-made excuses to take it. The Founders understood this when they wrote in the Declaration of Independence that mankind is "endowed by their creator with life." Life is one of those "unalienable rights" that government can neither give nor take away except by due process of law. God gives life, so He can declare the conditions by which life can be forfeited or taken.

Even assuming the word *murder* was properly translated *kill* in Exodus 20:13 of the KJV, it would be absurd to take that one verse as God's final word on the subject, ignoring all the other biblical references to killing, murder, self-defense, and capital punishment. In the Anglo-American common law (and the statutes of all 50 states), *murder* is defined as the illegal, intentional killing of a human being. It is an illegal form of generic homicide, which is the legally undesignated killing of a person. Homicide can be lawful or unlawful, or as statutes put it, justified (as in self-defense), excused (as in the insanity defense), or unjustified (as in murder or manslaughter).

When discussing the death penalty, we should keep in mind that most advocates on both sides of the issue agree in their respect and appreciation for the value of human life. Both sides argue from that starting point. For those who claim to live their lives according to the Bible, the paramount question must be how God wants us to respect, appreciate, and protect lives. The second question is whether God has authorized the death penalty as a way to respect and protect innocent life.

Death penalty opponents use Exodus 20:13 as their basis for argument. These individuals fall into two camps: those who have misunderstood this verse and those who willfully disregard the Scripture. Their argument runs: "God is love. His love is so complete and absolute that He would never allow one human to kill another for any reason. Therefore, 'Thou shall not kill' is God's blanket condemnation of all killing for any reason, including self-defense and capital punishment. Therefore, we should imprison murderers for life and leave their punishment to God."

Their opinion stems from genuine compassion and concern, but this uninformed and emotional argument does not go far. It is recitation of slogans without study, citation without context, and application without authority. Some people think "cleanliness is next to godliness" is in the Bible, but it is not. Paul says we are to destroy "speculations and every lofty thing raised up against the knowledge of God," and we must take "every thought captive to the obedience of Christ" (2 Corinthians 10:5). If this verse means anything, it says we shouldn't guess at what God means. Instead, we should research all He has to say on a certain subject. If He has addressed the subject, then we should not make pronouncements of policy that contradict His revealed will. Death penalty opponents have a lofty goal: mercy for murderers, regardless of their actions. But their "speculations" about the meaning and use of Exodus 20:13 is "against the knowledge of God."

The Death Penalty before the Time of Moses

Genesis 4:1-15 records the story of the first murder: Cain murdered his brother, Abel. God refused to accept Cain's offerings because Cain brought crops whereas Able sacrificed the *best* animals from his flock. This was apparently against God's instructions. Cain became jealous of and angry at Abel. God counseled Cain on what to do and how to deal with his anger (verses 6-7). Instead of repenting and mending his ways, Cain chose to eliminate his problem by murdering Abel. God gave Cain a chance to confess and repent (Where is your brother? What have you done?). Instead, Cain denied responsibility or knowledge. Finally in verse 14, Cain recognized the consequences of his action and naturally assumed that others would justly want to kill him for his crime. Notice he was not remorseful for his crime but only for the justice he anticipated. Even in his degenerate mind, he instinctively knew what the proper societal response demanded for the shedding of innocent blood (verses 13-15). Yet God did not kill him, nor did He allow anyone else to kill Cain. Instead, God cursed Cain to wander the earth, which would no longer yield crops to him. I can hear the death penalty opponents now:

"See? SEE? God wouldn't allow the death penalty on Cain or allow others to execute it. So there!" Again, if that were God's last word on the subject, I would be inclined to agree. However, that is not God's last word on the subject.

Reading further in Genesis 4:23, we see the result of God's forbearance. Five generations down, Lamech boasted to his wives that he had killed a man for wounding him and a boy for striking him, though he indicates that he knew both killings were unjustifiable. Then in verse 24, Lamech inferred that he would be protected from harm just like God said Cain would be protected even though he was a double murderer (referring to Genesis 4:15). Lamech's cynicism is apparent. He said, in effect, "If God protected my great-great-great granddaddy for one murder, then no one would dare touch me for killing *two* men! I can do as I please, and who's going to stop me?" God extended His love and forbearance to Cain and apparently did not punish Lamech. But why? We can only guess because there is no record of conversation about it between Lamech and God. He certainly hoped for both Cain and Lamech to repent. God says in Ezekiel 18:23-32 that He takes no pleasure in the death of the wicked and would prefer that they repent and live. In 2 Peter 3:10b, Peter tells us that God doesn't wish for anyone to perish but intends that all come to repentance. Perhaps God wanted early man to see that He valued life more highly than anything except righteousness, and therefore hoped that mankind would also revere life and refrain from violence in all forms. That very reasoning is one of the essential suppositions of the position of death penalty opponents: "Life is precious; can't we all just get along?" But God's extension of mercy did not work, as Lamech's sociopathic behavior and declaration show. The mercy shown to Cain acted as an incentive for Lamech to murder rather than as a deterrent. Moreover, by the time of Noah, "the wickedness of man was great on the earth, and that every intent of the thoughts of his heart was only evil continually" (Genesis 6:5). So what was the result of God's forbearance on the death penalty? Had man's innate goodness evolved into a non-violent utopia? Just the opposite: "Now the earth was corrupt in the sight of God, and the earth was filled with violence" (Genesis 6:11).

Let me suggest that the reason (besides hope of repentance) God did not institute the death penalty before the flood was to establish that mankind cannot control itself solely on the basis of grace. The absence of a death penalty gave everyone an implied license to kill. Unlike James Bond, the pre-flood citizens did not limit themselves to killing bad guys for the common good; they killed whenever and for whatever reason they chose, be it perceived need or whim. There was no moral or societal brake. The strong ruled. The weak were devoured. "Where there is no vision (revelation), the people cast off restraint, but blessed is he who keeps the law" (Proverbs 29:18). So the Lord told Noah that His grace and patience had come to an end: "My Spirit shall not strive with man forever ..." (Genesis 6:3a). "The end of all flesh has come before Me, for the *earth is filled with violence because of them,* and behold, I am about to destroy them with the earth" (Genesis 6:13, emphasis mine) because "the intent of man's heart is evil from his youth" (Genesis 18:21c).

I believe that God held back his wrath from Cain, Lamech, and all pre-flood people to show that, without a punishment equal to the abomination of murder, mankind would choose selfishness over the interests of others, up to the complete breakdown of society. Utter chaos resulted, wherein no good thing had a chance to thrive because life had no worth. Paul describes this process of degeneration in Romans 1:28-32. Without the "cruel and unusual punishment" of the death penalty, Man himself became cruel and unusual. I believe that God meant us to learn that without a death penalty society falls apart and the sanctity of life becomes meaningless. God wanted us to realize just how bad the world can get. If God ever let go of control of this world, we would soon turn it into Hell.

The most significant support for my thesis on God's intent for withholding the death penalty pre-flood is that His third command to Noah after he got off the ark (after be fruitful and multiply and not to eat flesh with blood) was to institute the death penalty:

And surely I will require your lifeblood; from every beast I will require it. And from every man, from every man's brother I will require the life of man. Whoever sheds man's blood, by man shall his blood be shed, for in the image of God He made man (Genesis 9:5-6).

Verse 6 is as plain as it gets: a 180-degree turn from His pre-flood policy. When you see the universally disastrous result of the pre-flood policy, God's policy change makes perfect sense. God was not surprised that a grace-toward-murderers policy failed. Being omniscient, He knew what the outcome would be, given man's fallen nature. On the contrary, He wanted to show us how bad the world would become if we deny human nature and leave the punishment of murderers until the hereafter (especially if like the pre-flood people, we live 600-900 years and think we are never going to die anyway).

"Whoever sheds man's blood, by man shall his blood be shed" (Genesis 9:6). The word *shall* in a statute always means *must*. The command is concise, sensible, and totally clear as to the reason for it: "[F]or in the image of God He made man." From Adam on, God intended that we should reflect His image. Not physically, of course; God is Spirit and has no body (John 4:24a). Rather, God intends for us to reflect His character: His love, compassion, forgiveness, and kindness, as well as His righteousness and justice, which He enforces through His own power and human agents throughout the Bible. If the Bible teaches us anything, it teaches that ideas and actions have consequences, and we, as individuals, are personally responsible for our ideas and actions. This is true from Genesis to Revelation. Therefore, even if it were proven that the death penalty is not a deterrent to murder, it does not matter because God made us and knows what is best for us. He says that the death penalty is good and right for us. Murder is a personal insult to God, who gave the victim his life and character. Therefore we have no right to quibble with His command to execute murderers. "Know that the Lord himself is God. It is He who has made us, and not we ourselves. We are His people and the sheep of His pasture" (Psalms 100:3).

Mosaic Law and the Death Penalty

God gave the Ten Commandments to Moses and Israel at Mount Sinai (Exodus 19:1-6). He did not stop with ten, though. He issued a system of laws for running their society, including criminal laws with a death penalty. The purpose of those laws was to make Israelite society a model of order, wisdom, and goodness to other nations (Exodus 15:26; Deuteronomy 4:5-8). They were to be the showcase of God's wisdom. Later prophets denounced Israel for making a mockery of God by disobeying His will and ruining their good example (Ezekiel 36:16-23). Part of that good example was forbidding murder and prescribing the death penalty for those who were convicted of it. Those who would have Exodus 20:13 mean "No killing, no how, no time!" don't have to look far to find that that interpretation was simply not God's intent or command. In just the next chapter, only twenty-five verses over from "Thou shall not murder," we find God ordering the death penalty in this verse: "He who strikes a man [with intent to kill] so that he dies shall surely be put to death" (Exodus 21:12). That torpedoes the assertion of death penalty opponents. It is not an anomaly, either. Verse 14 says, "If, however, a man acts presumptuously toward his neighbor, so as to kill him craftily, you are to take him even from my altar that he may die." (And that doesn't mean he dies of old age in prison.)

So premeditated or stealthy murder is to be punished by death. It was a tradition in most ancient cultures that a person running from the law or from the family of the victim could find immunity from punishment by laying his hands on a god's altar. In the Middle Ages, a person entering a church under the same circumstances could claim sanctuary from civil authorities. Yet God commands in Exodus 21:14b that murderers should enjoy *no* such sanctuary. They are to be removed from the altar and executed. This exact thing happened to Joab, the commander of David's armies, when Solomon became king. On his deathbed, David ordered Joab's execution for murdering Abner, Saul's general, after David had made peace with Abner and had declared the civil war over.[3] On David's death, Joab backed Solomon's brother Adonijah to succeed David, but David had declared Solomon his rightful heir. Having added treason to murder, Joab fled to the altar of the Tabernacle but was arrested there and executed (I Kings 2:28-35). God said Joab's blood was on his own head because he killed two righteous men without cause or order from David (verse 32). Exodus 21:14b indicates the church must not provide sanctuary or support to murderers; instead, it must let the civil authorities do their job and execute God's command. To do otherwise is sin.

Exodus 21 continues with more capital punishments for certain crimes. The death penalty is prescribed for kidnapping (verse 16), cursing parents (verse 17), and letting a known savage ox free so that a person is killed (verse 29). That is a total of five death penalties just in the next chapter from Exodus 20:13. Reading Exodus 21 reduces the death penalty opponents to one argument. They can only argue that God forbade the death penalty in Exodus 20:13 but then reversed Himself in Exodus 21. Certainly, God knew what He was doing to forbid murder, and then put teeth in the command.

Exodus 21 further clarifies the issue because it differentiates between murder and accidental killing without evil intent. Modern statutes call this kind of killing second degree murder, manslaughter, or criminally negligent homicide. God did not require the death penalty for unintentional killing. In verse 13, God says "But if he did not lie in wait, but God let him [the victim] fall into his hand [an accident], then I will appoint for you a place to which he may flee." These are the Six Cities of Refuge described primarily in Numbers 35:9-15, 22-28. A person who accidentally killed someone could flee there to escape "the avenger of blood" [the next-of-kin]. In practice, the congregation of the refuge city would judge between the slayer and the avenger (in other words, hold a trial) wherein the priests and Levites acted as judges (Deuteronomy 21:5). On a finding of no criminal intent, they would allow the slayer to reside in a refuge city until the death of the current high priest. When that high priest died, the slayer could return to his home and no one could touch him.

Similarly, accidental injury to a pregnant woman that caused her to miscarry was punished by a fine (Exodus 21:22). Once again, intentional, malicious killing was punished by death under the Mosaic Law. But as for the intentional murderer, God refused sanctuary in a city of refuge:

> But if there is a man who hates his neighbor and lies in wait for him and rises up against him and strikes him so that he dies, and he flees to one of these cities, then the elders of this city shall send and take him from there and deliver him into the hands of the avenger of blood, that he may die. You shall not pity him, but you shall purge the blood of the innocent from Israel, that it may go well with you (Deuteronomy 19:11-13).

So the judicial execution of murderers purges the nation of the guilt of innocent blood. "That it may go well with you" surely means that by killing murderers, Israel would avoid descending into pre-flood evil and chaos.

We must understand that God, starting at Sinai and throughout the rest of Exodus, Leviticus, Numbers, and Deuteronomy is setting up a civil and criminal legal system, complete with due process and procedure, courts and judges, and evidentiary laws and statutes. This contradicts those who, in ignorance of Scripture or in justification of their own vengeance, quote "an eye for an eye and a tooth for a tooth" (Exodus 21:23-25). The Mosaic Law can *never* be read as a system of personal vengeance. For example, Numbers 35:29-34 says:

> These things shall be for a statutory ordinance to you throughout your generations in all your dwellings. If anyone kills a person, the murderer shall be put to death at the evidence of witnesses, but no person shall be put to death on the testimony of one witness.

> Moreover, you shall not take ransom for the life of a murderer who is guilty of death, but he shall surely be put to death.

> You shall not take ransom for him who has fled to his city of refuge, that he may return to live in the land before the death of the priest.

> So you shall not pollute the land in which you are; for blood pollutes the land and no expiation can be made for the land for the blood that is shed on it, except by the blood of him who shed it.

> You shall not defile the land in which you live, in the midst of which I dwell; for I the LORD am dwelling in the midst of the sons of Israel.

One of the reasons God set up this system was to eliminate forever the vengeful, multi-generational blood feuds that still plague many cultures today. An eye was only taken for an eye after adjudication by civil authority, based on evidence of guilt and intent, with differences in punishment for negligence. Note that the eye would be taken by the judges, not by the injured party (Exodus 21:18-36). This ensured that the law's penalty was truly equal. The victim then had no chance to "twist the blade" (give more than he got).

Earlier, I divided the death penalty opponents into the deceived and those who willfully disregard Scripture. The most casual reading of Exodus 20 and 21 makes their scriptural positions untenable. God says that murder demands the life of the murderer after a judicial determination of guilt. The death penalty opponents might disagree but without a basis in Scripture. God warns us that "Fools mock at making amends for sin ..." (Proverbs 14:9a). The death penalty is God's way for the murderer to make amends. The conclusion, based on evidence from the Scriptures, is that God established and endorses the death penalty for certain crimes.

25

The Godly Person's Role in the Death Penalty

Moses relayed God's conditions (blessings and curses) to the Israelites: if they obeyed God, they could stay and prosper in Canaan or if they disobeyed, they would be punished and ejected. Three of the curses on the land are these: "Cursed is he who strikes [murders] his neighbor in secret …" and "Cursed is he who accepts a bribe to strike down an innocent person." "Cursed is he who does not confirm the words of this law by doing them. And all the people shall say, Amen" (Deuteronomy 27:24a, 25a, 26). Notice that, not only is the murder by stealth and for hire cursed, but also anyone who does not *enforce* the law against such cursed individuals. We are to be "our brother's keeper." As Jeremiah warned them:

> Do not trust in deceptive words, saying "This is the temple of the Lord, the temple of the Lord, the temple of the Lord." For if you truly amend your ways and your deeds, if you truly practice justice between a man and his neighbor, if you do not oppress the alien, the orphan, or the widow, and *do not [knowingly, intentionally] shed innocent blood in this place,* nor walk after other gods to your own ruin, then I will let you dwell in this place, in the land that I gave your fathers forever and ever (Jeremiah 7:4-7, emphasis mine).[1]

Murderers are the antithesis of God's entire purpose for mankind. They have no respect for anyone God created in His image or for His wish that they bless the world. As Creator, God is the only one who has blanket authority to take life or authorize man to do so. He has a plan for each person, and the ultimate part of that plan is that each person should come to know God through His Son, Jesus (John 3:16-17). The murderer arbitrarily cuts short that life process for his victim, and all the potential for good the victim might do for himself and others is snuffed out. The murderer has also prevented any good the victim's potential descendants might have done for society. To take illegally the life of one He created to reflect His character is the ultimate blasphemy against God.

Therefore, it is incumbent on the righteous in society to execute judgment on the lawbreaker. I have heard some say, "Well, I'm *for* the death penalty, but I personally couldn't throw the switch. After all, I'm a Christian and that would not go with living a holy life." Nothing could be further from the truth! When Moses came down from Sinai and found the people worshipping the golden calf, he called for whoever was on the Lord's side to come to him, and the men of the tribe of Levi (the priests, set aside for holy duties) responded.

> And he said to them 'Thus says the Lord, God of Israel, Every man of you put his sword upon his thigh, and go back and forth from gate to gate in the camp, and kill every man and his brother, and every man and his friend, and every man and his neighbor' [who had worshipped the golden calf]. So the sons of Levi did as Moses instructed, and about three thousand men of the people fell that day (Exodus 32:27-28). Then Moses said, 'Dedicate yourselves today to the Lord – for every man has been against his son and against his brother – *in order that He may bestow a blessing upon you today'* (Exodus 32:29).

The people as a whole were blessed and forgiven because the Levites executed God's judgment on the idolaters. Had they gone unpunished, not only would God's punishment on idol worship have been disobeyed (Deuteronomy 27:15), but Israel would have had that core group of disobedient people to lead them astray again. Remember these were not just people who were tempted and led astray; these were inventors of a replacement god, rejecters of the true God, who were determined to lead and even force others to share in their rejection of God. The Levite executioners were blessed for ridding the nation of them. Thus, they avoided the curse of Deuteronomy 27:26, "Cursed is he who does not confirm the words of this law by doing them."

Phineas was another holy executioner. His story is found in Numbers 25: 1-8. He was a priest and grandson of Aaron. At Peor, near the borders of Canaan, the Israelites began to worship the local Moabite god (Baal-Peor) and to have sex with and marry the Moabite women (verses 2-5). One Israelite even brought one of these girls back home. Right in front of Moses and the elders, he took her into his tent (verse 6). In Deuteronomy 23:3-5, God ordered that the Hebrews must not marry any Moabite or Ammonite. When Phineas saw this flagrant violation of God's law against idol worship, fornication, and intermarriage, he seized a spear, went into the tent and, finding the couple in an embrace, ran them both through. God had sent a plague among the Israelites who had worshipped Baal-Peor and fornicated with the Moabites, killing 24,000 of them. As soon as Phineas executed the two lovers, the plague stopped (Numbers 25:1-9). Then the Lord told Moses:

> Phineas has turned away My wrath from the sons of Israel, in that he was jealous with My jealousy among them, so that I did not destroy the sons of Israel in My jealousy. Therefore I say, 'Behold, I give him my covenant of peace; and it shall be for him and his descendants after him, a covenant of perpetual priesthood, because he was jealous for his God, and made atonement for the sons of Israel' (Numbers 25:10-13).

Phineas was a holy executioner; he blessed his nation, himself, and his descendants by his action.

In Psalms 149: 5-7, Israel was commanded to execute judgment on criminals, and it was an honor for godly people to do so: "Let the godly ones exult in glory. Let them sing with joy on their beds, let the high praise of God be in their mouths, and a two edged sword in their hand. To execute vengeance on the nations, and punishment on the peoples." Don't miss the guiding principle here. Where God decides and designates that some deserve death, it is incumbent upon obedient people to execute that judgment. Their obedience benefits us all. Society is blessed by not reverting to pre-flood chaos. People are warned and deterred from committing murder. Potential victims are blessed by not being victimized. When a murderer is killed, he, at least, will never kill again.

But enough about men; what about angels? What if God ordered an angel to execute someone? Would an angel say, "Wait, God, I can't kill anyone. I'm a holy angel"? King Hezekiah of Judah was attacked by the Assyrians under King Sennacherib. The story is told in Isaiah 36 and 37. Sennacherib's envoys publicly insulted God, scoffing at His ability to save Jerusalem. They stated that He was like the useless, false gods of all the other nations Assyria had conquered and could do nothing to help Judah. God replied through Isaiah that He would save Jerusalem. "Then the angel of the Lord went out, and struck 185,000 in the camp of the Assyrians, and when men arose early in the morning, behold, all of these were dead" (Isaiah 38:36). God used an angel as a holy executioner to save and bless His people.

In the Old Testament, God used angels and men as executioners. The fact that they executed His judgement did not diminish His holiness or theirs. Rather, they responded as obedient servants to the sovereign will, knowledge, and justice of a

Holy God. The execution itself is a holy act. Therefore, no Christian should think that carrying out God's command to execute murderers, whether by judicial order or in self-defense, is contrary to a holy life.

From the Old to the New Testament, God says that intentional murder causes a man to forfeit his own life. The killer has ended any chance of his victim ever fulfilling his ultimate destiny and thus forfeits his own future. He has insulted God by killing a fellow human made in God's image. His executioner, in God's view, has done a holy and beneficial act for mankind. "If a man sheds man's blood, by man shall his blood be shed" (Genesis 9:6).

God also explains the death penalty requirement by introducing the concept that shedding innocent blood pollutes the land. Let us re-examine what God said through Moses:

> And these things shall be for a statutory ordinance to you throughout your generations and in all your dwellings. If anyone kills a person, the murderer shall be put to death at the evidence of witnesses, but no person shall be put to death on the testimony of one witness. Moreover, you shall not take ransom for the life of a murderer who is guilty of death, but he shall surely be put to death. And you shall not take ransom for him who has fled to a city of refuge, that he may return to live in the land before the death of the priest. So you shall not pollute the land in which you are; for blood pollutes the land and no expiation can be made for the land for the blood that is shed on it, except by the blood of him who shed it (Numbers 35:29-33, emphasis mine).

What does "pollute the land" mean? Obviously, God is not concerned with spilled blood affecting the environment. The KJV uses the word *defile* to mean any act that makes a person, or thing, unsuitable for holy uses (for example, touching or eating unclean animals (Leviticus 15:25-31); bleeding from disease (Leviticus 15:25-31); rape (Genesis 34:2); priests touching the dead (Leviticus 21:1); and leaving an executed criminal to hang overnight (Deuteronomy 21:22-23). If a society allows murderers to go without punishment, individuals of that society eventually become callous about human life. The land is polluted by the cheapening of life's worth. Without justice for murderers, the nation's psyche is polluted by the nagging suspicion that there is no justice and, ultimately, no safety. Life is precious, but the murderer has polluted the land by spilling innocent blood. From that point, the murderer's life is no longer precious to God or to man, but is an abomination. His continued existence is an affront to a holy God, to an ordered society, and to the lost life of the victim.

Shedding innocent blood pollutes a society's thinking. A society that does not stop murder will become as callous as Israel did, so God expelled them from the Promised Land until they learned their lesson. In other words, to implement the death penalty is to value innocent life.

Shedding innocent blood pollutes the land, and John Donne was right when he said that when the bell tolls, it tolls for us all. Remember, "[T]he fear of the Lord is the beginning of wisdom; a good understanding have all those who do His commandments; His praise endures forever (Psalms 111:10).

What Good is the Death Penalty?

In Psalms, God's attitude towards murderers and evildoers is readily apparent. I will cite just a few examples. "The face of the Lord is against evildoers, to cut off all memory of them from the earth. Evil shall slay the wicked, and those who hate righteousness will be condemned (Psalms 34:16&21). "[He] who conceives mischief, and brings forth falsehood. He has dug a pit and hollowed it out, and has fallen into the hole which he has made. His mischief will return upon his own head, and his violence will descend upon his own pate" (Psalm 7:14(b), 15 and 16).

There is a reason why the wicked should be slain. Remember the discussion about the 5th commandment? Killing murderers not only stops their murdering, it cuts off a sinful example to others who might emulate them (especially without a death penalty). Furthermore, many mass murderers kill to be known and remembered.[2]

The main societal reason for the death penalty is that it deters murder. In John Lott's book *Freedomnomics*, he discusses the effect of executions on the murder rate since 1950. He explains that after the Supreme Court withdrew its 1968 moratorium on the death penalty in 1976, it took about 15 years for the appeals to finish and the execution lines to start moving. According to Lott's findings, murder rates fell dramatically until leveling off in 1998 at 1965-1968 levels.[3] When the death penalty was abandoned or rarely used, murderers were encouraged. Blood polluted the land.

How do murderers think? Psalms 10:3-11 describes the attitude of sociopaths. These scriptures tell us that they see ordinary citizens as food, as a resource only. More importantly, they believe that they will never be brought to justice. David asks God to break the wicked man's arm and to wipe out his wickedness (Psalms10:14-15) so that the weak might be encouraged and protected. Without a death penalty, society lives in fear. There are similar passages in Psalms, but I cite those in my discussion of self-defense.

The book of Proverbs provides examples of godly life principles and the thought processes of good and evil men, so an examination of these is profitable for our subject. On the death penalty, Solomon first personifies Wisdom and makes the comment, "For he who finds me [Wisdom] finds life, and obtains favor from the Lord. But he who sins against me injures himself, and those who hate me love death" (Proverbs 8:35-36). This introduces a constant theme of Psalms and Proverbs: the wicked bring about their own destruction. In regard to criminals, no one disputes the common wisdom seen in the movies of the 30s and 40s in the line, "He asked for it," or the famous Texas truism, "He needed killin'." Here are some examples: "but the wicked will be cut off from the land ..." (Proverbs 2:22a); "A man's own folly ruins his life, yet his heart rages against the Lord" (blaming God for his own wrong choices, Proverbs 19:3); "The Lord works out everything for His own ends, even the wicked for a day of disaster," (Proverbs 16:4); "A man who remains stiff-necked after many rebukes will suddenly be destroyed without remedy," (this certainly refers to the career criminal and his possible demise at the hands of a prepared victim, the efficacy of habitual offender laws, or the death penalty (Proverbs 29:1), "Stern discipline is for him who forsakes the way, he who hates reproof (correction) will die," (Proverbs 15:10); "Those who forsake the law praise the wicked (think of the death penalty opponents who constantly want to show how murderers have *rehabilitated* themselves) but those who keep the law strive with [resist] them," (Proverbs 28:4); "[T]he income of the wicked, punishment" (Proverbs 10:16b); "The way of the Lord is a stronghold for the upright, but ruin to the workers of wickedness" (Proverbs 11:5(b); "[H]e who pursues evil will bring about his own death," Proverbs 11:19(b); "When it goes well with the righteous, the city rejoices, and when the wicked perish, there is glad shouting" (Proverbs 11:10); and finally:

There are six things which the Lord hates, yes seven which are an abomination to Him: haughty eyes, a lying tongue, and hands that shed innocent blood, a heart that devises wicked plans, feet that run rapidly to evil, a false witness who utters lies, and one who spreads strife among brothers (Proverbs 6:16-19).

Therefore, God hates criminal acts (not criminals) in general, intentional murder in particular, and He requires the life of the murderer and punishment for lesser criminals. "An evil man is bent only on rebellion, so a cruel messenger [the executioner] will be sent against him" (Proverbs 17:11). If God's attitude is so clear, why do opponents of the death penalty attempt to stand up for murderers on biblical grounds?

According to Lott's findings, murder rates fell dramatically until leveling off in 1998 at 1965-1968 levels. When the death penalty was abandoned or rarely used, murderers were encouraged. Blood polluted the land.

Criminal Procedure and the Death Penalty

In Ecclesiastes 8:11, Solomon says: "Because the sentence against an evil deed is not executed quickly, therefore the hearts of the sons of men among them are given fully to do evil." The wisest man who ever lived (inspired by the Holy Spirit) tells us two things here. First, that punishment of evildoers *is* a deterrent to others doing evil. Second, the deterrent effect is enhanced by the swift execution of the sentence. My own state, Alabama, is one of the top states (third after Texas and Florida) in frequency of executions. Yet, because of the appeal process, murderers are usually not put to death until 12 to 20 years after their convictions. Moreover, it can easily be 2 years or more from the commission of the crime until the trial.

This raises a real problem with our judicial system whose earliest roots arise from the Bible. "Innocent until proven guilty" is God's concept, given to the Jews through the Law. God also ordained procedures and rules of evidence, all designed to protect the rights of the accused as well as those of society. Law in our society is a product of this tension between the rights of the individual and the right of society to be protected from evildoers. While not perfect (no manmade institution is), the law is a reliable, time-proven mechanism for delivering justice to both the guilty and to the innocent. Until recently, the advantage was mostly on the side of the State. Since the 1950s, the U.S. Supreme Court, state supreme courts, and legislatures have found new rights for the accused in the Bill of Rights. Most folks have no problem with things like discovery, which allows a defendant to know not only much of the evidence the state intends to introduce against him but also any evidence that would tend to show his innocence.[1] This is only fair. Yet, many citizens are frustrated by the seemingly endless tiers of state and federal appeals available to a convicted murderer. Even more protest the reversal of a conviction based on legal technicalities. Yet, these technical rules of evidence and procedure are considered essential for a fair trial and have been developed for good reasons over centuries. Let me assure you, reasonable judges, lawyers, legislators, and citizens differ and agonize over the application of these rules. This is how law develops over time. Otherwise, we would still have trial by combat or throw the accused in a river to see if they float.

Defense lawyers are often asked, "How can you defend a guilty person?" I reply that lawyers often do not know whether their client is guilty. About 95 percent end up pleading guilty (but that is later in the process). Some of the accused are innocent or the evidence against them is very weak, making the prosecutor's job difficult at trial. The main job of a defense counsel is to make sure that the state proves each element of the crime beyond a reasonable doubt. If the state were not forced to do so every time, then police and prosecutors could use false evidence and lying testimony to assure a conviction. If defense lawyers do their jobs, then honest citizens need not fear the knock in the night that citizens of other countries dread. Good defense lawyers keep the process and its participants honest. If after doing their best, the defense loses, and the judge sentences the guilty to 30 years in prison, we can all sleep soundly, knowing the accused was truly guilty and the state had to work hard to prove its case honestly beyond a reasonable doubt.

Some rules for appeal require reversal when mistakes are made by the defense attorneys, prosecutors, and judges. The appellate courts act as referees. Most of these rules assure the time-tested basis of a fair trial. Some cases or sentences are reversed when, after trial, a higher court changes the law and requires reversal, such as when the Supreme Court declared a moratorium on executions in 1968. But there is no excuse for convictions and subsequent reversals of convictions based on intentional misconduct by prosecutors and police. Lying, suborning perjury, and manufacturing evidence have *no* place in the courtroom! Society's right to defend itself does not mean the end justifies the means! Mosaic Law did not allow any conviction on less than competent evidence. Such illegal behavior destroys confidence in the system and merely gives ammo to the arguments of the death penalty opponents. Instead, we need to take God's prescription for lying under oath seriously.

> If a malicious witness rises up against a man to accuse him of wrongdoing, then both men who have the dispute shall stand before the Lord, before the priests and judges who will be in office in those days. And the judges shall investigate thoroughly, and if the witness has accused his brother falsely, *then*

*you shall do to him just as he had intended to do to his brother. Thus you
shall purge the evil from among you. And the rest will hear and be afraid, and
will never again do such an evil thing among you. Thus you shall not show
pity:* life for life, eye for eye, tooth for tooth, hand for hand, foot for foot.
(Deuteronomy 19:16-21, emphasis mine)

Moreover, reliable DNA evidence should be retroactively applied to every
conviction possible. That will help insure that our prisons do not house or execute
innocent people. The entire ins and outs of the appeal system are beyond the
scope of this book. There is much good, but some wrong, about it. The problems
can be solved by honest and informed voters, legislators, and the legal profession.
Yet God's Word stands! Delays in punishment detract from the deterrent effect
(Ecclesiastes 8:11). Our duty is to make sure that any delays are only necessary
and legitimate ones.

Some death penalty opponents might say, "You argue that the death penalty
is a deterrent to murder, yet everyone knows it is not." However, the death
penalty opponents are wrong. In fact, studies prior to the Supreme Court's 1968
moratorium on the death penalty concluded that a one percent increase in the
U.S. execution rate per year yields a four to seven percent decline in the overall
murder rate the next year.[2] Studies since then have shown even higher per capita
reductions of the murder rate.

In his excellent book *Freedomnomics,* John Lott affirms these studies. From his
research, Lott concludes that a murderer is 20 times more likely to be executed
than a cop is to be killed in the line of duty in any given year.[3] He notes that while
the Supreme Court reinstated the death penalty in 1976, because of appeals it was
not until the early 1990s that executions really increased. Lott affirms, "Between
1991 and 2000, there were 9,114 fewer murders per year, while the number of
executions rose by seventy one." Studies showed that executions during the 1990s
contributed to a 12 to 14 percent drop in overall murders. Moreover, of the 12
studies done by economists since the mid-1990s, nine studies concluded that
executions lowered murder rates. Three studies said that executions were of no
effect, but none found that the death penalty increased murder rates.[4]

Execution of death sentences were not the only factor though. Murder and
other violent crime rates had peaked in 1993, but by 2005 they had fallen to
1968 levels.[5] Why the drop? Lott gives three major factors: imposition of the death

Studies showed that executions during the 1990s contributed to a 12 to 14 percent drop in overall murders. Moreover, of the 12 studies done by economists since the mid-1990s, nine studies concluded that executions lowered murder rates. Three studies said that executions were of no effect, but none found that the death penalty increased murder rates.

penalty; increased incarceration rates along with longer sentences for subsequent felonies (3 strikes and you're out); and finally, right to carry laws.[6]

These facts are secondary, however, to the revealed will of God. Whether we can perceive the benefits of obeying God or not, we must still obey and trust in His wisdom. It does not matter if the death penalty is a deterrent or not. If God says to put murderers to death after due process, then we are wise to obey.

Throwing Out the Baby with the Bathwater

Now, I want to share my own thoughts on the drawn-out process in capital cases. We lawyers are no less susceptible (and perhaps more so) than other professions to think that a subject in our purview is our exclusive domain. I perceive us viewing capital murder cases and the death penalty with a kind of intellectual blinders. Doing so allows us to isolate the subject in the legal realm without comparing it to other human experience. If we do so, we endow the legal process of trying, sentencing, appealing, and executing a death case with a sanctity it does not deserve.

You see, a capital case is considered a *higher* kind of criminal case by the legal system because the defendant could lose his life. The broad discovery, the increased funds for defense lawyers, experts, and forensic tests, along with the ability to file multiple appeals are not afforded to any other defendant for any other kind of crime. In Alabama, for instance, there is no limit to the bill an appointed attorney can submit in defending an indigent client in a capital case. We justify this by comparing the indigent defendant's resources with the seemingly limitless resources of the state. In all other criminal cases, defense fees are limited by scaling the appointed lawyer's pay to the severity of the crime. The less severe the crime, the lower the statutory fee allowed. We all realize that *equal justice under law* is not an absolute rule, but an ideal for the conduct of courts. If it were the former, then a misdemeanor shoplifter would be entitled to all the advantages given in defense of the capital murderer. As a result, that case would drag on without resolution for as long as a death penalty case does. Finality in criminal adjudications would disappear, as would the deterrent effect of sentencing. In effect, because society has finite resources, the speeder, the shoplifter, the car thief, the drug trafficker, the armed robber, the child molester, and the non-capital murderer receive less justice than the capital murderer does.

A common sense reason exists for this inherent inequality. Though the awesome wealth and power of the state or federal government is stacked against the criminal defendant in every case, to allow the criminal defendant the same resources that back the policeman and the prosecution in every sort of case would financially ruin our society. Of course, this is one of the major strategies of the death penalty opponent defense bar: to justify and demand more and more of the state's time and resources in death cases until it is simply too expensive to execute a death sentence. Who has not heard the cost/benefit argument that it is far cheaper for the State to incarcerate for life than to execute? This argument is the result of a conscious, widespread tactic by death penalty opponents to make the cost of the death penalty too high for society to bear. Anyone with the temerity to ask whether *some* of the safeguards for a fair trial or appeal should be removed is met with a contemptuous, "But the State is trying to take the man's *life!*" Then they will claim the death penalty is not a deterrent anyway. How can it be a deterrent if it takes 25 years from sentence to execution?

What happens when we compare the vast difference in resources allotted to a shoplifter case versus capital murder? Death penalty opponents say, "Where a murder defendant's life is at stake, no expense is too great, no delay too long, no argument is too redundant to save it." My question is, why? If the trial has resulted in a legal guilty verdict, an experienced judge has sentenced death, and the appellate courts find no violation of law or procedure in the trial, then why allow so many "bites at the apple," state and federal, on appeal? In what other field of human endeavor do we go to such lengths, at such cost, by so many to first eliminate every possible reason to proceed before we perform the required action?

Suppose a murderer has just killed a man with an axe. He raises it again and advances on his victim's wife, who kills him with a bullet to the brain. There would be only a brief police investigation and two funerals. The murderer would not get (after two years of preparation and legal wrangling) a trial, which he would have received after successfully murdering both his victims. He would not get a sentencing hearing to present mitigating and aggravating factors in his life so that the jury could fix punishment at death or life without parole. A sentencing hearing would have allowed the jury to hear how his father molested him, his mother was a prostitute, and his I.Q. is two points below average (mitigating factors). The wife who shot him did not need to know about his sad upbringing or that he had a record of (among many other things) a prior attempted murder, a rape that left his victim crippled, and a crack habit (aggravating factors). In contrast, the victim's husband did not have the benefit of multiple appeals to courts to stop the axe in mid-swing. Nor did he have the chance to say goodbye to loved ones and put his affairs in order, as his killer would have had. Yet the wife's shot to the head is all the due process the murderer will get, and society is perfectly happy with that.

Had the wife not had a gun, he would have killed them both. When apprehended, the killer would have had the super process of trial, of presenting his good and/or unfortunate side to the sentencing jury, and of multiple appeals. The privilege to place mitigating factors before a jury is not available to a criminal defendant in any other crime! Not only that, but he has an advantage on appeal that no other kind of criminal defendant has: the "plain error rule." In an appeal for any other kind of conviction, many procedural traps can negate a defendant's appeal. The biggest is the preservation rule. The judge, prosecutor, defense attorney, police, or even the jury can make an error in a non-capital trial that is clearly against the law and that would cause the trial to be reversed (either for a new trial or dismissed completely). However, the error must be preserved by defense counsel's objection and the judge's adverse ruling (overruled). That objection and the adverse ruling must also be on the record in order for the appellate court to consider the error on appeal. The preservation rule must be enforced, or reversals and trials would be endless because few trials are conducted perfectly. Society cannot afford the lack of finality.

But in capital cases, the "plain error rule" not only negates this preservation-of-error requirement, it also requires appellate courts at each level to search the record for any mistake, adverse ruling, or procedural error that could reverse a capital case. This "plain error rule" stands as the goalie before the capital defendant's net through every retrial and every appeal in every appellate court, state or federal, up to and including the U.S. Supreme Court. If the defendant's counsel was inexpert or asleep at the wheel, the "plain error rule" saves counsel from the need to preserve the error by an objection and an adverse ruling. Moreover, time or cost limits are rarely set on the process no matter how redundant. (Congress has recently enacted a federal habeas corpus limitation on numbers of those type appeals, but I refer to the appellate process as a whole.) After all this scrutiny and all of these reviews, the "plain error rule" ensures that the chance an innocent man will be executed is *extremely* small.

Now we return to the ax-murderer and the armed wife. If she kills her attacker, society consents to the timely dispatch of the murderer by his intended victim as the only legal process he is due. If he kills her, society demands that no time, resources, or expense be spared before the sentence is implemented by the state. Why this contrast? In both cases, "A man's life is at stake." Why in the one instance should the threat of judicial extinction require a Herculean effort on his behalf to preserve his guilty life when, on the other hand, his immediate extinction by his intended victim is perfectly acceptable? What if a policeman had come in just as he raised the axe to strike the husband? The law in every state allows the officer to use deadly force against the attacker to prevent either death or permanent maiming injury to the intended victims. The result is a minimal process: one funeral.

What if after being shot, the attempted capital murderer survives as far as the ER? After hours of heroic effort to no avail, doesn't the medical team cease their efforts at some point and declare him dead? Will they not make a cost/benefit analysis on spending any more time on his hopeless cause when their time and resources could be better used to save those who can be saved? It is called *triage*. Every Boy Scout learns this in first aid.

You see the analogy. Many people die in our country every day, most of them innocent. They die from hundreds of different causes, yet we as a society agree that those losses are both inevitable and acceptable. How many will die in car wrecks today? Should we stop driving until cars and trucks are so safe that no innocent person can die in one? Or should we say it is better that 300 million should walk rather than one child be killed in a car wreck? Let me assure you, the day we build a perfectly safe vehicle, it will be so expensive that no one will be able to afford it. Realizing that, society has decided that the advantages of having cars far outweigh the cost of innocent life. Each day we accept a certain level of imperfection that causes loss of innocent life because those things benefit everyone beyond the inevitable unfortunate losses. For instance, in 2007, four times more people died nationally of complications from medical or surgical care than from firearms accidents.[7] So where are the outraged cries to ban doctors and hospitals? There are none, because we all know that even with its imperfections, modern medicine's benefits far outweigh the price its innocent victims sometimes pay. In short, we intuitively know and accept that *no* human process, machine, or practice can be perfect. Then why do we expect perfection from a death penalty case?

How often have you heard the old shibboleth: "Better a hundred guilty men walk free than one innocent man lose his life." How so? If we agree that perfection in any endeavor is not possible in this world, why should we attempt the impossible in a death penalty case? I am not advocating deliberate or negligent convictions and executions of the innocent. After a guilty verdict in a capital case, the jury can recommend a sentence of life-without-parole or the death penalty. If, after hearing all the facts, they decide on life-without instead of death, they have acted justly and we should have no complaint with it. Exodus 23: 6-7 says: "You shall not pervert the justice due to your needy brother in his dispute. Keep far from a false charge, and do not kill the innocent and the righteous, for I will not acquit the guilty." American (and Mosaic Law) requires that a jury be convinced of guilt beyond a reasonable doubt (that is 98 percent certainty of guilt). No matter how solid the evidence, most murderers maintain their innocence their entire lives. Just because one of them *might* be telling the truth against all evidence and reason does not justify a system that releases troops of guilty predators to continue their criminal careers. On a cost/benefit basis, the benefit of exterminating 99 evil murderers at the cost of one innocent is a no-brainer. This is the same cost/benefit basis upon which society bases all its other decisions. How is it better if 99 guilty murderers go free to keep from accidentally or mistakenly killing one innocent man? So each of those 99 can then go out and murder one more victim? What if only one of the 99 returns to his old ways and murders someone? What if his victim was the one wrongfully accused guy that the system saved while letting the 99 go free? What if his victim was your child or wife? Why is the life of the unjustly executed more important than any other victim of murder? We know that two-thirds of the Taliban and al-Qaeda POWs we let go will return to fight against us. What if out of every 99 we release, 66 come back with atomic suitcase bombs? What do we say to the hundreds of thousands they kill? What do we say to the families of the soldiers they kill in conventional combat?

The Mosaic Law did not demand perfection, just proper procedure and lack of malice, bribery, and perjury. We should not require perfection from our criminal justice system either, but we should do the best we can. This logic is neither cold-hearted nor unusual. If we inadvertently execute an innocent man on rare occasions, it is exactly the sacrifice we expect and receive when a good soldier gives his life for his country so that the evil enemy might be defeated and his fellow citizens might survive. The desired end is also the same: the preservation of a good society by the sacrifice of an innocent in order to destroy evil. So from now on, let us have a sense of perspective and proportion toward the death penalty in context with all human experience. Given the slim chance that an innocent will be executed versus the ruinous expense of the appellate process and realizing the deterrent effect of the death penalty, is it not time for society to consider the cost/benefit of our present capital appeals system?

Ezekiel lets us in on God's attitude about the death penalty. Chapter 18 confronts Israel over their assertion that He was unfair in meting out punishment. They thought that God had punished them with exile to Babylon for the sins of their ancestors rather than their own. Therefore, they wanted to punish the sons for their fathers' sins at law, claiming the policy reflected God's justice. God pointed out that they were in exile for their own sins, and then proceeded to show them His policy for punishment (Ezekiel 18:30).

He first established His sovereignty saying "[A]ll souls are Mine ... The soul who sins will die" (Ezekiel 18:4). Then He said that each person is responsible for his own actions: "If a man is righteous, and practices justice and righteousness ... he is righteous and will surely live, declares the Lord God" (Ezekiel 18:5, 10b). But, if that man has "... a violent son who sheds blood ... he [the son] will surely be put to death; his blood will be on his own head" (Ezekiel 18: 10a, 13b). "'Do I have any pleasure in the death of the wicked,' declares the Lord God, 'rather than that he should turn from his ways and live?' " (Ezekiel 18:23). " 'For I have no pleasure in the death of anyone who dies' declares the Lord God. 'Therefore repent and live' " (Ezekiel 18:32; 33:11a).

The Death Penalty in the New Testament

Death penalty opponents will say, "Yes, the Old Testament endorses the death penalty, but God's attitude as revealed by Jesus in the New Testament is entirely different. The God of the Old Testament seems vengeful, angry, and harsh in His judgments. But Jesus preaches love, forgiveness, and grace, and now we are under grace. Surely God does not endorse the death penalty through Jesus?"

While this attitude is sincere, it is also inaccurate. Scripture is clear that our loving God, the "God of the Old Testament," was always rich in mercy and repeatedly forgave individuals and Israel of their sins (see Jonah). Those who hold that God has a different personality in each testament have not thoughtfully read the Bible, from beginning to end, as they would any other book. Though His methods and means of dealing with mankind may change, "Jesus Christ is the same yesterday, today and forever" (Hebrews 13:8). His purpose, character, nature, love, forgiveness, and justice have not changed. He never says (in either Testament) that sin is okay, should be overlooked, or that people should not have to bear its consequences. Consider the consequences of David's sins with Bathsheba (Old Testament) as well as the consequences over the sins of Ananias and Sapphira (New Testament). Did God's sense of judgment change? God struck Herod Agrippa dead because he murdered the Apostle James, attempted to murder Peter, and blasphemed (Acts 12:20-24). As surely as there are gravitational results to stepping off a ten-story building, there are earthly consequences to disregarding God's laws throughout the Bible.

Applying Criminal Law Penalties under Grace

So what do Jesus and the apostles have to say about crime and punishment, including the death penalty? Starting in 1 Timothy 1:3-7, Paul addresses the problem that some are teaching "strange doctrines ... myths, which give rise to mere speculation ... wanting to be teachers of the Law, even though they do not understand either what they are saying or the matters about which they make confident assertions." Today these false teachers include death penalty opponents who mistakenly teach that "Thou shall not kill" forbids execution of murderers and pacifist Christians who claim pacifism is a biblical doctrine. Paul's purpose in verses 3-7 is to refute false teachers, such as Gnostics who held that any sin done in the body did not harm the spirit, which they considered separate. Apparently, some of the false teachers were saying that since Christians were under grace, any behavior was allowable because God loves to forgive. Paul refutes this in Romans chapter 5 and 6, stating that even under grace, God's moral stance does not change. However, a second teaching of this passage is that some moral sins are universally recognized as crimes at all times in all societies, and that society's duty is to judicially control these crimes for its own good (Romans 13:1-7).

We must remember that when Paul wrote his epistles in the mid-first century A.D., the Jews had been under Roman law for a hundred years. The Mosaic Law applied fully only while Israel was a theocracy – from the time of Moses to Samuel. Once they had kings or were ruled by foreign powers, they were subject to the civil authority and the statutes those authorities enacted. For instance, the Romans forbade the Jews to execute anyone under Mosaic Law without their approval (John 18:29-31). The felon had to be turned over to Roman Authority. The accused could only be punished if he had broken Roman law and only to the extent that Roman law allowed.[1]

In 1 Timothy 1:8-11, Paul points out that these penalties are not "for [controlling] a righteous man" (verse 9a). Rather, they are to deter those who refuse to obey the law: "For those who are lawless and rebellious" (verse 9b). Some in his list were Roman crimes and are still crimes today, including "those who kill their fathers or mothers, for murderers, ... kidnappers, liars [identity thieves, giving false ID to a cop, con artists, check forgers] and perjurers [such as those who lie under oath or swear falsely to obtain false legal process] (verses 9d and 10a). Paul did not mean for this to be an exhaustive list of crimes or sins, because he started in verse 8 with the general terms "lawless and rebellious" and ends in verse 10 with "and whatever else is contrary to sound teaching." He thereby covers any other crimes listed in the state's criminal code.

Now think carefully: is there any verse where Jesus or another New Testament writer says any of these crimes in Paul's list are now acceptable under grace? Murder was wrong before Cain killed Abel even though God had set no command forbidding it. It didn't suddenly become wrong with Exodus 20:13 anymore than kidnapping or assault was okay before Abraham and Moses! These crimes have always been and will always be wrong, and any society that tolerates them will destroy itself sooner or later.

Paul discusses the Christian's responsibility to government in Romans 13:1-7. He calls government "[A] minister to you for good. But if you do what is evil, be afraid; for it does not bear the sword for nothing; for it is a minister of God, an avenger who brings wrath on the one who practices evil."[2] The clear meaning here is that the government stands as the God-ordained enforcer of the law between the criminal and his victims, and that it bears the power of the death penalty (the sword) on God's behalf for certain crimes. The God-given job of all governments is to defend society from criminals. The sword Paul refers to here is the Roman *gladius*, the standard sidearm of the Roman legionary. Designed primarily as a stabbing weapon, it created wide, deep wounds that would lead to massive internal damage, bleeding, and swift death. It clearly does not fall in the category of what today are called intermediate or non-lethal force weapons: tazers, stun-guns, pepper spray, batons, and high-tech sound or microwave heat transmitters. When a Roman legionary drew his gladius on you, your only choice was to yield or to die. We can be certain that Paul meant by this reference that God means for government to have the right of capital punishment to control crime.

In Acts, we are told how Paul returned to Jerusalem after his last missionary journey. While there, the Jews conspired to kill him, so he appealed to the Roman authorities (as a Roman citizen) for a trial before the Roman governor of Judea. The Jews were seeking the death penalty. Paul knew Christianity and its doctrines as well as any of the apostles. He had been personally taught by Jesus (Galatians 1:12-17). If Jesus had taught him any tenet opposing the death penalty, this was the perfect time to elaborate on it, based on Scripture and the inspiration of the Holy Spirit. Instead, Paul tells Festus, the governor, "If then I am a wrongdoer, and have committed anything worthy of death, *I do not refuse to die*; but if none of those things is true of which these men accuse me, no one can hand me over to them" (Acts 25:11, emphasis mine). Paul was willing to accept the death penalty under both Roman and Jewish law, so long as the capital charge was true. He never quibbled on Scriptural or other grounds whether capital punishment was wrong. He accepted it as a good and proper governmental penalty upon legal conviction of certain crimes. Paul, therefore, accepted that the State, rather than the Mosaic Law, defined crimes on a secular basis instead of a religious one

Paul discusses the Christian's responsibility to government in Romans 13:1-7. He calls government "[A] minister to you for good. But if you do what is evil, be afraid; for it does not bear the sword for nothing; for it is a minister of God, an avenger who brings wrath on the one who practices evil."

(Romans 13:1-7) Then as now, those who violate statutory criminal law must bear the penalties of the law. If their crimes happened to coincide with crimes under the Mosaic Law, fine. But if acts that were sins under that law are not crimes under a civil code, then logically they are of no legal effect.

Finally, Jesus addresses the death penalty in the same way. When Pontius Pilate asked Jesus, "You do not speak to me? Do you know that I have the power to release You, and I have authority to crucify You?" He replied, "You would have no authority over Me, unless it had been given you from above, for this reason the one who delivered Me up to you has that greater sin" (John 19:10-11). Like Paul, Jesus had a perfect opportunity to expound on and condemn the death penalty as an obsolete-now-because-of-grace concept, as He had done with other Mosaic laws throughout his ministry. In the Sermon on the Mount, He compares the man-made laws and interpretations (with which the Jews had corrupted the Divine law given to Moses) to what God really intended. ("You have heard it said … but I say to you …" Matt. 5:21-22, 27-28, and so forth). Instead, He acknowledged that Pilate's power came from a God-ordained, duly constituted government, and that Pilate had the right to execute Him and to do so by crucifixion, a truly cruel and unusual means of punishment if ever there was one.

Jesus even endorsed the death penalty when addressing the Pharisees in Mark 7:6-13:

And He said to them, "Rightly did Isaiah prophesy of you hypocrites, as it is written 'This people honors Me with their lips, but their heart is far away from Me. But in vain do they worship Me, teaching as doctrines the precepts of men' "Neglecting the commandments of God, you hold to the tradition of men." He was also saying to them, "You nicely set aside the commandment of God in order to your keep tradition. For Moses said, "Honor your father and your mother," and, "He who speaks evil of father or mother, let him be put to death.", but you say, "If a man says to his father or his mother, 'Anything of mine you might have been helped by is Corban" (that is to say, given to God), "You no longer permit him to do anything for his father or his mother, thus invalidating the Word of God by your tradition which you have handed down, and you do many things such as that.

Jesus quotes Exodus 20:12 (honoring parents), then Exodus 21:17 (requiring the death penalty for cursing parents) to point out the Pharisees' hypocrisy.[3] They taught that a person could relieve himself of any responsibility for his aging parents by piously claiming that any of his excess cash had been pledged to the Temple. In effect, they taught that one could curse his parents by turning his back on them without penalty. Jesus tells them they deserve death under the Law for doing and teaching so.

Jesus tells the Pharisees that they have circumvented God's required punishment and His law requiring that parents be obeyed and cared for. Jesus hereby endorses the death penalties of the Mosaic Law and condemns the Pharisees for invalidating it. Remember, until Jesus hung the Law on the cross, all its rules and penalties still applied. Therefore, we can infer that He still supports the death penalty through modern legal means, since "Jesus Christ is the same yesterday, and today, yes and forever" (Hebrews 13:8).

When speaking to His disciples of coming persecution, Jesus said, "They will make you outcasts from the synagogue, but an hour is coming for everyone who kills you to think that he is offering service to God" (John 16:2). Again, Jesus refrains from condemning the death penalty; rather, he mentions it merely as one of the dangers His followers would have to endure. He does not imply that the punishment is per se unjust, but rather unjust for its application to the innocent for the wrong reason. In fact, John tells us in Revelation that the blood of martyrs will be required of those who killed them unjustly (Revelation 6:9-11). Yet again, John gives no hint of God's displeasure with the death penalty itself. Speaking of Revelation, what are Hell and the Lake of Fire but the ultimate death penalty, administered by a totally righteous and just God?

Finally, Peter gives us perspective about Christians who break the law: "Act as free men, and do not use your freedom as a covering for evil, but use it as bond slaves for God .... For what credit is there if, when you sin [commit crimes] and are harshly treated, you endure it with patience? But if when you do what is right and suffer for it you patiently endure it, this finds favor with God" (see generally 1 Peter 2:13-20). In other words, Peter says that Christians should not break the law, but if we do break the law and get caught and sentenced, we are not to gripe about it. Notice he does not specify whether the punishment is death or something less. He says, "If you did it, and the shoe fits, wear it!"

When you think about it seriously and look at it biblically, there is simply no basis to condemn the death penalty on scriptural grounds. Opponents of the death penalty condemn it only by pulling Scripture out of context to supply a pretext for their preconceived notion. In an honest study of the Bible and self-defense, though, the Bible's consistent endorsement of the death penalty from Genesis to Revelation is irrefutable. The conclusion is clear: God has granted society the ultimate means of self-defense against murderers through the death penalty.

Throughout the Bible, God lets us complain that the world is not as it should be. But then He shows us how we could make it better if we would just work with Him. In that cooperation, our armed vigilance and the death penalty leave no room for criminals and murderers to act or survive.

Epilogue

epilogue

The Greatest Act of Self-Defense

He was quite mellow now, though the last few days had been immensely exciting. For the hundredth time, he closed his eyes to relish the memories. All week, his anticipation had grown as he whispered in Judas' ear. He'd felt his skin prickle as the traitor reached his decision, negotiated with Caiaphas and his cronies, and took the 30 pieces of silver.

"Humans," Satan mused. "They insist it's about principle, but in the end it's about money."

He recalled his own mirth when James, John, and Peter couldn't stay awake to pray at the Mount of Olives. He had become intoxicated with Jesus' anguish as the Son prayed for another outcome. Forced to sneak away when ministering angels appeared, he had returned in time to see the priests arrive with the Temple guards. By that time, he was positively giddy. Jesus was determined to sacrifice Himself for the filthy animals who had rejected His Father and mistrusted Him! How could He hope His gesture of self-sacrifice would be any more effective? Didn't Jesus realize He would be just another martyr, soon forgotten by half-wits scrabbling for survival, fame, and power?

"Oh the irony of it! Satan chuckled. The "all-knowing" Father can see no further than this? Pathetic. I've overestimated Him all these years. This time, His baffling commitment to blood sacrifice will be His downfall!" Then Satan quietly exclaimed, "I've won! His Messiah is dead!" This declaration made him feel more alive than all his previous triumphs combined, more than all his victory howls across the centuries!

Replaying the drama in his head, he recalled his glee at the mock trial, which violated 1400 years of Jewish law, evidence, and procedure. Then there was Pilate, the quintessential politician, who, true to his breed, was always willing to arrange sins of omission when those of commission might prove embarrassing.

Such a perfect example of humanity! Despite his meddling wife, Pilate came through. Such politicians were exceptions to the rule that all bipeds have spines! Their purses saw to that.

And the soldiers! How enthusiastically they saw to their work! The "Hail, King of the Jews!" scene was priceless, but the real fun began with the serious torture. Satan proudly recalled briefing the scourgifier about Jesus being the source of all slanders spoken against him by the Jews. *That* guy laid it on with a vengeance; the Roman *flagrum* was the perfect instrument! By the time he finished, you could see a few of Jesus' ribs. Delicious! How his demons had capered and howled with joy! When they drove in the nails and raised Jesus up, their exultations redoubled! Satan had thrown his own head back and howled above them all. Victory! "So long in the coming but well worth the wait! What a victory! And the crowning glory was that Jesus had trapped Himself!"

Yet Jesus' quiet dignity throughout was disturbing. He had always been a cool customer. Satan thought back to their showdown in the desert early in Jesus' ministry. "There He was after 40 days of fasting: lips cracked, eyes bulging, sunken face, trembling slightly, yet He rejected every bait I dangled. I tried to cross Him up by misquoting His own Scripture, and He parried me with verses of His own. Despite His physical extremity, He was decisive. He spoke with ... finality ..." Satan's reverie trailed off as he shook his head, bringing himself back to the present revelry.

"What a party!" he observed, brightening. The feast was first rate. Wine for all from the blood of history's greatest hypocrites, the lesser tables feasting on history's greatest criminals, while the gourmet feast on the dais featured the greatest tormentors of the Jews (minus himself, of course): Pharaoh and his father from the time of Moses, who threw Hebrew boys in the Nile; Ahab and Jezebel, what a faithful pair; Jeroboam, who led Israel astray, never to return to Jehovah; Rehoboam, whose arrogance split Israel forever, condemning the Northern Kingdom to idolatry and both kingdoms to hundreds of years of civil war, resulting in the extinction of Israel; Ben-Hadad of Syria, who tormented Israel for years; Herod the First, killer of wife, son, and infants: a paranoid for the ages; and the gem of them all, Antiochus Epiphanes, who slaughtered Jews and forced conversion to his Greek gods. 'Epiphanes,' snorted Satan, 'the-living-image-of-God.' What a narcissist! Just the way I like them! His detractors called him 'Antiochus Epidemes' (Antiochus-the-nutcase). How droll. How true. Humans and their conceits," he snorted.

Satan leaned back in his throne, feet on the table, recalling how each of these guests of honor were brought alive and unaware to the table, only to be ripped apart in the demonic feeding frenzy, their horrific screams only adding to the joy of the moment. Demons at the head table tossed quivering flesh into their slavering maws with gusto, but this created no satiation (nothing in Hell ever did). In a few days, these morsels would reconstitute from the demonic excrement to resume their torments and contemplate whether they would become the stars of the next banquet. Satan chuckled at the ghastly humor of it all as he picked his teeth with one of Epiphanes' toenails.

In his self-satisfaction, Satan began to review the highlights of his long war with the Father. What had the Father said in the Garden? "I will put enmity between you and the woman, and between her seed and your seed. He shall crush your head, and you shall bruise his heel." "Nonsense!" he thought, "Who's crushed now, Father?" Since Jesus died, had he not heard his minions sing his praises? They were still bragging about their own "outstandingly vital" roles in his ultimate victory, as they retold the history of his march to triumph. Jehovah had tossed His last die with His Son, and Satan had killed the Son and won the pot. Henceforth, mankind would live to dread the grave until the end of time. They will never be able to recover from their predilection to disobey Jehovah. They will live in fear, violence, and ignorance, spending brief lives one-upping each other. There would always be a few Jehovah fanatics, but compared to his heroes, they'd be drowned out in the world history that he would write.

Why, just look at the dedicated champions he had on earth. The Emperor Tiberius, that dear murderous pervert! He would be here soon, and sure to be delightfully tasty. He was teaching Caligula perfectly. Talk about a devotee with potential! As for the Jews, why, between the self-centered Pharisee party and the violent Zealots, he could foresee an imminent rebellion against Rome. Perhaps he could finally arrange the national suicide he had nearly achieved several times before. Now that he'd eliminated God's son, the future was pregnant with possibilities.

Morality, honesty, self-control, kindness, goodness, justice, and love would become increasingly rare until snuffed out. He'd see to that. Whatever God called "good," he would pervert. "The future is delightful," Satan told himself with a contented sigh. "Truly, it is better to rule in Hell (and on Earth) than it ever was to serve in Heaven."

"I must share my vision," he decided, removing his feet from the table and sitting up. He was about to call for silence, when a side door burst open. A breathless Abraxas stumbled up to the dais. The stench about him was not the familiar odor of hellspawn but the reek of contact with Jehovah's angels. The hideous burns on his face and body revealed spiritual conflict. Something unlooked for and terribly wrong had brought the guardian of Hades to Satan. "What does this mean, Abraxas? Speak!"

"He has attacked!" gasped Abraxas. "He has freed the captives!"

"He? Who? Out with it!" demanded Satan.

"My lord, when the Accursed One gave His spirit to His Father, we all assumed He'd gone back home. All was quiet through Friday and Saturday until twilight at the Sabbath's end. Then suddenly, the Martyr appeared with Michael and Gabriel at the head of His army! They instantly took us captive and smashed the gates of paradise that the Jews call Abraham's Bosom. The Accursed One began preaching to them, and then He led them out to heaven! He turned them loose on me and my men! Abraham, Daniel, Job, Moses, and David led the charge. Their wrath was terrible. We were scorched and scattered! Gideon decapitated Baal. Joshua and Rahab gutted Ashtoreth. Michael disintegrated Molech with a glance, while Samson smashed Dagon to pieces. That one thief on the cross and Lazarus the Leper cut Isis and Osiris to ribbons. There were millions of them! Gabriel's trumpet paralyzed our troops with pain, as the Accursed One bound us in shimmering mazes of heavenly light! I only just now escaped to tell you!"

Satan's brow furrowed, his eyes aflame. Rage welled up. "Appollyon! Take this … incompetent, and give him to Basanites and his torturers for a thousand years!" Abraxas' protesting screams faded as Satan sought counsel from his princes on the dais. Borax, Zeus, Azmodius, Marduk, Ares and the others all began talking at once.

"War," declared Ares, "We attack Heaven at once!"

"Idiot," growled Satan, "that's always your solution. We've tried that tactic and lost. Recall the Father's power! Anyway, I don't need a strategy until I know what's happening! Analysis?"

"A mere raid?" offered Borax. "A retaliation for slaying His Messiah. Those in Paradise were never ours anyway. We still hold Tartarus, which contains far more numerous populations."

"I agree," belched Zeus, "this is just petulance on the Maker's part. He's a sore loser."

"Wrong," said Athena, sad, quiet, and thoughtful as always. "I believe this is but the first part of imminent disaster."

"What do you mean? Out with it!" ordered Satan.

"My Lord," Athena bowed her head slightly, "Consider what the Usurper said on several occasions: That He would give His life, but He would take it up again in three days. He said that no one *could* take His life from Him. He said He'd lay it down voluntarily, and take it up again at His Father's command."

"But *of course* His spirit would live on," objected Hades. "The spirit is eternal."

"No," Athena quietly replied. "We've assumed that, but I think now He meant His *physical* body. And he was specific about doing it on the third day after His death."

"But why?" asked Satan, his brow now showing concern rather than fury, the blaze in his eyes now smoldering doubt.

"Because both the Creator and His Usurper Son occasionally raise the dead, something, forgive me Lord Satan, that none of us are empowered to do. I fear that the Father intends to raise the Son as well."

"So?" scoffed Ares, "What's one Messiah walking around again. He didn't win but a small minority. He'll do no better by extending His mission."

Satan ignored Ares. "I still don't see your point, Athena."

"Remember this butcher-Creator's fixation with blood sacrifices," she argued, "yet He said the animal sacrifices couldn't absolve sin, but merely roll them ahead to some ultimate, expiating event."

"You can't mean …" said Hades, face turning white, his blood-smeared jaw dropping.

"Yes," affirmed Athena, "It was a trap. *We* kill Him, and God accepts His blood as the perfect sacrifice. It's quite possible that the sinful nature of humans can now be defeated!"

At last, Satan's face betrayed fear as the realization dawned on him. "So this raid is the second phase" said Satan, "He raises those who are His from Death and takes them to Heaven. But if He rises from the dead, He signals His intent to take all those who love Him out of death to be with Him eternally."

"Unhappily, my Lord, I believe you are correct. He means to destroy Death. And the third day will be upon us in a few hours." Athena's affirmation was barely a whisper. Hades fainted, his face splashing among Herod's entrails.

The horror of this possibility struck Satan like a blow. His thoughts flew. "Sin and Death destroyed! Unthinkable! The third day! He *must* be stopped!" Hiding his fear, he smiled slyly, looked up and down the table and growled, "But if He can't *rise*, He can't win." Standing, he assumed his command voice, bellowing to shake the foundations of the Netherverse. "To arms, hellions! *Every* demon will immediately cease his activity and report to the Usurper's tomb. *Now!*"

In the predawn darkness of that first day of the week, something odd occurred: Calm, Peace, Contentment arose, and Love overflowed the earth. Though briefly, mankind experienced a pinnacle of perceived personal well-being and regard for one another, unknown since before the serpent appeared in Eden. No one lusted after another's spouse. Con-men stopped in mid-scam and said, "Forget it." Muggers let their prey walk by unmolested. No one argued or fought. No one made unseemly remarks. Everyone loved his neighbor as himself.

The reason for this brief utopia? Satan and his minions had retreated from every corner of the world. Not one demon had the least interest in tempting or tormenting a single human. All evil influence was extinguished. Instead, Satan and all his myriads were stacked, piled, packed, and pinned to the wheel-like stone that covered the entrance to Jesus' tomb. All the malevolent energies of Hell concentrated on keeping that stone in place so the Savior could not emerge. Satan lay foremost against it, anchoring his steely fingers into the surrounding rock face. His veins stood in stark relief from his skin, every muscle straining. Now *his* sweat streamed from every pore in great drops of blood.

Naked fear gripped Satan as never before, fueled by the realization of what Jesus' victory would mean. One of his favorite pastimes had been tormenting humans with hypothetical horrible "what ifs." Since the beginning, Satan had tortured all humanity with doubt as they awaited and worried about life's various outcomes. Now *his* mind raced with possibilities of disasters visiting his realm if the Usurper achieved His goal. "It *can't* happen!" he screamed to himself. "I won't let it! *I* am the ruler of this world." Yet, neither his bravado nor the weight of his countless slaves upon him gave him any confidence. Seconds passed as slowly as eons as he strained to pin the stone in place.

—————

Had you been in Jerusalem the morning of that First Day just as the sky began to grey in the east, you might have been awakened by a small earthquake. Had you been one of the Roman squad on sentry duty at the tomb, you would have been struck into a catatonic state one second after the brief quake began, unaware of the angel shielding you from the cosmic force to be released one second later. The quake, in fact, was the earthly reflection of the titanic battle in the spiritual realm.

In that second, Satan glimpsed a blinding-white light blowtorching through the cracks between the tomb and its stone door. An instant later he felt a blow even more powerful than the blow that, so long ago, booted him all the way from Heaven to Hell. Blindness and searing pain from within and without became his world. Every cell of his being screamed agony into his brain as he heard the agonized howls of his defeated followers. His only other sensation was that of moving away from every other being at speeds faster than thought until he came to rest at the very rim of the universe, the closest galaxy a mere pinprick of light.

On the morning of that First Day, God achieved the Resurrection of His faithful Son. He had blown the legions of Hell off the tomb, scattering them to the farthest points of His creation with the merest flick of His little finger, as easily as a preoccupied man might shoo a fly off a picnic salad. His Son had defeated Sin and Death: their fate is sealed, and so is Satan's. Battles will still be fought, but heaven's victory is a foregone conclusion. God tricked Satan into killing His Son so that He could reply with the most devastating strike in history.

"For God so loved the world, that He gave His unique Son, that whosoever believes in Him should not perish, but have eternal life. For God did not send His Son into the world to judge the world, but that the world should be saved through

Him" (John 3:16-17). God, His Son, and His Spirit will now dwell in people's hearts, empowering them, at last, to defeat their natural temptation to sin. The God-sized hole that He built into each person can now be filled with Jesus. Now we can be whole, complete in Him. Through Jesus, we can now live life as God meant us to live it: triumphantly in a fallen world, all because Jesus committed the greatest act of defending others in the history of the world. He died for us and rose from the grave so that we might live.

John 3:16 is often quoted as the quintessential proof of God's Love. But have you ever noticed how John 3:17 illustrates it? John 3:17 means that if I were the only person who ever sinned or would sin, then Jesus would have become human and let me drive the nails into Him so I could have the opportunity to be forgiven and become His child. That's how much God loves each of us!

God has done everything He can, through His Son, His Spirit, His Word, and His people, to seek and save us from ourselves. Our job is to obey the Great Commission of Matthew 28:18-20: To go and make disciples of all nations. To accomplish this goal, God allows and blesses self-defense. Jesus means for us to preserve our own lives and the lives of innocents so we can get the job done, keeping others alive so they can hear, believe, and then baptized into the work of spreading the message.

Realizing our duty to fulfill Jesus' command to spread the Gospel brings us to one final contradiction in the position of pacifist Christians. Let's go back to the criminal charging into a fast-food restaurant and shooting everyone in sight. The pacifist has effectively decided to commit suicide. (Note that the Bible does not say suicide is an unforgivable sin. If you are in Christ, that one isolated act of rebellion would condemn you no more than if you told a lie and then died of a heart attack before you could repent.) The pacifist dies and appears before Jesus who then proceeds to show him how many people he would have witnessed to, taught, helped, and won to Christ if he had died at his natural time instead of on that day in the fast-food restaurant. Moreover, Jesus shows him all the blessings those he converted would have conferred on the world – not to mention the effect on his widow and children – had he just been there to win them to Christ. Then Jesus shows the pacifist how many lives he would have saved and how much sorrow and misfortune for friends and family would have been prevented if, when the wolf came, he had been armed and trained, a mentally and spiritually prepared shepherd instead of a sacrificial sheep. Maybe this is where our tears come from and what the verse means when it says God will wipe every tear from our eyes in Heaven (Revelation 7:17). Perhaps, in Heaven, we will all weep when we realize the missed opportunities and the neglected potential of our lives.

Jesus said "[T]he Son of Man has come to seek and save that which is lost." After all the study I have done over the years, I am convinced that Jesus did not use the word "save" in a purely spiritual context. If a person is in deadly peril by drowning, heart attack, or felonious assault, how can I save them spiritually if I don't first save them physically? James says, "[P]rove yourselves doers of the word, and not merely hearers who delude themselves" (James 1:22). James illustrates it in this way:

> What use is it, my brethren, if man says he has faith, but he has no works? Can faith save him? If a brother or sister is without clothing and in need of daily food, and one of you says to them "Go in peace, be warmed and filled," and yet you do not give them what is necessary for their body, what use is that?...For just as the body without the spirit is dead, so also faith without works is dead (James 2:14-16, 26).

Do you get it? God requires that I render the physical help that James says "is necessary for [the preservation] of their body." Likewise, if I am the one being assaulted, I must try to preserve my life to fulfill the Great Commission, let alone to finish being the husband and father that God has blessed me to be. Remember, Jeremiah tells us that Jesus' plans for our lives are for good, not evil, with the aim for our welfare (Jeremiah 29:11). God's goal for my life is that I do good to others, refrain from harming them (spiritually or physically), and teach them how to pass on the knowledge His Word teaches us.

Passing that knowledge on has been the point of this book. I have applied 36 years of study in the law, tools and methods of self-defense, and 32 years of relating Biblical principles to my understanding of the law so that others can benefit from these principles. If you find the points I have made on the Scriptures and law to be valid, please apply this knowledge to your own life and pass it on to others. My prayer is that if you ever come to that horrible place where deadly force is necessary, you will not hesitate in fear; instead, you will demonstrate power, love, and sound judgment (2 Timothy 1:7). Regarding Power: Use the force necessary to save the innocent. Regarding Love: Protect the innocent, your nation, and all that is good, and show love in the aftermath, doing your best to heal the victims, trying to win the criminal over. Regarding Sound Judgment: Be assured going in that God says what you are doing is good and it complies with the civil law, the customs of war, and biblical morality. The knowledge that you fight righteously will insure that you come out alive and victorious over evil; that knowledge will also insure your spiritual, legal, and mental soundness on the other side of combat.

May you never need to use force, but if you do, remember all the Bible heroes who used force when nothing else would stop evil. Remember Solomon, inspired by the Holy Spirit, who said, "There is an appointed time for everything. And there is a time for every event under heaven .... A time to kill, and a time to heal .... A time for war, and a time for peace" (Ecclesiastes 3:1, 3, 8). Self-defense, defense of country, and defense of third parties is righteous. Self defense is blessed by God, just as He blessed Abram when Abram rescued Lot. Legal defense of others is part of our godly duty on earth. It ensures our survival and our witness to the gospel. Its necessity is blessed by God, who said, "There is a time to kill."

Endnotes

Preface

[1] See Leviticus 19:16, Psalms 82:4, Proverbs 3:27-28; 24:11-12, and Matthew 5:39; 26:52.

[2] Elizabeth Tenety, "America Fails Religion Pop Quiz," *The Washington Post,* September 27, 2010.

[3] See generally, Deuteronomy 6:4-9; Psalms 119:97-112; Ecclesiastes 12:13-14; 2 Timothy 2:15; and Revelation 2:29

[4] John Lott, *More Guns, Less Crime,* 3rd ed. (Chicago: University of Chicago Press, 2010), 324.

Chapter 1

[1] Ala. Code § 13A-7-6 (b) (LexisNexis 1975).

[2] Bill Langlois, *Surviving the Age of Fear* (Waco, TX: WRS Publishing, 1993), 183-190.

[3] Ala. Code §13A-3-23(a)(3) (LexisNexis 1975).

[4] Ala. Code § 13A-7-5 (LexisNexis 1975).

[5] Ala. Code § 13A-7-6 (LexisNexis 1975).

[6] Ala. Code § 13A-7-7 (LexisNexis 1975).

[7] Mitch and Evan Vilos, *Self-Defense Laws of All 50 States* (Centerville, UT: Guns West, 2010).

[8] Massad Ayoob, *In the Gravest Extreme* (Concord, NH: Police Bookshelf, 1980) 58-60.

[9] Ibid, 1.

[10] See generally Kent Scheidigger and Michael Rushford, "Social Benefits of Confining Habitual Criminals," *Standard Law and Policy Review 11,* (Winter 1999).

[11] James D. Wright and Peter H. Rossi, *Armed and Considered Dangerous: A Survey of Felons and Their Firearms* (New York: Aldine DeGruyter, 1986) 145-149, 154.

[12] Massad Ayoob, *The Truth About Self Protection* (New York: Bantam Books, 1983) 327, 347.

[13] Victor David Hanson, *The Wars of the Ancient Greeks* (London: Cassell, 2000), 62.

Chapter 2

[1] Edward Earle, *Makers of Modern Strategy: Military Thought from Machiavelli to Hitler* (Princeton: Princeton University Press, 1971), 103.

[2] Massad Ayoob, *The Truth about Self-Protection* (New York: Bantam Books, 1983).

[3] Jeff Cooper, *The Principles of Personal Defense* (Boulder, CO: Paladin Press, 1972).

[4] Bill Langlois, *Surviving the Age of Fear* (Waco, TX: WRS Publishing, 1993).

[5] For information on Massad Ayoob's classes, go to www.massadayoobgroup.com.

[6] Ala. Code § 13A-8-42 (LexisNexis 1975).

[7] Roy Huntington, "Add It Up," *American Handgunner* 38, no. 1 (January/February 2013):104.

[8] Gary Kleck, *New Perspectives on Gun Control* (New York: Prometheus Books, 2001), 292.

Chapter 4

[1] Ala. Code §13A-3-23(d) (LexisNexis 1975).

[2] H. Black, *Black's Law Dictionary* (St. Paul, MN: West Publishing, 1979), 519.

[3] Call the National Rifle Association at (703) 267-1500 to find an instructor in your area.

[4] John Lott, *More Gun, Less Crime* 1ˢᵗ ed. (Chicago: University of Chicago Press, 1998), 11.

[5] Richard Poe, *The Seven Myths of Gun Control* (Roseville, CA: Prima Publishing, 2011), 105.

[6] Chip Foose, *Overhaulin*, The Discovery Channel, 2007.

[7] See also Proverbs 13:3; 15:23; 16:21 and 24; 25:11.

[8] Harper Lee, *To Kill a Mockingbird* (New York: Harper Collins, 2002), 33.

Chapter 5

[1] See *Callogrides v. City of Mobile*, 475 So. 2d 560 (Ala. 1985); *Garrett v. City of Mobile*, 481 So. 2d 376 (Ala. 1985); and the U.S. Supreme Court case, *Castle Rock v. Gonzales*, 545 U.S. 748 (2005) for the holding that police forces have no duty toward or to rescue any individual.

[2] Chris Bird, *The Concealed Handgun Manual*, 2ⁿᵈ ed. (San Antonio, TX: Privateer Publishing, 2000), 19-23.

[3] *The Holy Scriptures According to the Masoretic Text* (Chicago: The Menorah Press, 1973).

Chapter 6

[1] Homer, *The Iliad,* Translated by Richard Lattimore (Chicago: University of Chicago Press, 1951); Herodotus, *The Persian Wars,* Translated by George Rawlinson (New York: The Modern Library, 1942); 2 Samuel 2:12-17; and R.L. Fox, *Alexander the Great* (New York: Dial Press, 1974), 99.

[2] Ala.Code §13-3-23(c) (3) (LexisNexis 1975); See also Mitch and Evan Vilos, *Self-Defense Laws of All 50 States* (Centerville, UT: Guns West Publishing, 2010). No U.S. state allows dueling.

[3] See Moses against the Amalakites, Exodus 17; Joshua at Jericho, Joshua 6; Gideon, Judges 7; Barak, Judges 4; Samuel at Ebenezer, 1 Samuel 7; Saul at Jabesh-Gilead,1 Samuel 11; Jonathan at Michmash, 1 Samuel 14.

[4] William E. Simon, *A Time for Truth* (New York: Berkley Books, 1979), 229.

[5] Victor David Hanson. *A War Like No Other* (New York: Random House, 2005), 92; Peter Connolly, *Greece and Rome at War* (Englewood Cliffs, NJ: Prentice-Hall,1981), 49.

Chapter 7

[1] Ala. Code § 13A-3-23 (a) (LexisNexis 1975).

[2] Ibid, (a) (1) (3) & (4)

[3] *Brown v. United States*, 256 U.S. 335 (1921).

[4] F. Lee Bailey and Henry B. Rothblatt, *Crimes of Violence, Homicide and Assault* (New York: The Lawyers Co-operative, 1973), 528, 614. And Supplement 628.7.

[5] *Beard v. United States*, 158 U.S. 550 (1895).

[6] Jon Peters, *Defensive Tactics with Flashlights* (Ventura, CA: Reliapon Police Product, 1982), 156-159.

[7] Ala. Code §13A-3-23 (d) (LexisNexis 1975). A person who uses force, including deadly physical force, as justified and permitted in this section is immune from criminal prosecution and civil action for the use of such force, unless the force was determined to be unlawful.

[8] *Ray v. State*, 580 So. 2d 103 (Ala. Crim. App. 1991).

[9] Ala. Code § 13A-6-20(1) (LexisNexis 1975).

[10] Ala. Code § 13A-1-2(14) (LexisNexis 1975).

[11] Ala. Code § 13A-3-23(a) (3) (LexisNexis 1975).

Chapter 8

[1] *Tennessee v. Garner,* 471 U.S. 1 (1985).

[2] In this section from Romans, Paul is quoting from Proverbs 20:22; 24:29; Deuteronomy 32:35; and Psalms 94:1.

[3] *The Holy Scriptures According to the Masoretic Text* (Chicago: The Menorah Press, 1973).

[4] G. Fletcher, *A Crime of Self-Defense: Bernhard Goetz and the Law on Trial* (Chicago: University of Chicago Press, 1990), 161.

[5] Paxton Quigley, *Armed and Female* (New York: St. Martin's Paperbacks, 1990), 136.

Chapter 9

[1] James D. Wright and Peter H. Rossi, *Armed and Considered Dangerous: A Survey of Felons and Their Firearms* (New York: Aldine DeGruyter, 1986), 54.

[2] Richard Poe, *The Seven Myths of Gun Control* (Roseville, CA: Prima Publishing, 2001),105.

Chapter 10

[1] See also Titus 3:1; Daniel 4:32, 34-35; 1 Peter 2:13-17; I Timothy 2:1-4.

[2] Will Durant, *The Story of Civilization: Caesar and Christ* ,Vol. III (New York: Simon and Schuster, 1972), 139-140.

[3] Ibid., 324.

[4] N. Lewis and M. Reinhold, *Roman Civilization, Sourcebook II: The Empire* (New York: Harper Torchbook Edition, 1966), 195.

[5] J.I. Packer, Merrill C. Tenney, and William White, Jr., ed., *The Bible Almanac* (Nashville: Thomas Nelson, 1980), 22.

[6] Ala. Code § 13A-3-27 (f) (LexisNexis 1975).

[7] Ala. Code § 13-11-75 (LexisNexis 1975).

[8] John Lott, *More Guns, Less Crime* 3rd ed, (Chicago: University of Chicago Press), 240-241.

[9] Ibid., 240-251.

[10] Ibid., 324.

[11] Ibid., 94-95; 259-274.

[12] Ibid., 324.

[13] James Wright and Pete Rossi, *Armed and Considered Dangerous: A Survey of Felons and Their Firearms* (New York: Aldine De Gruyter, 1986), 301.

[14] Ibid., 147.

[15] Ibid., 302.

[16] Ibid., 147.

[17] Ibid., 303.

[18] See Leviticus 19:16; Psalms 82:4; Proverbs 3:27-28 and 24:11-12.

[19] Roy Huntington, "Add It Up," *American Handgunner* 38, no. 1 (January/February 2013):104.

[20] Lott, *More Guns,* 241-252.

Chapter 11

[1] Massad Ayoob, "Post-Shooting Trauma," (Concord, NH: Police Bookshelf, 1990), DVD.

[2] See also Isaiah 51:4-6; 52:13-15; 54; 55:3-11; 56:6-7; 57:19; 65:1-2; Jeremiah 3:15-18; Joel 2:28-32; Amos 9:11-12; Zechariah 2:10-11; 8:20-23.

[3] Ala. Code § 13A-11-7(a)(5) (LexisNexis 1975).

[4] See Paul's instructions to Timothy about gently persuading those Christians who sin in 2 Timothy 2:24-26.

Chapter 12

[1] Ala. Code §13A-3-25(a) (LexisNexis 1975).

[2] *Matthews v. State*, 115 So. 2d 763 (Ala. Ct. App. 1928).

[3] Larry Schweikart, *America's Victories: Why the U.S. Wins Wars and Will Win the War on Terror* (New York: Sentinal/Penguin Group, 2006), 62.

[4] See generally Psalm 124; 140:7; 149:5-9; Proverbs 21:31; Ecclesiastes 9:18; and all the history books of the Old Testament.

[5] Victor Davis Hanson, *Soul of Battle*, (New York: Anchor House, 1999), 362.

[6] Charles Whiting, *Patton* (New York: Ballantine Books, 1968), 158.

[7] See also Proverbs 24:11-12; 3:27-28.

[8] See Deuteronomy 22:8 (a fence on the rooftop to prevent falls); Exodus 21:29 (a known dangerous bull who kills someone); and Deuteronomy 19:10 (cities of refuge for those who kill accidentally, so they are not killed in revenge).

[9] See also 2 Samuel 7.

[10] See Gideon (Judges 6-8), Barak (Judges 4-5), Samson (Judges 13-16), Jepthath (Judges 11-12), David (1 Samuel 17), Samuel (I Sam.7) and various prophets (Hebrews 11:32). See also the list of David's heroes who saved Israel many times over in 2 Samuel 23.

[11] See Judges 5:8 (Canaanites) and 1Samuel 13:19-22 (Philistines).

Chapter 13

[1] Dr. Alexis Artwohl and Loren W. Christensen, *Deadly Force Encounters: What Cops Need to Know to Physically and Mentally Prepare for and Survive a Gunfight* (Boulder, CO: Paladin Press, 1997), 38-42.

[2] Ibid, 179-185.

[3] Dave Grossman, *On Killing: The Psychological Cost of Learning to Kill in War and Society* (New York: Little Brown, 2009), 30.

[4] Ibid, 3.

[5] Ibid, 233-242.

[6] Artwohl and Christensen, *Deadly Force Encounters*, 179-185.

[7] Eugene H. Peterson, *The NASB/The Message Parallel Bible* (Grand Rapids, MI: Zondervan, 2004), 2134.

Chapter 14

Ala. Code §13A-3-23 (a) (1) (3) (LexisNexis 1975).

[2] See generally Mitch and Evan Vilos, *Self-Defense Laws of All 50 States* (Centerville, UT: Guns West Publishing, 2010).

[3] Ala. Code § 13A-6-43(b) (LexisNexis 1975).

Chapter 15

[1] See Psalms 2; 24:1; 46:8-10; 139.

[2] See also Proverbs 14:6; 15:31; 22:15; 29:15 and 19.

Chapter 16

[1] See also Deuteronomy 4:2, 12:32 and Revelation 22:18.

[2] See also John 14:6-12.

[3] See also Matthew 12:25 and Luke 5:22; 6:8; 9:47.

[4] See also 1 Corinthians 10:14-33, Romans 14:4, and Galatians 6:1-3.

Chapter 17

[1] Ian Wilson. *The Bible is History* (Washington, DC: Regnery, 1999), 44. Per-Atum and Avaris are probably the cities listed as Pithom and Raamses in Exodus 1:11.

[2] Werner Keller. *The Bible as History* (New York: William Morrow, 1981), 101. On was the original name for the capital city of Thebes.

[3] See also Numbers 12:6-8 and Deuteronomy 34:10.

[4] Vilos, *Self-Defense Laws*. Arizona, 53; Colorado, 79; Idaho, 134.

Chapter 18

[1] Eric Metaxas, *Bonhoeffer: Pastor, Martyr, Prophet, Spy* (Nashville: Thomas Nelson, 2010) 247.

[2] Eugene Peterson, *The NASB/The Message Parallel Bible* (Grand Rapids, MI: Zondervan, 2004), 1918.

Chapter 19

[1] Edward Gibbon, *The Decline and Fall of the Roman Empire* Vol.1 (New York: Random House, n.d.), 416-417.

[2] Ibid., 416.

[3] Gibbon, 416, note 103.

[4] N. Lewis & M. Rheinhold, *Roman Civilization, Sourcebook II, The Empire* (New York: Harper Torchbook Edition, 1966) 595-596.

[5] Will Durant, *The Story of Civilization: Caesar and Christ*, Vol. III (New York: Simon and Schuster, 1944), 667-668.

[6] Ibid., 651.

[7] Lewis & Rheinhold, 595.

[8] Adrian Goldsworthy, *How Rome Fell* (New Haven: Yale University Press, 2009), 179.

[9] Ibid., 180.

[10] Ibid., 183.

[11] Maurice Keen, ed. *Medieval Warfare: A History* (Oxford: Oxford University Press, 1999), 254-258.

[12] Stephen Mansfield, "Prologue: The Vigil at Arms," in *The Faith of the American Soldier* (New York: The Penguin Group, 2005).

[13] Louis B. Parks, "They're Ready to Fight for 'Onward Christian Soldiers,'" *Houston Chronicle*, May 31,1986.

[14] See also Mark 3:27 and Luke 11:21-22.

[15] Psalms 82:4; Proverbs 3:27-28, 24:11-12; and Leviticus 19:16.

[16] Vilos, *Law in 50 States*: Iowa, 159; Texas, 386 ; Utah, 400.

[17] See Matthew 5:19, 21; 19:18; 22:7; Mark 7:21; John 8:44

[18] See John 1:1-18; Romans 8:6-17; Philippians 2:5-11; Colossians 1:13-20; Hebrews 1:1-3; 3:1-4

[19] See Matthew 21:12-13; Mark 11:15-18; Luke 19:45-46.

[20] F. LaGarde Smith, *The Daily Bible* (Eugene, OR: Harvest House Publishers, 1984), 599.

[21] Durant, *Caesar and Christ*, 536-37.

Chapter 20

[1] See Jeremiah 7:1-7; Ezekiel 18; Micah 6:8; John 13:17; and James 1:22-25.

[2] See 1 Chronicles 24:19; 2 Chronicles 8:14; 31:2; Luke 1:8-9.

[3] See Luke 5:17-26; 6:1-11; 11:37-54; 13:10-17.

[4] See Leviticus 19:16; Psalms 82:4; Proverbs 3:27-28; 24:11-12; Micah 6:8

[5] *The Archaeological Study Bible* (Grand Rapids, MI: Zondervan, 2005), 1727.

[6] Ibid, 2015.

Chapter 21

[1] Chuck Swindoll, *The Inspirational Writings of Charles R. Swindoll: Improving Your Serve* (New York: Inspirational Press, 1998), 72-74.

[2] Larry Choninard, *College Press Commentary on Matthew* (Joplin, MO: College Press, 1997), 95.

[3] C.S. Lewis, *The ScrewTape Letters* (New York: New American Library, 1988), 32.

[4] W.E Vine. *Vine's Expository Dictionary*, (Nashville, TN: Thomas Nelson, 1997), 727-28.

[5] Ibid, 727.

[6] Ibid, 728.

Chapter 22

[1] See Exodus 21-22; 23:1-9; Leviticus 24:13-23; and Deuteronomy19.

[2] "The 'Right Hand' in Ancient Thinking," *The Archeological Study Bible* (Grand Rapids, MI: Zondervan, 2005), 1983.

[3] See Exodus15:6 and 12; Psalms 16:8; 18:35; 44:3; 60:5; Isaiah 41:10; 48:13

[4] Larry Choninard, *The College Press NIV Commentary on Matthew* (Joplin, MO: College Press, 1997) , 115-118.

[5] H. Lee Boles, *A Commentary on The Gospel According to Matthew* (Nashville, TN: Gospel Advocate, 1961), 148-149.

[6] Dave Grossman, "Terrorism and Local Police," *The Ohio Police Chief Magazine* (Summer 2002), 39.

[7] Ayoob, *The Truth About Self Protection*, 327, 347.

[8] Phillip Yancey, *The Jesus I Never Knew* (Grand Rapids, MI: Zondervan, 1995), 228-236.

Chapter 23

[1] See Luke 9:1-6; Matthew 10:5-15; and Mark 6:7-13.

[2] See Matthew 26:47-56; Mark 14:43-50; Luke 22:47-53; and John 18:1-11.

[3] See Acts 2:14-36, Peter's sermon at Pentecost, and 1 Corinthians 15:3-4.

[4] See also Mark 14:49 and Luke 22:37.

[5] Paraphrased from Matthew 26:50-56; Mark 14:43-51; Luke 22:47-51; and John 18:3-12.

[6] See Matthew 9:4; 12:25; Mark 2:6-8; Luke 5:22;6:8;11:17;24:38; and John 16:30.

[7] Paul McCartney and John Lennon, "Happiness is a Warm Gun," *The White Album* (Apple Records, 1968).

[8] See Matthew 16:21-23; 17:9, 22-23; Luke 9:22, 44-45; and John 16:18-22.

[9] See Mark 3:1 5 and Luke 13:10 17.

Chapter 24

[1] David Leiber, *ETZ HAYIM: Torah and Commentary* (New York: The Jewish Publication Society, 2004), 447.

[2] See also Deuteronomy 10:17-18, 32:39; Psalms 90, 139; Daniel 4:2-3, 34-35; Isaiah 42:5; Acts 10:34-35, 17:24-28; Ephesians 3:14-15; Colossians 1:13-20, 3:25; 1 Timothy 6:13-16, 1 Peter 2:13-14; and Revelation 4:11.

[3] See also 1 Kings 2:5-6 [David's order]; 2 Samuel 3 [civil war, Abner defected to David, Joab murdered him]; 2 Samuel 20:1-12 [Joab's murder of Amasa].

Chapter 25

[1] See also Leviticus 24:17, 21.

[2] Dr. Phil Challmers, *Inside the Mind of a Teen Killer* (Nashville: Thomas Nelson, 2009), 157.

[3] John Lott, *Freedomnomics* (Washington, DC: Regnery Publishing, 2007), 132-138.

Chapter 26

[1] *Brady v. Maryland*, 373 U.S. 83 (1963).

[2] John Lott, *The Bias Against Guns* (Washington, DC: Regnery Publishing, 2003), 118.

[3] John Lott, *Freedomnomics* (Washington, DC: Regnery Publishing, 2007), 133.

[4] Ibid, 134-137.

[5] Ibid, 112-117.

[6] Ibid, 132-144.

[7] Centers for Disease Control, "Deaths: Final Data for 2007," National Vital Statistics Report 58, no. 19 (May 20, 2010). There were 613 accidental firearms deaths versus 2,597 deaths from complications of medical and surgical care.

Chapter 27

[1] See Luke 23:1-4, 13-16 and Acts 22:22-29, 23:23-45, 25:1-12, 26:30-32.

[2] See also 1 Peter 2:13-17.

[3] See also Leviticus 20:9.

Bibliography

Aguiar, Ron. *Keeping Your Church Safe*. Xulon Press, 2008.

Artwohl, Alexis and Christensen, Loren. *Deadly Force Encounters: What Cops Need to Know to Physically and Mentally Prepare For and Surive a Gunfight.* Boulder, Colorado: Paladin Press, 1997.

Ayoob, Massad. *In the Gravest Extreme.* Concord, New Hampshire: Police Bookshelf, 1980.

—. "Post-Shooting Trauma."*DVD.* Concord, NH: Police Bookshelf, 1990.

—. *The Truth About Self-Protection.* New York: Bantam Books, 1983.

Bailey, F. Lee and Rothblatt, Henry B. *Crimes of Violence, Homicide, and Assault.* New York: The Lawyers Co-operative Publishing Co., 1973.

Beard v. United States. 158 U.S. 550 (1895).

Bird, Chris. *The Concealed Handgun Manual.* 2nd ed. San Antonia, Texas: Privateer Publishing, 2000.

Black, H. *Black's Law Dictionary.* St. Paul: West Publishing, 1979.

Boles, H. Lee. *A Commentary on The Gospel According to Matthew.* Nashville: Gospel Advocate, 1961.

Brady v. Maryland. 373 U.S. 83 (1963).

Brown v. United States. 256 U.S. 335 (1921).

Callogrides v. City of Mobile. 475 So. 2d 560 (Ala., 1985).

Castle Rock v. Gonzales. 545 U.S. 748 (2005).

Centers for Disease Control. "National Vital Statistics Report." *Deaths: Final Data for 2007.* Vol. 58. no. 19. May 20, 2010.

Challmers, Phil. *Inside the Mind of a Teen Killer.* Nashville: Thomas Nelson, 2009.

Choninard, Larry. *The College Press NIV Commentary on Matthew.* Joplin, Missouri: College Press Publishing, 1997.

Christensen, Loren. *Surviving Workplace Violence* . Boulder: Paladin Press, 2005.

Connolly, Peter. *Greece and Rome at War.* Englewood Cliffs, New Jersey: Prentice-Hall, 1981.

Cooper, Jeff. *The Principles of Personal Defense.* Boulder, Colorado: Paladin Press, 1972.

Durant, Will. *The Story of Civilization: Caesar and Christ.* Vol. III. New York: Simon and Schuster, 1972.

Earle, Edward. *Makers of Modern Strategy: Military Thought from Machiavelli to Hitler.* Princeton: Princeton University Press, 1971.

Fletcher, G. *A Crime of Self-Defense: Bernhard Goetz and the Law on Trial.* Chicago: University of Chicago Press, 1990.

Foose, Chip. *Overhaulin'.* The Discovery Channel. 2007.

Fox, R.L. *Alexander the Great.* New York: Dial Press, 1974.

Garrett v. City of Mobile. 481 So. 2d 376 (Ala., 1985).

Gibbon, Edward. *The Decline and Fall of the Roman Empire.* Vol. I. New York: Random House, 1944.

Goldsworthy, Adrian. *How Rome Fell.* New Haven, Connecticut: Yale University Press, 2009.

Grossman, Dave and Christensen, Loren. *On Combat: The Psychology and Physiology of Deadly Conflict in War and Peace.* 3rd. Warrior Science Publications, 2008.

Grossman, Dave. *On Killling: The Psychological Cost of Learning to Kill in War and Society.* New York: Little Brown & Company, 2009.

—. "Terrorism and Local Police." *The Ohio Police Chief Magazine,* Summer 2002: 39.

Hanson, Victor Davis. *A War Like No Other.* New York: Random House, 2005.

—. *The Soul of Battle.* New York: Anchor House, 1999.

—. *The Wars of the Ancient Greeks.* London: Cassell and Company, 2000.

Herodotus. *The Persian Wars.* Translated by George Rawlinson. New York: The Modern Library, 1942.

Homer. *The Iliad.* Translated by Richmond Lattimore. Chicago: University of Chicago Press, 1951.

Huntington, Roy. "Add It Up." *American Handgunner 1,* January/February 2013: 104.

Keen, Maurice, ed. *Medieval Warefare: A History.* Oxford: Oxford University Press, 1999.

Keller, Phillip. *A Shepherd Looks at Psalms 23.* Grand Rapids: Zondervan
  Publishing, 1970.

Kleck, Gary. *New Perspectives on Gun Control.* New York: Prometheus Books,
  2001.

Langlois, Bill. *Surviving the Age of Fear.* Waco, Texas: WRS Publishing, 1993.

Lee, Harper. *To Kill a Mockingbird.* New York: Harper Collins, 2002.

Lewis, C.S. *The ScrewTape Letters.* New York: American Library, 1988.

Lewis, N. and Rheinhold, M. *Roman Civilization, Sourcebook II: The Empire.* New
  York: Harper Torchbook Edition, 1966.

Lieber, David L., *ETZ HAYIM: Torah and Commentary.* New York: Jewish
  Publication Society, 2004.

Lott, John. *Freedomnomics.* Washington, D.C.: Regenery Publishing, Inc., 2007.

—. *More Guns, Less Crime.* 3rd. Chicago: University of Chicago Press, 2010.

—. *The Bias Against Guns.* Washington, D.C.: Regenery Publishing Inc., 2003.

Mansfield, Stephen. *The Faith of the American Soldier.* New York: The Penguin
  Group, 2005.

Matthews v. State. 115 So. 2d. 763 (Ala. Ct. App., 1928).

McCartney, Paul, and John Lennon. *Happiness is a Warm Gun.* Comps. Paul
  McCartney and John Lennon. 1968.

Metaxas, Eric. *Bonhoeffer: Pastor, Martyr, Prophet, Spy.* Nashville: Thomas Nelson,
  2010.

Mitchie's Alabama Code. Charlottesville, VA: Matthew Bender & Company, 2008.

Packer, J.I., Tenney, Merrill C., and White, William Jr., ed. *The Bible Almanac.*
  Nashville: Thomas Nelson, 1980.

Parks, Louis B. "They're Ready to Fight for 'Onward Christian Soldiers'." *Houston
  Chronicle,* May 31, 1986.

Peters, John. *Defensive Tactics with Flashlights.* Ventura, California: Realiapon
  Police Products, Inc., 1982.

Peterson, Eugene H. *The NASB Message Parallel Bible.* Grand Rapids, Michigan:
  Zondervan, 2004.

Poe, Richard. *The Seven Myths of Gun Control.* Roseville, California: Prima
  Publishing, 2001.

Quigley, Paxton. *Armed and Female.* New York: St. Martin's Paperbacks, 1990.

Ray v. State. 580 So. 2d 103 (Ala. Crim. App., 1991).

Scheidigger, Kent and Rushford, Michael. "Social Benefits of Confining Habitual Criminals." *Standard Law and Policy Review 11*, Winter 1999.

Schweikart, Larry. *America's Victories: Why the U.S. Wins Wars and Will Win the War on Terror.* New York: Sentinal/Penguin Group, 2006.

Simon, William E. *A Time for Truth.* New York: Berkley Books, 1979.

Smith, F. LaGarde. *The Daily Bible.* Eugene, Oregon: Harvest House Publishers, 1984.

Swindoll, Chuck. *The Inspirational Writings of Charles R. Swindoll: Improving Your Serve.* New York: Inspirational Press, 1998.

Tenety, Elizabeth. "America Fails Religion Pop Quiz." *The Washingon Post,* September 27, 2010.

Tennessee v. Garner. 471 U.S. 1 (1985).

The Archaeological Study Bible. Grand Rapids, Michigan: Zondervan, 2005.

The Holy Scriptures According to the Masoretic Text. Chicago: The Menorah Press, 1973.

Vilos, Mitch and Evan. *Self-Defense Laws of All 50 States.* Centerville, Utah: Guns West Publishing, 2010.

Vine, W.E. *Vine's Expository Dictionary.* Nashville: Thomas Nelson, Inc., 1997.

Whiston, W. *The Works of Josephus: The Antiquities of the Jews, Book 2.* Peabody, Massachusetts: Hendrickson, 2006.

Whiting, Charles. *Patton.* New York: Ballantine Books, 1970.

Wilson, Ian. *The Bible is History.* Washington, D.C.: Regnery, 1999.

Wright, James D. and Rossi, Peter H. *Armed and Considered Dangerous: A Survey of Felons and Their Firearms.* New York: Aldine DeGruyter, 1986.

Yancy, Phillip. *The Jesus I Never Knew.* Grand Rapids, Michigan: Zondervan, 1995.

Acknowledgments

First, all thanks and glory go to Jesus. Any good this book does is from You.

Thanks and love to my wife, Velvet: brilliant, beautiful, and patient with her expertise in the English language and her objectivity and hard work to make this all make sense. Next, to Ed Garner, editor: your real-world outlook and organizational skills brought order out of my chaos. I would have been lost without you. To Mark Sandlin for the thoughtful cover art. Also to Felicia Kahn for production design.

Thanks and honor to Mom and Dad, my heroes, who taught me God's ways. To Dave Jungen, who typed the first two chapters of the manuscript and who donated "The Holy Hand Grenade of Antioch" (the thumb drive that held the manuscript and all revisions). To Amanda Barnes, who deciphered my scrawl to finish typing the remaining chapters of the manuscript. To Jim Biard, my prayer partner. After I had been stuck for two years, you said, "Just start free writing." To all the Christian friends who prayed for and encouraged me throughout the creation of this book. To Judge John Patterson, who gave me my first legal job and taught me so much about thinking like a lawyer. To my friends at the Huntsville Police Department who helped inspire this book. Keep safe.

Finally, I owe a lifelong debt to the many authors and instructors who inspired me to teach others to stay safe. Foremost, my thanks go to Massad Ayoob, whose writings started me thinking about self-defense in a legal, moral, and ethical manner. For Lt. Col. Dave Grossman, who helped me understand the spiritual and psychological aspects of this subject. And to so many others: John Lott, Jeff Cooper, Evan Marshall, Bill Langlois, Alexis Artwohl, Loren Christensen, Jim Grover, and Ed Nowicki. As Isaac Newton said, "If I have seen more clearly than others, it is only because I have stood on the shoulders of giants."

About the Author

Greg Hopkins received his first firearms training as an auxiliary police officer in his hometown of Waverly, Ohio, where he also served on the city council. He earned his law degree at The Cumberland School of Law in Birmingham, Alabama, and served as a City Magistrate there. After graduation, Greg clerked at the Alabama Court of Criminal Appeals, and he was admitted to the bar in 1989. Greg served as City Prosecutor for Huntsville, Alabama, and trained the Huntsville Police Department and its detention officers in legal use-of-force. He received training for police advisors at the FBI Academy in Quantico, Virginia, and completed Level One of Massad Ayoob's Lethal Force Institute in Pearl, Mississippi. After leaving the City Attorney's office, Greg practiced criminal defense law, served as a City Court Judge, and became a court-certified expert witness in firearms and self-defense law. He regularly consults on self-defense and firearms cases to analyze and reconstruct crime scenes. Greg is a nationally certified instructor in Use-of-Force and Pepper Spray by the National Criminal Justice Training Council of Twin Lakes, Wisconsin. He is a Life Member of the National Rifle Association and has been a certified NRA Pistol Safety and Personal Protection Instructor since 1991. Greg has trained police and civilians in use-of-force law for 21 years. He teaches legal seminars on self-defense law, effects of violence on witnesses, and effects of Post Traumatic Stress Disorder (PTSD). Greg has taught Bible classes to adults since he was 18.

www.bibleselfdefense.com